C000134604

'The story of Lyn's House is a mast   f
life-enhancing friendships where ak   ι
encounter, not bunkers of separate   ?
communities, Lyn's House offers a r   t
of each other where all learn, all giv   l
talents, their strengths and vulnera   ?
for one another. Is this not what a loving God asks of us and guides us to?
Find the answer in these wonderful pages.'

       – *Mary McAleese, President of Ireland (1997–2011) and Professor of*
             Children, Law and Religion, University of Glasgow

'Anyone under the influence of Jean Vanier who might be tempted to a
romantic conception of community needs to read this book. These honest
essays describe the hard mental and physical work necessary to make Lyn's
House work and work it does. It is wonderful work, however, that helps free
those associated with it from our endemic self-fascination. Hopefully this
book will be widely read not only by those working to create Vanier-inspired
homes of hospitality but by all seeking what it means to be "church".'

       – *Stanley Hauerwas, Gilbert T. Rowe Professor of*
          Theological Ethics, Duke Divinity School, North Carolina

'This beautiful series of reflections from people involved with Lyn's House
illuminates both the practicalities of the venture and its potential influence
on shapers of tomorrow's society. This is an inspiration to model Christ and
express true Christian community.'

       – *Justin Welby, Archbishop of Canterbury*

'In this marvellous book we are inspired by the genesis and vision of a small
prayerful community within the context of Cambridge, offering friendship
rather than care to those with learning difficulties. Blessed by Jean Vanier,
it is a variant of L'Arche that allows members to continue their careers
and which has the potential to spread worldwide with new variations and
improvisations. In a culture obsessed with individual status, Lyn's House is
a flare of hope, a sign of God's love.'

       – *Micheal O'Siadhail, poet and author of* The Five Quintets

'Lyn's House is an experiment, just as L'Arche is – a place where we are tested
against the radical call of Jesus. This book takes us through the stages of a
brave experiment, from testing the water through to making community
work in a particular context – Cambridge. It shows how people with learning
disabilities can make it possible for a complex community to be shaped
and to live well together, and draws out some valuable lessons for all of us
from this practical experience.'

       – *Tony Gibbings, Community Leader, L'Arche Ipswich*

'Jean Vanier was one of the few authentic prophets of our time. His visions were not laminated but embodied in the communities he founded and in which he lived. One of the tests of authentic prophecy is its power to live on and be fruitful beyond the earthy life of the prophet and to take new forms as the landscape changes. The increasing regulation and professionalisation of care for those whom the law describes as "vulnerable adults", has led to a fresh interpretation and embodiment of Jean's vision in the life of Lyn's House described in this book. I hope that the picture given here will serve to introduce an even wider circle of people to the living spirit of Jean Vanier.'

– Richard Chartres, Bishop of London (1995–2017)
and member of the House of Lords

'What an utterly remarkable book. I open the pages and am welcomed into a house that is a small haven amidst a world grown too big. Page by page, and the house opens to its smallest detail, room and furniture, residents and guests, core meals and close talk, housework rules, care and love among some who write books and some who cannot speak, sharing together deep friendship and prayer. Page by page, and I find another universe, where human beings do not seek to know too much or possess too much but learn to know the joy of deeper friendship and to risk telling us readers about it. That we may know just enough to want to grow small havens.'

– Peter Ochs, Edgar M. Bronfman Professor of
Modern Judaic Studies, University of Virginia

'This book powerfully captures the spirit and practical wisdom of how to create a space in which all are welcome and valued – not for what they achieve, but for the innate gifts they bring. Such spaces are rare indeed. The lessons of Lyn's House, and the experience of Jean Vanier's lifelong commitment to seeing and hearing those who the world overlooks, are lessons of life for us all. They speak refreshingly to a world which talks about inclusivity and equality, yet misses many of its essential hallmarks. This book launches us on a journey of radical hospitality, in which we learn from those who walk that walk: how to host, and how to be another's guest. It does not shy away from the challenges – but honestly lays out a blueprint for living to our own and others' God-given potential. A vision for radical friendship across unlikely borders, modelled perfectly by Jesus. Doing this in the academic context of Cambridge is a celebration in itself. Those whose lives are orientated towards achievement discover new rhythms of life in all its fullness.'

– Sarah Snyder, Archbishop of Canterbury's Special Adviser for
Reconciliation and Director, Rose Castle Foundation

'Is it possible to live Jean Vanier's vision outside of L'Arche? Lyn's House shows that it is. *A Kind of Upside-Downness* tells the remarkable story of a house which announces in the heart of a city of world-renowned academic achievement that "God has chosen what is foolish in the eyes of the world to confound the wise" (St Paul to the people of Corinth). In Lyn's House those who are intellectually disabled teach the intellectually able to ask not "How do I rate you?" but rather "How do I love you?" Such a vision of "upside-downness" will be Jean Vanier's lasting legacy; this book and Lyn's House are a most worthy testament to that.'

– Nicholas Hudson, Auxiliary Bishop,
Diocese of Westminster (Roman Catholic)

'This remarkable book unsettles us with demonstrations of unconditional love and service to humanity. Readers are challenged to stay connected to the least, the last, the immobilised, the scarred, the weak, the sacred. We are challenged daily to love all souls, regardless of physical difference and perceived ability. Jean Vanier was a lighthouse shining the path forward. Lyn's House emerges as a bright spot in time, a community of people who slow down and imbibe love: friends, housemates, volunteers, parents, siblings, and others. Let's celebrate this revolution of upside-downness!'

– Jerry White, Professor of Practice, University of
Virginia; shared the 1997 Nobel Peace Prize

'Justice and human rights matter hugely, and their implementation by law and regulation are indispensable: but they do not and cannot tell the whole ethical story. Lyn's House, and the L'Arche communities that inspire it, keep alive an older. broader and indispensable ethical tradition in which inclusive community and culture, giving and sharing, are central. They remind us of what matters.'

– Baroness Onora O'Neill, Emeritus Professor of Philosophy,
University of Cambridge and Chair of the Equalities and
Human Rights Commission (2012–2016)

'When Jean Vanier received the Templeton Prize in 2015, I well remember the way he leaned over the podium, looked at the attendees, and said "Community life is hard." Here was a man who embodied the best of communal living, acknowledging that sharing spaces and food and daily life with others is very hard to do. *A Kind of Upside-Downness* is a deeply meaningful testament to the beauty of community life and the challenges one might face. In the end, you will walk away from this book with a sense of hope in Jean Vanier's vision and a better understanding of what it means to realise that vision in today's context. The book is both inspirational and extremely useful.'

– Heather Templeton Dill, President, John Templeton Foundation

'Community is a hard thing to comprehend. We can spend forever trying to describe it, but in the end we only know it when we see it and feel it. Jean Vanier spent his life helping us to see what community looks like and to feel the importance of the presence of others for the recognition and living out of our shared humanness. The L'Arche communities help us to move beyond our cultural individualism and into a new world of kindness, love and belonging. This book puts Jean Vanier's thinking into action in fresh and new ways and opens up the possibility that in the midst of the violence, alienation and dislocation that threatens to overwhelm this world, there is hope. If we listen to the message of this book we will be changed.'
– John Swinton, Professor in Practical Theology and Pastoral Care, School of Divinity, History and Philosophy, King's College, University of Aberdeen and Director, Centre for Spirituality, Health and Disability

'Once you have established the theological priority of being with, you need detailed examples and practical wisdom that make clear how being with transforms discipleship, ministry and mission. Those are precisely what this inspiring book provides. These pages offer a vivid and moving witness to what truly incarnational living means and to the rewards it offers.'
– Samuel Wells, Vicar of St Martin-in-the-Fields and author of A Nazareth Manifesto

'This is a genuinely inspirational book. It offers an intimate depiction of how a few dedicated individuals, motivated by compassion and Christian vision, have created and are sustaining a life-enhancing community – enfolding into it, especially, those often marginalised by their learning disabilities. This is inspired by the ideas and practical vision of Jean Vanier – surely one of the most saintly figures of the late 20th century. William Blake wrote that those who seek to do good must do it in "minute particulars". This is Vanier's approach and that of the Lyn's House community.'
– Martin Rees, Astronomer Royal, President of the Royal Society (2005–2010)

'A Libyan sage once told me, "Son, what you need is 'the way of the crippled'!" I asked, "What is the way of the crippled, Sidi?" He said, "The way of the crippled is the way of Sidi Ahmed Rifa'i. Sidi Rifa'i promised, 'I am the Sheikh of the crippled! Come to me limping and broken.'" In Jean Vanier, I had the honour of meeting a Christian sage who was a practitioner of this very way of life.

This collection of essays, including some by friends close to Jean Vanier, gives us a glimpse of life at Lyn's House and how his ideals have shaped a community. The essays are nothing short of inspiring. The brokenness that we encounter in others becomes a reflection of our own brokenness and in turn, through all its travails, a light that guides us to God and to a more authentic commitment to life itself. As Jean Vanier said, "We are not called by God to do extraordinary things, but to do ordinary things with extraordinary love".'
– Aref Ali Nayed, Founder and Director of Kalam Research and Media and former Ambassador of Libya to the United Arab Emirates

A Kind of Upside-Downness

Learning Disabilities and Transformational Community

Edited by
DAVID F. FORD, DEBORAH HARDY FORD
and IAN RANDALL

Foreword by FRANCES YOUNG

Jessica Kingsley *Publishers*
London and Philadelphia

'Admiral of Arks' by Michael O'Saidhail is reproduced from *Collected Poems* (O'Saidhail 2013) with kind permission from Bloodaxe Books.

The lines from 'Lough Derg' by Patrick Kavanagh are reprinted from *Collected Poems*, edited by Antoinette Quinn (Allen Lane, 2004), by kind permission of the Trustees of the Estate of the late Katherine B. Kavanagh, through the Jonathan Williams Literary Agency.

First published in 2020
by Jessica Kingsley Publishers
73 Collier Street
London N1 9BE, UK
and
400 Market Street, Suite 400
Philadelphia, PA 19106, USA

www.jkp.com

Library of Congress Cataloging in Publication Data
A CIP catalog record for this book is available from the Library of Congress

British Library Cataloguing in Publication Data
A CIP catalogue record for this book is available from the British Library

ISBN 978 1 78592 496 5
eISBN 978 1 78775 139 2

Printed and bound in Great Britain

Contents

Foreword by Frances Young 9

Introduction 15

In Memory of Jean Vanier 23
David F. Ford

Part 1: Called into Community

1. Jean Vanier and a Community in Cambridge 27
   Deborah Hardy Ford

2. Becoming a Community 39
   Judith Gardom

3. Living in Community that Embraces Others 61
   E.S. Kempson

Part 2: A Wisdom of Community

4. Building Community Beyond Us and Them 83
   Daniel Smith

5. Wisdom's Call 103
   Suzanna R. Millar

6. The Spirit Speaks to the Church: Shabbat Wisdom 125
   Deborah Hardy Ford

Part 3: Discerning Community Today

7. Community as a Sign of Hope 141
   Philip S. Powell and Ian Randall

8. Experiments in Friendship 161
Patrick McKearney

9. Why L'Arche? Why Lyn's House? What Next? 179
Theresia L. Paquet and David F. Ford

Appendix 1: Lyn's House Practicalities. 203
James Gardom

*Appendix 2: Our Accumulated Wisdom
for Welcome and Community* 213
E.S. Kempson

Bibliography 225

The Contributors. 231

Foreword

This book, and the project it describes, belongs to the legacy of Jean Vanier. How else could I have begun, writing as I am in the immediate aftermath of his death? At this very time people all over the world are giving testimony to all that he has meant in their lives. One of my correspondents, Sister Claire Rolf, sent words which are so true to the experience of so many of us that I dared to ask permission to quote:

> Jean has gone to be with his dearest and most beloved friend, Jesus.
> Jean, the friend of the poor
> the friend to so many
> to each one of us.
> He befriended us in our weakness and poverty and said, 'You are
> loved exactly as you are, you do not have to be anything else.'
> Jean was, for me, a living icon of our Lord. He revealed the kind,
> tender, respectful, welcoming, human, loving face of Jesus.
> I will spend the rest of my life receiving the gift.
> How blessed we have all been.

What Jean embodied, and L'Arche exemplifies, is evidently present yet again in Lyn's House.

Indeed, in important ways, Lyn's House is a fresh embodiment, neither exactly L'Arche nor exactly Faith and Light, though recognisably belonging to the same family, a new creative improvisation on what Jean initiated, undertaken with his encouragement. This book about it is an invitation to try out ever more new improvisations, for it provides at the same time both insight into Jean's prophetic vision and loads of practical advice from hard-won experience and steep learning curves. It will prove illuminating for all kinds of readers – those already in the L'Arche loop, and those still to discover the powerful challenge of that gentle, humble giant, Jean, the friend of Jesus, whom some of us were so privileged to know.

So, what is distinctive about Lyn's House? Let me not anticipate all the rich surprises in store – I leave the reader to discover the story for themselves, and to enter into the fascinating reflections provided by the chapters which follow. Here let me just briefly highlight, and then explore a bit further, three distinctive elements to look out for:

- the primary focus on friendship and hospitality, rather than providing care

- the explicit intention to embrace the context – Cambridge/the University – so as to find a way for young adults to balance participation in a L'Arche-like experience with continuing preparation for academic or professional career-paths

- the commitment to creating an open community, not in spite of, but because of the explicit Christian confession lying at its heart.

Friendship

Living with persons with learning disabilities has always been the vision of L'Arche, providing homes and workplaces where assistants live a simple life in all its everyday ordinariness alongside core members. But persons with learning disabilities are vulnerable adults, and statutory requirements in the UK and elsewhere mean there is constant pressure to professionalise the care provided and, as far as possible, to support people to live independently rather than in group residential homes. But neither professional care, nor ongoing parental care, can ever be the same as friendship.

The character of adult friendships in our society, and the inevitability of those with learning disabilities being excluded from such relationships, is explored in a key chapter of this book. Friends usually gather to share meals, offer hospitality, participate in fun and games, go places together, enjoy common pursuits. This kind of friendship is what Lyn's House set out to foster from the beginning. The 'housemates' share a communal home, but their commitment is to facilitate welcome and hospitality, a gathering-space for 'core friends' (the persons with learning disabilities), together with volunteers, to share meals, to join in fun and games, to pray together.

One of the things I always noticed about Jean was his capacity to give total attention to a person – that was how so many had the experience described above in Sister Claire's words, the sense of being 'befriended' by Jean. The welcome and hospitality so many of us have received from L'Arche communities was inspired by Jean's very way of being, as well as his prophetic call to welcome each and every one, especially those who are different, the excluded, the marginalised. The multitudinous testimonies of assistants to their discovery of mutual joy in relationship with core members proves that in L'Arche the caring relationship has often become friendship. But caring responsibilities can so easily become top-down control – yes, for the good of the vulnerable person, no doubt... But that quickly corrupts the casual delight of friends in just being together. Perhaps Lyn's House provides a model in which Jean's welcome to each one can be more effectively and consistently enfleshed because this kind of friendship, not the demands of sharing the nitty-gritty of caring and domestic life, lies at the heart of both vision and reality. Here is the context where it is possible to let go of 'us' and 'them' without denying the difference, to enter into 'upside-down' friendships.

Balance

The novelty of Lyn's House is the placing of its 'upside-down' reality in the intellectual hothouse of Cambridge. High-flying academics discover here that there are values in life beyond the kind of success demanded by the society of which they are a part; they receive the capacity to slow down with their intellectually challenged friends, just to be, while their abilities, ambitions and anxieties are healthily de-centred.

Upside-downness always lay at the heart of Jean's challenge: the challenge of the Beatitudes, the challenge to go down the ladder, to reject the success values of our society. But this can so easily be heard as a call to abandon career goals and commit to a lifelong 'upside-downness', a withdrawal from society, from status or potential leadership roles. I have met some, especially women, who, for all their acknowledgement of the remarkable vision and rewards of living in community with persons with learning disabilities, have found claustrophobic the radical and sacrificial commitment to the caring and domestic role which is inevitably demanded of L'Arche assistants – after all, too many women have been trapped in that role over the centuries!

Of course, the truth of the matter is that the L'Arche model has consistently sent out assistants into work in the world: as Henri Nouwen observed:

> ...many assistants came and went... They often came for one or two years to explore a new direction in life... A few found their permanent vocation in L'Arche, but most of them went on to become lawyers, social workers, therapists, nurses, or businessmen and women.[1]

The particular feature of Lyn's House is its radical embrace of Jean's vision without seeming to deny the importance of intellectual endeavour or the challenges of the adult working world – it's a case of finding the right balance. For the L'Arche experience has the potential to have significant wider impacts. As I recently wrote in a different context:

> ...commitment to making the world a better place lies at the heart of Christian service, and service means something other than imposing top down control... We need people who are receptive to others to be the servants of all in our public life.

Lyn's House, with young housemates who are potentially influential players in the world's most important social, political and educational institutions, has an important formative role to play. Furthermore, as many of the chapters in this book demonstrate, along with L'Arche, Lyn's House inspires research and intellectual engagement with all kinds of social and theological dimensions.

Open because Christian

The Spirit of Jesus was at the heart of Jean's inspiration, and Jesus was both his friend and the source of his embrace of the whole of humankind. I have long found it interesting that Jean never wrote 'disability theology'; rather he explored 'theological anthropology' – what the L'Arche experience means for all humanity.

In our increasingly secular society, it is easy in practice for openness so to dilute the originally Christian character of an organisation that its source and vision are compromised. Worldwide, L'Arche keeps exploring anew what its mission is in an ever-changing world, and how to live true to its sources when the communities have become

---

1   Henri J.M. Nouwen, *Adam. God's Beloved* (London: DLT, 1997), p.54.

highly pluralist, often more humanist and secular than Christian. Lyn's House was conceived as a place where the tension could be creatively handled: the housemates were to be committed Christians, living together as an explicitly Christian praying community; but their welcome would be for all, 'and the creed, and the colour and the name won't matter' – whether for volunteers, guests or core friends. This book provides plentiful evidence of how this goal has been realised and how it has brought depth to the whole project, depth to the relationships fostered by its prayer-heart, depth to discernment of what is actually going on – indeed, deeper insights into the value, meaning and wisdom of the Lyn's House way.

The editors originally had in mind that Jean Vanier could write this Foreword. It has been a privilege to stand in for him. As it happens it's not the first time. Circumstances meant that I had spent a little time previously with Faith and Light in Moscow. So, when they wanted to celebrate their twentieth anniversary in 2010, and Jean had already stopped undertaking such travels, it was me they invited to share with them.

The question I was asked most often was whether they were like other Faith and Light groups. What was so lovely, to my mind, was their improvisation on the norms of Faith and Light – the way in which they had 'encultured' into an Orthodox environment the characteristic pattern of simple and inclusive sharing, caring and praying. The music was a wonderful mixture of Taizé songs, choruses and Orthodox chants. The cloth laid at the centre of the circle as a focus for prayer was not only spread with candles, flowers, twigs, stones and other beautiful objects, but there in the midst was an icon.

At the residential centre where we all stayed that icon was everywhere: the ancient Coptic depiction of Jesus with his arm around his friend, the martyr-saint, St. Menas – they stand side by side, with Jesus' fingers clearly visible resting on his friend's shoulder. Time and again I heard of someone with learning disabilities pointing to the icon and saying, 'There's my friend.'

Asked if there was anything I'd like to take back with me, I requested one of those icons. The answer came, 'Of course. We just print them off the internet and stick them on cardboard.' Increasingly battered, my cardboard icon from Moscow sits beside my bed, and I too can look and feel Jesus' hand of friendship on my shoulder.

Maybe this icon of friendship could become a badge for Lyn's House, a symbol embracing the heart of what it's all about. For Lyn's

House enshrines and bequeaths Jean's way of befriending each and every person, just as they are, a way of being which ultimately stemmed from his friendship with Jesus.

Frances Young, May 2019
Emeritus Professor of Theology, University of Birmingham,
Methodist minister and mother of Arthur, who was born with
profound learning disabilities in 1967, and author of *Arthur's Call* (SPCK 2014); *Brokenness and Blessing* (DLT 2007); and editor of *Encounter with Mystery* (DLT 1997)

Introduction

Jean suddenly gripped me by the arm: 'You should start a L'Arche in Cambridge!' As soon as he said it, I knew he was right. In a place where people rely so heavily on their intellectual abilities (and are often very fearful of their 'weakness' and fragility), there needed to be a way to discover the 'upside-down' secret and mystery of L'Arche – a way for people to discover the gentleness and joy of loving and being loved whoever they are and whatever their abilities/disabilities.

(Deborah Hardy Ford, Chapter 1)

This book tells the story of what, twenty years later, followed from that meeting between the late Jean Vanier and Deborah Hardy Ford, and is still continuing today in the Lyn's House community in Cambridge. Besides telling the story, and giving vivid testimonies to what has been experienced by people who have taken part in it, we also reflect on what we have learned.

That learning is partly some practical lessons about how to shape a new community centred on people with and without learning disabilities who come together in friendship. But, in addition, it is the discovery of a sort of wisdom, which we are convinced is of great importance far beyond this little community. Each chapter opens up aspects of that wisdom, and the climax of the book in Chapter 9 connects it with the thinking of Jean Vanier and others involved with the L'Arche communities that he began over fifty years ago. And, because we see Lyn's House being able to help to inspire further communities that embody a similar wisdom of friendship, we conclude that chapter by imagining future possibilities.

All the editors and contributors have been part of the wider Lyn's House community, and several of them have also had extensive involvement with L'Arche communities. We are all aware that there has been very significant work done, within the wider context of reflection on disability, on the issues we discuss. Throughout this book references will be made to important literature. Yet what is offered here begins with lived experience, and intensive conversation around it, more than with reading, and tries to interweave all three together in the search for wisdom. We are Christian thinkers keenly concerned both with disability and with the wisdom-seeking that has been going on, with increasing scope, rigour and depth, in disability theology, which outlines and critiques theological tradition and the Christian responses to disability.[1] Within this theological enterprise there is often the aim of making a difference to practice, and case studies may be included.[2] There are rich reflections on basic themes, such as what it means to be human, and contemporary spirituality.[3] Other books speak more directly out of personal contexts, such as the writings of Frances Young.[4] We are most grateful to Professor Young for writing the Foreword to this book. Within that large and growing literature this book is most akin to the writings of Jean Vanier and those influenced by him.[5]

Lyn's House, Cambridge

The Lyn's House project was inspired by Jean Vanier in person, as Deborah Hardy Ford explains in Chapter 1, but (with encouragement from Vanier and others in L'Arche) it has not followed the L'Arche model entirely. At present it has no formal affiliation with L'Arche UK, although there are strong connections. The Lyn's House community differs from established L'Arche communities around the world in that those with and without learning disabilities do not live together in Lyn's House.

This book also differs from what has been written by parents and carers of those with learning disabilities. While that important body of literature might often speak about or come from experiences which many readers will never have, this book describes the kind of community which could be established in many different contexts and is open to very broad membership. Such potentially wide-ranging communal initiatives as ours can provide opportunities for relationships with those with learning disabilities to be built by people who might otherwise never experience these relationships.[6]

In the period covered by this book, a period of six years, there has been a small core community of four people who have lived together and prayed together in a house in Cambridge (a house which once belonged to Lyn, as will be explained) and they have acted as hosts for those with learning disabilities, who are known as 'core friends'. These friends are invited round to Lyn's House for meals two or three times a week on rotation, with each person visiting every fortnight, allowing the building of deeper friendships. There are also larger tea parties once a month, which are a chance for the wider community, including those who support the house in various ways, to spend time all together, and there are other events in the house from time to time.

Those who live in the house, who up till now have been mostly young adults who have jobs in Cambridge or are doing research at Cambridge University, speak of having been profoundly changed by the experience. They themselves have come from different countries and a range of Christian traditions. Our book seeks to convey something of what has happened over time, and to draw in several voices. There are the voices of the core friends who come to the house. There are the voices of those who have lived as residents in the community: they give their testimony and seek to explore what has been learned for the future about how best to build a loving, hospitable community and make the space to receive and get to know guests well. Lyn's House also includes a group of dedicated volunteers who regularly join the meals that are hosted, often cooking and leading prayer or reflection. And there are members of the steering group, which includes the three editors. So the book combines these varied voices, each of which has attended to the others. The intention is that all of this should contribute to ongoing reflection and, ideally, to fresh initiatives: it is not simply the telling of the story of one project.

The Content of This Book

A word of explanation needs to be given about the title of the book, with its rather enigmatic 'A Kind of Upside-downness'. This comes from a poem dedicated to Jean Vanier, called 'Admiral of Arks' (a reference to Vanier's early years in the British Navy, and to L'Arche), in which Micheal O'Siadhail describes the origins and character of this community life:

To trust the grooves and habitats of love.
Soup, apples from village neighbours.
Raphael and Philippe. One tap and one stove.
    Slobber of dailyness. Tasks begun and rebegun.
Small humdrum of the wounded,
Seizures, tears, rushes of anger or affection.
    More listening than wanting to do things for,
Fecundity of nothing accomplished,
Ordinary unhurried to and fro of rapport.
    No mask or echelons, a kind of upside-downness,
Osmosis of bare and broken
Takers and givers in a single fragile caress.[7]

Commenting on this poem in a sermon he preached in November 2013 in Trinity College, Cambridge, Professor David F. Ford, one of the editors of this book, stated: 'Perhaps most striking is the way "takers and givers" come together, with "More listening than wanting to do things for."' This, he said, is not about people with abilities and skills 'doing good to' those without them. Instead, there is a more fundamental mutuality that does away with that division of 'us and them.'[8]

The book is in three parts. In the first part, 'Called into Community', there is a scene-setting opening chapter by Deborah Hardy Ford, also a co-editor of the book, who is an Anglican priest and psychotherapist in Cambridge and has been the co-ordinator of the steering group which serves Lyn's House. She relates what led up to Lyn's House over a period of twenty years, and how a 'complex community' has developed. There is a focus in this chapter and throughout the book on the theme of community. Deborah Hardy Ford highlights that the vision of Lyn's House has been for 'a deep sense of courtesy, generosity, solidarity, grace.'[9]

The next two chapters trace some features of the story of Lyn's House. Judith Gardom, who is a member of the steering group for the House and is involved in academic life in Cambridge, has traced aspects of this story, and she features in particular the voices of the core friends; of volunteers; and of parents and carers. The aim of this chapter is to present a picture of the life that has developed. For this purpose, photos and drawings are included. Several of the drawings are the work of Daisy Prior, who is a volunteer at Lyn's House. The chapter also features observations, seeking to see what has been learned as the material has been gathered.

A chapter then follows by Emily Sumner Kempson. She has been a member of the community living in Lyn's House, while she was completing her PhD. Her main focus is on the life of the residents in Lyn's House, and the chapter is written with a particular concern for any others who might want to be in such a community. She has helpfully drawn from work that has been done previously on the life of the residential Lyn's House community over the years. Loraine Gelsthorpe, a professor in Cambridge and another member of the steering group, has contributed to this chapter.

Part 2 of the book, 'A Wisdom of Community', offers wider reflections, which are connected with – and in important ways arise from – Lyn's House, but extend further. In Chapter 4, Daniel Smith, who lived in Lyn's House for two years while undertaking his PhD, writes on 'mutuality in community'. 'Inclusion', as he notes, is an important word today, but our society and our churches are still often defined by divisions, barriers and value judgements which shape how we respond to people we perceive as 'different' from ourselves. This is true for people with intellectual disabilities and this chapter suggests that in 1 Cor. 12:22–24 St Paul's discussion of how we should treat 'weaker' members is a place from which to explore mutuality. He explores letting go of 'us and them' divisions without denying difference.

Suzanna R. Millar, who lived in the house for two and a half years while writing her PhD, examines the role of 'Wisdom' in relation to those with learning disabilities. She points out that in common usage 'wise' can be taken to mean 'clever', or 'learning-abled', so that the 'disabled' are not included in that category. However, she argues that the message of the Bible turns the whole idea of 'wisdom' upside down, and with it, the very foundations of how we think, of what 'understanding' is. The experience of knowing the friends at Lyn's House has brought fresh insights into biblical wisdom, as outlined in that chapter.

In Chapter 6 Deborah Hardy Ford takes up the topic, 'The Spirit Speaks to the Church: Shabbat Wisdom'. In this chapter she explores the insight that there is something very close to the Jewish tradition about what happens in Lyn's House. There is something about its quality of time, relationship, celebration and joy that is deeply 'Shabbat'. The chapter looks at the themes of welcoming a mystery; being more at home; being reshaped; and 'resetting our clocks' and finding our balance again. It concludes with an invitation to the church to be open to new possibilities, and in particular to the wisdom of Shabbat.

In Part 3, 'Discerning Community Today', the focus is on opening up ideas that can be taken further. Chapter 7 draws from themes in Jean Vanier's *Signs of the Times*: 'from exclusion to encounter', 'from isolation to community' and 'from strength to vulnerability' seem especially appropriate. In the first section, Ian Randall outlines some historical developments in communal living in relation to those with learning disabilities. The second section offers some experiences in church life, in theological communities and in the area of vocation. The third section, by Philip S. Powell, who lived in Lyn's House for three years while working for a charity in Cambridge, recognises vulnerability in community, but at the same time aspects for celebration and for healing.

Patrick McKearney, who lived and worked in a L'Arche community, then later was part of the Lyn's House community, and whose PhD in social anthropology was related to L'Arche, writes about friendship. He reports on research on the place of friendship as imagined and practised in British social life, and examines the role it plays in the lives of those with intellectual disabilities. He argues that the individual-focused care provided by 'Supported Living' can only go so far in enabling people with such disabilities to form intimate friendships. But something like Lyn's House can enable this to go further. The space it creates is one where those with learning disabilities are not in a dependent relationship with either family or carers, and are able to develop long-term mutual relationships in the adult world.

Finally, in Chapter 9, Theresia L. Paquet and David F. Ford go to the heart of the main inspiration for Lyn's House, Jean Vanier and the L'Arche communities. With the help of a week spent in Trosly-Breuil with Jean Vanier and others involved with L'Arche, they explore the deep rationale for L'Arche, and its relation with Lyn's House. Jean Vanier himself, and in addition a professor in economics and social sciences who has spent years doing research on L'Arche, and a philosopher who has known L'Arche close-up over decades are among those who contribute. Among the issues that emerge are some to which Lyn's House is making a distinctive contribution, such as the tension between L'Arche's Christian roots and its openness towards those of many faiths and none. Overall, Lyn's House is seen as an improvisation on L'Arche with particular emphases on the potential of the Cambridge context; on shaping a new sort of complex community that still embodies the L'Arche vision; on combining a primary quest for Christian depth with engagement with the depths of other traditions; on creating special times and social spaces for friendships; and on exploring what sort of commitment all this requires. The chapter concludes by suggesting further improvisations on L'Arche.

There are appendices on practical issues by James Gardom, also a member of the steering group and Dean and Chaplain of Pembroke College, and by E.S. Kempson.

An Invitation to Look Forward

Although we have spoken about the third part of the book as forward-looking, the intention of the whole book is to be outward-looking and forward-looking. There is an invitation to readers to consider ways in which established movements such as L'Arche can be contextualised and translated into different contexts. It is the hope of those who have contributed that what is included here might be of interest to parents, carers and friends of persons with learning disabilities, to people involved in church ministry and others involved in Christian communities or interested in setting up their own inclusive communities, and to theologians.

Awareness of changes brings with it an awareness of vulnerability. This includes the vulnerability of Lyn's House itself. We are working to establish it in a way that will last. As this book has been in process of production, a new possibility for the location of the House has emerged. The new setting is to be a house within the grounds of the Margaret Beaufort Institute of Theology (MBIT) in Cambridge, which is one of eleven constituent institutions within the Cambridge Theological Federation. The community and the friendship that has marked Lyn's House, as described in this book, will continue, and the expectation is that through the partnership with MBIT what is offered will be enhanced.

A Final Note

In conclusion, we want to note the use of pseudonyms and of terminology, and to express thanks. It is common safeguarding practice in books like this to use pseudonyms rather than actual names, and we have followed that practice. Terminology and language in relation to those with learning disabilities is continually changing, and often an earlier generation's terms become unfashionable or even objectionable.[10] We have mostly used 'learning disabilities', sometimes 'intellectual disabilities' or on occasions the more general 'learning difficulties' or other terms. The main point is not the terminology but the fact that we are speaking of our friends, of '*people* with learning disabilities'. Jean Vanier makes the point: 'They are truly *people*, with all the implications that this word holds. Each person is unique and important. Yet there is a difference... The important thing in language is to signify difference while respecting the person.'[11]

As editors, our thanks go to all who have been involved in Lyn's House and who have played a part in this book. Our thanks also to Jessica Kingsley Publishers for their commitment to the book: in particular, we are indebted to James Cherry, Sean Townsend, Victoria Peters, Louise Massara and William Baginsky for their unstinting help in the process of its production.

David F. Ford, Deborah Hardy Ford and Ian Randall, editors

Endnotes

1   For an overview, see Brian Brock and John Swinton (eds), *Disability in the Christian Tradition: A Reader* (Grand Rapids, MI: William B. Eerdmans, 2012).

2   For example, Roy McCloughry and Wayne Morris, *Making a World of Difference: Christian Reflections on Disability* (London: SPCK, 2002).

3   For spirituality, see William C. Gaventa, *Disability and Spirituality: Recovering Wholeness* (Waco, TX: Baylor University Press, 2018).

4   Frances Young, *Face to Face: A Narrative Essay in the Theology of Suffering* (Edinburgh: T & T Clark, 1990) and Frances Young, *Arthur's Call: A Journey of Faith in the Face of Severe Learning Disability* (London: SPCK, 2014).

5   See Anne-Sophie Constant, *Jean Vanier: Portrait of a Free Man* (Walden, NY: Plough Publishing House, 2019), for a biography by a close friend of L'Arche and Jean Vanier. The story of L'Arche appears in several places, for example in Kathryn Spink, *The Miracle, the Message, the Story: Jean Vanier and L'Arche* (London: Darton, Longman and Todd, 2005); Michael Hryniuk, *Theology, Disability, and Spiritual Transformation: Learning from the Communities of L'Arche* (Amherst, NY: Cambria Press, 2010); Jean Vanier, *An Ark for the Poor: The Story of L'Arche* (Ottawa: Novalis, 2012). See also Frances M. Young (ed.), *Encounter with Mystery: Reflections on L'Arche and Living with Disability* (London: Darton, Longman & Todd, 1997).

6   There are of course wide-ranging books, such as Stanley Hauerwas, Jean Vanier and John Swinton, *Living Gently in a Violent World: The Prophetic Voice of Weakness* (Downer's Grove, IL: InterVarsity Press, 2008).

7   Micheal O'Siadhail, *Collected Poems* (Tarset: Bloodaxe Books, 2013), p.580.

8   See http://trinitycollegechapel.com/media/filestore/sermons/FordVanier171113.pdf.

9   See H. Reiners, *Receiving the Gift of Friendship: Profound Disability, Theological Anthropology, and Ethics* (Grand Rapids, MI: Eerdmans, 2008).

10 For example, 'mentally retarded', 'mentally handicapped', 'mentally deficient'.

11 Jean Vanier, *The Heart of L'Arche: A Spirituality for Every Day* (London: SPCK, 2013), p.14.

In Memory of Jean Vanier

David F. Ford

Shortly after this book was submitted to the publisher, Jean Vanier died on 7 May 2019. He had encouraged us to write it, and he had also agreed to write the Foreword, but his health did not permit it. These are some personal thoughts and memories written soon after his death.

What a person! I cannot think of anyone who has rung so true. Hearing of his death, in that stillness of trying to take it in, one memory and reflection after another came up. Here are a few of them.

I spent a good deal of time talking with Jean about the Gospel of John. I sometimes think that part of the reason he spent so much time in his later years writing his extraordinary commentary on the Gospel of John, *Drawn into the Mystery of Jesus through the Gospel of John*, writing other books on John, doing a TV series on it, and giving regular retreats on it, was in order to leave L'Arche, and everyone else, with his own Farewell Discourses. He was acutely aware that the commitment of L'Arche to its core members is permanent, so there had to be continuity beyond himself as founder. It was moving to watch over many years as he encouraged and self-effacingly helped the process of his own succession. The text that occurs to me is what Jesus says: 'It is to your advantage that I go away...' (John 16:7). Now Jean has gone away, and he has left an organisation that has learned, far better than many I know, how to sustain and develop its life and work for the sake of coming generations.

For me, that commentary on John is his greatest writing, distilling the wisdom of love and faith that he longed to share. It interweaves what he has learned from following Jesus with his experience in

L'Arche, but it goes even further: it offers a whole way of living – thinking, praying and acting – for the twenty-first century.

I have been especially moved by how he discovers a triple deepening of love through John's Farewell Discourses. In John 13 there is love through service, when Jesus sets the example by washing his disciples' feet. Foot-washing has now become the distinctive ritual of L'Arche.

In John 15 there is love between friends, as Jesus prepares to lay down his life for his friends. One of the most striking marks of the testimonies given by Jean and by others who have lived in L'Arche communities is how often they speak of surprising and life-changing friendships with people with learning disabilities.

Then in John 17 comes what Jean calls 'the summit of love' – utter unity in love with God and with other people for the sake of the whole world. I see that chapter, the final prayer of Jesus, as the deepest and most challenging in the whole Bible. In his commentary on it, Jean plumbs those depths and helps readers meet the challenge, and in the process he reveals, perhaps more than anywhere else, the deepest secret of his own life of faith and love.

That faith and love were also inextricable from peace. Jean passionately longed for peace in the fullest sense, with abundant life, joy, and celebration, yet he was also utterly realistic about all that can go terribly wrong, not least within ourselves. My final thought is about Jean's prophetic message and example for our century. I find it best expressed in his short book (how good that most of his books are short!), *Signs of the Times: Seven Paths of Hope for a Troubled World*. The essential insight of that book is summed up in one thing he said in Trosly-Breuil during the week described in Chapter 9 of this book: 'I believe there is a treasure of peacemaking. A vision where the weakest and the most excluded change us.'

That is a wisdom which he himself exemplified most beautifully.

PART 1

Called into Community

— CHAPTER 1 —

Jean Vanier and a Community in Cambridge

Deborah Hardy Ford

'Will you be my friend?'

As Jean Vanier turned to leave, after visiting a residential home for men with intellectual disabilities[1] in rural France, a voice suddenly cried out to him: 'Will you come back? Will you be my friend?' Something in its tone compelled Jean to respond and was the beginning of a lifetime's vocation dedicated to seeking ways in which people with and without intellectual disabilities might discover the mystery and gift of life in one another.

It led to an extraordinary movement, known as 'L'Arche' ('the Ark' or 'the Covenant' – 'rainbow' in French), which gradually grew and found its expression in different cultures all over the world. Today (2019) there are over 150 different communities in an International Federation: from Argentina to Australia; Belgium to Bangladesh; Denmark to the Dominican Republic; from Egypt to Edinburgh; Ipswich to the Ivory Coast; Mexico to Manchester; from Uganda to the Ukraine; Palestine to the Philippines; Syria to Switzerland...

'Faith and Light' began to grow, too – overflowing out of a pilgrimage to Lourdes. The essence of Faith and Light is that local groups of families, friends and individuals with intellectual disabilities meet regularly to share friendship, worship and celebration. By contrast with L'Arche, there are no residential communities involved. There is, however, a strong link with L'Arche in that Jean Vanier, with Marie-Hélène Mathieu, co-founded the Faith and Light movement. It, too, now spans the world. L'Arche in the UK began in Kent in 1974.[2] There are now twelve communities in the UK.

But back in 1993, I was oblivious: I had never heard of any of them, although I had heard of Jean Vanier and begun to discover a language which spoke and resonated deeply with my own life and spirituality in the writings of Henri Nouwen.[3] Something about how Nouwen spoke (wrote) helped me begin to face my own fragility and brokenness with compassion and hope. It was not just his personal wisdom and experience that spoke, but the mysterious healing and transformation he had encountered through getting to know and love people with intellectual disabilities.

One day, my husband David told me he was going to meet Jean Vanier while he was visiting Cambridge. 'Why don't we invite him here, so you can meet him, too? It's a great opportunity.' 'OK' I replied: 'When?' – relishing the possibility of some stimulating adult conversation as life beyond motherhood began to open up again. We had moved to Cambridge from inner-city Birmingham a few years earlier and I was finding it very difficult. Our second baby had died not long before and it was all beginning to catch up with me. Whilst beautiful in many ways, Cambridge is a challenging place to live: especially if you are an 'outsider' and not feeling strong. People's vulnerability is often deeply buried and guarded. 'Will you be my friend?' was the question I was asking deep down, too: 'Does anyone care about me enough to be my friend? And hear my pain as well as my joy?'

So, I prepared carefully for the 'important person' coming for lunch: I tidied the house, prepared a tasty meal, laid a beautiful table... The doorbell rang; I scooped our son, Daniel (an infant), into my arms and opened the door: the precise moment at which Daniel decided to produce a very smelly nappy. 'Hello! It's so good to meet you... please come in and make yourself at home: I'm afraid I'm just going to have to go and change Daniel's nappy,' I explained. 'Oh, I'll change him for you!' replied Jean; 'I'd be happy to,' lifting Daniel into his arms – before I'd even finished my sentence. And off they went. I couldn't quite believe it: it was wonderfully 'upside down'. No man (apart from David) had ever offered to change any of my children's nappies. And, what's more, there was not even a murmur from Daniel (who would usually protest vociferously if a stranger tried to pick him up). But that's the sort of person Jean Vanier was: he had the knack of seeing what really mattered. And he looked and saw very attentively and tenderly. The result was that you wanted to open up and talk to him: he invited it in you.

We talked about a lot of things, including what I might be being called to in this next chapter of my life. Jean suddenly gripped me by the arm: 'You should start a L'Arche in Cambridge!' As soon as he said it, I knew he was right. In a place where people rely so heavily on their intellectual abilities (and are often very fearful of their 'weakness' and fragility), there needed to be a way to discover the 'upside-down' secret and mystery of L'Arche – a way for people to discover the gentleness and joy of loving and being loved, whoever they are and whatever their abilities/disabilities.[4]

Sharing a Vision

Twenty years later, the moment was ripe. David and I had had ongoing contact, visits and conversations with Jean and others in L'Arche over the years, and it had been a central part of my own journey into healing and formation as an Anglican priest and psychotherapist. And whilst I never would have chosen the long years spent grappling with deep and relentless questions about all sorts of things (God, meaning, suffering, identity, belonging etc.) I can now see they were crucial preparation in terms of finding deep ground and roots in preparation for what was yet to come. Vocations can be a long time in the making.

I now felt at home in Cambridge and enjoyed training and working as a hospital chaplain, a psychotherapist and spiritual director. And I remained convinced that Jean was right: Cambridge needed a L'Arche precisely because it is Cambridge. People with intellectual abilities and disabilities need each other.

Quite apart from the potential of L'Arche for personal trans-formation and growth, Cambridge is full of people in various processes of formation and discernment: most of them highly successful (although often deeply insecure); many going on to positions where they will voice, shape and influence society at all levels and all over the world; people who need to experience 'upside-down' wisdom and ways of doing things. Cambridge is very powerful, competitive and hierarchical in its (often very ancient) traditions and institutional life. It is also full of life, energy, vision and young people from all over the world who can write, articulate and give voice to those on the margins.[5]

The final prompt came out of a place of pain and disillusionment. Yet again, I was hurt and angry about the dominant patriarchal and hierarchical patterns of power I was experiencing in the systems and organisations of which I was part – this time, the Church. It was time to put faith into action: time to live and nurture a different way; time to start a L'Arche in Cambridge.

I mentioned it to a colleague, James Gardom, the dean of one of the Cambridge colleges. He and his wife Judith had recently begun to learn about L'Arche and wanted to know more – curious that there was nothing in the Cambridgeshire area. Their daughter, Clare, had been living and working with L'Arche Inverness and had been profoundly moved by her time there. She later wrote:

> For me, L'Arche was a shock. I went to Inverness just after my degree, looking for community and a co-operative environment. I met people who were very different from me and to begin with felt completely uncomfortable and out of place. I had lots of ideas about how community should be (I had read *Community and Growth*[6]) and was disappointed that it wasn't perfect. Gradually things changed – the house had been short-staffed, and we got more assistants. A few people left. I was no longer new. I made friends. Spring came. I began to notice God in the real experiences and people around me. I started to learn from the people with disabilities – to enjoy small celebrations; to accept what the day brought; to laugh, forgive and ask for forgiveness, over and over again.
>
> I left reluctantly, to start a course I'd applied for at the beginning of my time in L'Arche. Returning to an academic context without a strong sense of community was a difficult adjustment. The intellectual conversations I had missed felt exhausting and overstimulating. For a long time, I wanted to return to L'Arche, but other aspects of life kept me in the south. I am still learning to balance the head and the heart.
>
> The first discussions about Lyn's House began the year I returned from L'Arche. I appreciated the chance to articulate and process what I had experienced, and it has been great to see the reality taking on a life of its own beyond our first theoretical discussions.[7]

Testing the Waters

Our conversation grew, with a group soon meeting regularly to pray and talk more about starting a L'Arche community in Cambridge. We googled and networked to try and learn whether others had tried anything here: nothing emerged. Jean encouraged us: 'Talk to L'Arche UK – L'Arche is changing and having to adapt: be open to something new. Getting the spirit of L'Arche at the heart of what you do is the most important thing: right from the start.'

An early meeting with John Sargent (then National Coordinator of L'Arche in the UK) spelled out the challenges L'Arche UK were facing with their 'traditional' model of community at that time: a model based on residential homes where people with and without intellectual disabilities lived together; and those without disabilities were employed as service providers by the local authority. The challenges they were experiencing were primarily about the increasing demands of local authority regulation and bureaucracy, as well as a trend towards providing more independent or supported living for those with intellectual disabilities, a trend which has its own difficulties.[8] 'Why don't you try something different?' he suggested, 'Have a look at what others are doing and consider alternative models.' A key member of the group had lived and worked in L'Arche for many years. She was now living and training in Cambridge and longed for a model that would enable her to live in community whilst continuing to work and study. Inspired by the patterns of 'Shared Lives' in L'Arche Melbourne (Australia),[9] we began to develop a vision for a model where those without intellectual disabilities might live together and create a welcome home to offer friendship and hospitality to those who did.

At that point, we knew hardly anyone with learning disabilities in or around Cambridge, but began to gather in someone's home for monthly tea parties and tested our ideas with wider networks and contacts within the city; people started to come and the circle gradually grew. The pattern has been that the work has largely expanded through personal contacts. People encouraged us to keep going – many of them offering professional time and expertise if or when we needed it.

It emerged that a local Faith and Light group had met in Cambridge for many years, but had recently folded because it was just too hard: it was run by parents – already exhausted by the demands of caring for our families and children with intellectual disabilities. One of those involved spoke of how 'we wanted to, but we simply couldn't do it any more: we needed others to take a lead and provide something our children could participate in.'[10]

The vision soon became a project with a life and energy of its own, stretching us to keep up with it: developing and maturing a community of friendship and hospitality. The key elements were:

1. A Christian house (hopefully acting as a 'hub house')

2. A maximum of four to six people

3. Located in Cambridge

4. Living and sharing meals together

5. With a commitment to hospitality (for those of all faiths or none)

6. Building community with people with learning disabilities

7. Working with a group drawing inspiration from L'Arche

All we needed now was somewhere for it to happen: something easier said than done with the cost of housing in Cambridge. But within weeks a close friend of someone in the group died. Her daughter caught the vision and suddenly the vision became a reality. The house was a pure gift: a beautiful Victorian house to rent quite close to the centre of Cambridge, with a ready-made community room, which the owner (an artist) had built and used as her studio. After weeks of serious house clearing, cleaning and preparation, we were ready to go!

It was not all smooth sailing: almost immediately, there were moments of deep disagreement – particularly about expectations and patterns for those living in the house: about leadership; about sex; about power and authority. We agreed to differ on some issues, and a couple of people no longer wanted to be involved. Others moved on and away from Cambridge. But a stable and consistent cohort survived, with external partners remaining committed and keen to collaborate.

Launch and Development

The house first opened its doors with a tea party one Sunday afternoon.

As one of the guests arrived, he suddenly realised he had been there before: when Lyn was alive, and he had enjoyed visiting her from time to time with his carer and dog. 'It's Lyn's House!' There was no doubt about it: and from that moment, Lyn's House was born and is still the name of the house at the time of writing. The life and energy kept growing: our job was to try to navigate and keep up with it. The vision was for a Christian community (open to those of any denomination), with prayer and shared faith at its heart, which was open to all: friends and volunteers of other faith traditions or none. 'Go deep' – advised Jean, during an early visit. 'Don't have too many people: concentrate on building trust and developing deep and meaningful relationships.' The subsequent growth in the number of friends with learning disabilities was largely through personal contacts. The word about Lyn's House has spread in this way.

A Community

The first four members of the residential community moved into the house in the summer of 2013: all involved in post-graduate study in various disciplines: two of them training for ordination at one of the local theological colleges.[11] The priority for the first term was to establish patterns and rhythms for living and growing in community together: developing a quality of warmth, home and friendship into which to invite and welcome others – together with the roles and systems which that would involve. Central to this was prayer, a weekly community night and sharing meals together.

The pattern now is for two or three 'core friends' (our friends with learning disabilities) and a few volunteers and/or members of the steering group to gather with members of the house (in the same 'clusters' each time), to pray, share a meal and spend the evening together several times a week. The wider community meets as a whole at a monthly tea party, with time simply to enjoy one another's company and to sing and pray (for more, see Chapter 2) and lots of other 'ad hoc' meetings between various individuals and groupings (initiated outside the house) happen regularly too. So Lyn's House increasingly became a 'hub house' for other dimensions of community life spinning out in different ways and directions: it has become a cumulative community.

Steering and Governing

For the first five years, the life and work of Lyn's House has been supported, overseen and guided by a steering group, meeting regularly with house members and sometimes others (including core friends). Each year has brought new developments, challenges and opportunities and we are now in the process of reviewing our governance and the various roles, responsibilities and structures needed to take the project forward and into the longer-term future. The dynamic of the community as a whole is of a simultaneous deepening ('intensity') and broadening ('extensity') over time.

Complex Community

Lyn's House is a complex community of people involved in different ways and levels – both residential and extended: house members; core friends; volunteer members; steering group members; parent members and so on. It is not dissimilar to certain religious orders, with 'first' and 'second' order members (men or women living the traditional residential model of religious/monastic life in community); and 'third order' members (lay members living and working separately), where their numerical order is nothing to do with ranking, but simply signifying the order in which they came into being.[12]

Those living in Lyn's House are not living in intentional community simply for the sake of it: they are serving a very particular mission: creating a welcoming home and space where those with and without intellectual disabilities can get to know one another and grow in mutuality and friendship. Jean Vanier makes the distinction between a community and a group:

> The difference between a community and a group that is only issue-oriented, is that the latter see the enemy outside the group. The struggle is an external one; and there will be a winner and a loser. The group knows it is right and has the truth and wants to impose it. The members of a community know that the struggle is inside of each person and inside the community; it is against all the powers of pride, elitism, hate and depression that are there and which hurt and crush others, and which cause division and war of all sorts. The enemy is inside, not outside.[13]

Living in community is about facing and living with difference (for more, see Chapter 4); and with whatever that brings up in us: whether it's difference in intellectual ability; gender; faith; philosophy of life; socio-economic values; theology; age; race; culture (and so on). It means being able to risk being real, honest and open – about ourselves as well as others – especially when it's about things we find difficult. It means managing hopes and expectations, as well as disappointments and disillusionment. It takes time. It means keeping on talking, listening and trying to understand one another, even when it feels impossible. It means managing conflict and trying to find ways to be gently assertive without being aggressive – something the British do not always find easy. The second year in the house was a difficult and painful one in many ways (for a whole set of different reasons). But we have come through to deeper and richer relationships as a result.

Developing a community based on 'upside-down' values raises all sorts of other issues, too: models and styles of leadership; organisational structures and procedures; how to develop systems that help rather than hinder; how to genuinely listen and include the voices of those with disabilities; establishing and maintaining appropriate boundaries; dealing with turnover, change and house members moving on; and sometimes having to take difficult and painful decisions (such as when and how we might need to exclude someone). How can we develop 'best practice' and a certain 'professionalism' in the way we go about things, without becoming stuck in or stifled by the very things that we set out to avoid?

From the beginning, we sought to maintain an equal gender balance of those living in the house – partly to offer friendship and meet the needs of both female and male core friends. Sometime this has been possible, but it has been more difficult to recruit men than women, so we have been careful to try and redress any imbalance by having other male members of the community (primarily volunteers and steering group) present whenever possible.

Lyn's House is deeply ecumenical: members of its wider community include Baptists, Anglicans, Quakers, Russian Orthodox, Roman Catholics, United Reformed and Pentecostals; and, among these, contemplatives, charismatics, liberals, conservatives and Anglo-Catholics, as well as those of other faiths and of none. It is sometimes a challenge to find ways to pray together and to hold our differences in creative tension but this has also been hugely enriching and enhancing.

So far, there is no identified 'leader' amongst those living in the house, and the leadership style of the steering group is to encourage, enable and facilitate. There are no 'parent figures' to give orders and/ or to blame, even when it sometimes feels as if that would be a much easier option than having to tolerate the levels of uncertainty and anxiety aroused without them. The leadership within the steering group is also shared, with no formal leader, although we are certainly open to learning and discerning if a recognised leader might be a helpful thing.

As well as developing gifts within, we rely regularly on the wisdom, insight, support (and money!) of others who are well 'outside' the Lyn's House community. Now, in our sixth year, Brother Sam, SSF (the Society of St Francis) is acting as an external mentor to those living in the house and helping us think about our wider community life together. And we have employed an experienced project manager on a part-time basis to help with administering and developing the project to its full capacity.

Identity and Wider Belonging

Lyn's House has a wide range of other friends, supporters and 'partners', too: locally, nationally and internationally: university colleges; theological colleges; churches of many different denominations; religious orders; other faith communities; prison communities; other universities; charities for those with learning disabilities…and is keen to cultivate these and more. It is often through these networks that those who become involved hear about Lyn's House.

Whilst Lyn's House has not (as yet, anyway) taken the route of becoming a 'Fresh Expression'[14] (of church) or 'New Monastic Community',[15] we are certainly open to new possibilities. We did explore the possibility of being recognised as a L'Arche Project.[16] From the start, we were keen to be in touch with L'Arche – and we have been. Several members of the wider Lyn's House community have lived and/or worked in different L'Arche communities (in the UK and abroad); others have visited projects and communities, made friends and kept/keep in regular touch.

L'Arche has already grappled for years with various questions: what makes an improvisation in the spirit of L'Arche, 'L'Arche' enough? What is the 'essence' of L'Arche? What criteria are needed to measure and discern it? What other dynamics might be at play? What have they, and we, to lose or gain? One deeper issue, perhaps, is about ecumenism and how 'receptive' L'Arche is able to be.[17] What might it need to learn from others? Who and what helps it to recognise its own blind spots and opportunities for growth? How might L'Arche, as well as Lyn's House, need to reconceive itself and retell its story?

Calling Others into Community

Just as Jean Vanier took the initiative in prompting a L'Arche in Cambridge all those years ago, we have been proactive in discerning, inviting and 'commissioning' others to get caught up in the life and spirit of Lyn's House too. For me personally, this has been a new and surprising phenomenon. I have always been rather tentative and wary about 'selling things' and asking others to take up responsibilities or get involved in things. But Lyn's House has been different: there is something very urgent and necessary and *good* about it and we *need* people to help it to flourish. Engaging with our core friends and seeing the depth of transformation and life the project brings to everyone involved (in all sorts of different ways) has somehow liberated me from my qualms: there's absolutely nothing to lose and absolutely masses to be gained (so watch out!).

Inevitably, some people have been more committed than others, but the majority have become more, not less, engaged and involved as the years go by and despite regular turnover of those living in the house, there have gradually been more people wanting to stay on for longer than an initial year. And those who have been involved tend to stay involved (whether it be by social media, returning to visit when they can, and/or taking on a new role within the community). The monthly tea party that has taken place as I have written this chapter included visits from four former house members (now living locally with new jobs and responsibilities) together representing every year in the life of Lyn's House to date...as well as six new young people, studying or working in Cambridge.

We have developed certain Lyn's-House-shaped customs and rituals – ways to mark significant events in our life together and to tell and retell our story/stories as we go deeper into it/them together. And we rely on others to teach and help us see, discern and be honest about things we might miss: what is really going on. The venues for offering and sharing hospitality beyond Lyn's House itself grow each year, with a 'to and fro' of shared times (meals, parties, weddings, films, outings) initiated and organised in all sorts of different places (homes, pubs, theatres, colleges, churches, cinemas, etc.) by members of the wider community (core friends; steering group; volunteers; house members; and parents alike) throughout the year.[18]

There is a wonderful sense of 'overflow', and underlying everything else, a deep sense of courtesy, generosity, solidarity and grace. Once again, I am reminded that over and above (or way underneath) anything we plan or try to do or make happen, the Lyn's House project has always had a life and energy of and beyond its own. It's part of something much, much bigger: a life and energy that has somehow swept us up into its adventure – full of ups and downs (as good adventures are), but with a quality of life, energy and joyful surprise which is open to all. For those of us trying to 'steer', even with all hands on deck, we have certainly sometimes felt at very full stretch

– but 'the wind blows where it wills'[19] and our main task is to keep focused and alert: anticipating and watching for its signs, sails at the ready, calling out and inviting others to join in:

This love that is forever is in motion…
now and here nothing will stand still
…human and fallible we
trust the love that is surrender to the flow…[20]

Endnotes

1   The Introduction notes the different uses of language and terminology over time and in different contexts, as well as in this book.

2   In countries where there are more than two L'Arche communities, they are governed internally; when there are two or less, they are governed by L'Arche International.

3   A Dutch Catholic priest, writer and theologian, much influenced by Jean Vanier and L'Arche.

4   It is not the purpose of this book to write about L'Arche itself: many others have done this. See note 5 in the Introduction for references to key texts – to which I would add, Henri J.M. Nouwen, *Adam, God's Beloved* (Maryknoll, NY: Orbis Books, 2007).

5   A more recent challenge to L'Arche UK has been the recruitment of new assistants, many of whom have previously come from different parts of Europe.

6   Jean Vanier, *Community and Growth* (New York: Paulist Press, 1989).

7   Clare Gardom (2018), now living and working in Oxford.

8   We were already well aware from those we knew, that although many people with intellectual disabilities often find this a very attractive model/option, the reality in time is that they often find it much lonelier than anticipated, with little continuity in the care provided by professional care/support workers.

9   See larche.org.au/larche-communities/Melbourne.

10   One parent, during an early conversation.

11   In the years since, members of the house have often included those working at post-graduate level (who, despite the Cambridge college system, are often quite isolated/lonely), together with those working in various other capacities within Cambridge.

12   As in the current order of Anglican Franciscans – although the Roman Catholic equivalent has adopted different terminology, to avoid any assumptions about 'rank'.

13   Vanier, *Community and Growth*, pp.29–30.

14   See http://freshexpressions.org.uk.

15   See www.ianmobsby.net/category/new-monasticism.

16   A formal three-year period of mutual discernment to explore becoming a L'Arche community.

17   See www.dur.ac.uk/theology.religion/ccs/projects/receptiveecumenism/about.

18   The midweek meals and monthly tea parties in the house take place mostly during university term times, with other occasional events at other times.

19   'The wind blows where it chooses, and you hear the sound of it, but you do not know where it comes from or where it goes. So it is with everyone who is born of the Spirit' John 3:8 (NRSV).

20   From Micheal O'Siadhail, 'Rhapsody', *Collected Poems* (Tarset: Bloodaxe Books, 2013), p.261.

CHAPTER 2

Becoming a Community

Judith Gardom

Welcome sign made by Lyn

For the first year or two of the project, our experiment in shared hospitality was carried out from our own homes. When we opened a resident community, the physical house itself, with its particular architecture and atmosphere, began to shape how the form of life and patterns of welcome developed. A small room off the kitchen with no other obvious use became a prayer room. The housemates' rooms (i.e. for the resident community) could be reached by a separate door, giving them an important degree of privacy. We were excited that the house had a beautiful, rather untamed garden. Lyn, whose daughter rented the house to us, had been an artist, and her studio, together with the extended kitchen-dining room and broad passageway opening into the garden, gave us space for large gatherings.

Some of the pictures, furniture and books that had been in the house for decades were kept. Lyn had a gift for finding ordinary objects, and placing them together in unlikely ways alongside the art she collected and her own paintings and drawings, which were often variations on her own symbolic themes. From what might have just looked like muddle, beauty and meaning glowed, which could stand as a metaphor for what her house has become in this new phase of its life. This poem, written just after her death, attempts to capture something of her vision of the world, expressed through her art and her house. Having known her personally, I remain deeply grateful for the way she taught me to look again, and look differently.

> A cracked ploughshare placed against the light
> is flame or finger; dead driftwood grows curled
> leaves; mirrors befriend and unfold our shadows.
> Patterns of your vision grow familiar:
> the open upturned hands; heart that is
> artichoke enclosed by layered leaves; cross-centred
> branching life; the soul that is a child
> contained in womb-space. You knew how many
> winding paths we all travel, alone and together.
> In your hands, tree roots circling the moon
> could tap the wise earth's blood. Now I begin
> to see how you saw, reading between your lines.
>
> (Judith Gardom, May 2013)

This chapter is the work of many people who have contributed their words through conversations and written reflections, or indirectly through the innumerable acts of shared hospitality and friendship that make up the shared life of the house. The aim is to convey something of what it is like for us to belong to the Lyn's House community, and the sections are intended to suggest the shape of a year, from September to July – our year is the Cambridge academic year, with a new start at harvest time, and farewells in the summer. Between these annual points of transition spreads a patchwork of activities, planned and unplanned, whose variety is summed up by one of the non-resident members of the community:

We cook for one another, draw pictures, laugh at jokes, notice silly socks and stamp collections and favourite colours, play croquet in the summer, sing for birthdays, sing along with musicals, sing carols at Christmas, sing for no reason at all, mourn losses, pray together, navigate conflicts and challenges, build frighteningly tall Jenga towers, share joys ranging from new films and family holidays to finishing dissertations and growing families, and generally support each other through life's minutiae and monuments.

These things are Micheal O'Siadhail's 'fecundity of nothing accomplished': ordinary things through which, as we experience them together as a community of people with and without learning disabilities, we are recipients of a distinctive kind of grace, made up of the mundane and the surprising. A resident of the house reflects: 'It has been, for me, like the surprise of seeing Jesus fill up twelve baskets when there was so little to begin with: where has all this goodness come from?' Although the answer ultimately remains a mystery, what follows is an attempt to describe some of the fragments that fill the baskets.

Welcome into the Story

The 'scroll' telling the story of the project

'Genuine welcome is an energy of peace,' said Jean Vanier. 'To welcome...is not only to open one's door and one's home to someone, it is to give space to someone in one's heart.'[1]

It is three o'clock on a Sunday afternoon in late September. I have invited you to the first tea party of the year. As we arrive outside a

Victorian semi-detached house in Cambridge on a wide, quiet street, you can hear the shouts of a student rowing coach from the river nearby. We head for a side door, past an old school bench, a couple of half-finished stone carvings, and five or six bikes. I pull an old, knotted piece of string that hangs by the door, and a bell jangles inside the house. On the door a faded home-made sign says 'Welcome'.

The door rattles open and we are greeted by a young man who, I explain to you, lived in the house a couple of years ago, and still visits when he is in Cambridge. As you step inside you brush past a geranium plant that grows from floor to ceiling by the door, releasing a sharp scent. We are in a stone-floored passage, a kind of conservatory between the main house and the studio, with the afternoon sun shining through the roof. Gardening tools are propped against the wall, and you can see the garden through the open door at the other end of the passage. A variety of shelves hold coloured glass bottles, pots, carved figures, dried flowers, stones and plates. Coats overflow a coat stand. Someone's washing is drying in a corner. People stand talking in twos and threes.

To your left, an open door leads to the kitchen. Someone is carrying a plate of food and a glass of lemonade from the kitchen across the passage to the studio. She stops to say hello and puts the plate down so that she can shake your hand. She repeats your name carefully and tells you hers, and asks if you would like a cup of tea. The bell jangles again above our heads, and I open the door to a smiling woman pushing a walking frame, who shouts 'Hello!' joyfully. Outside, a taxi is drawing up, while someone else parks another bike against the garage.

A little later, after more introductions in the kitchen, offers of tea, cake and popcorn, we move to join the others in the studio, a light, square room with doors open to the garden. People sit on the three sofas; a group is playing a noisy game of Jenga; an older man is drawing, with great concentration, at a table; others are writing on coloured cards that are being passed round. There are two pianos, a grandfather clock, and shelves full of cookery books, board games and craft materials. Photographs of faces are strung like bunting. As you hesitate by the door, people move to make space for you and find you a chair, as the tower of Jenga blocks topples with a crash amid plates of cake.

'Welcome!' says Miriam, and you are included by name as a newcomer. Over the years, rituals of beginning have evolved. The four new housemates of the house are introduced, each name followed by cheering, shouts of 'Hello!', and handshakes and patting on the shoulder from those who are sitting nearest to them. They are given cards to welcome them, which are then taken back to recirculate so that everyone can sign them.

The story of the development of the project from the beginning is told through the unrolling of a scroll of wallpaper, on which everyone involved is represented by the outline of their hand, alongside drawings and symbols representing L'Arche, the world, Cambridge, the house, and parties. As Miriam retells the story, she points to the names of people: 'Do you remember Jerome?' 'Ryan, who still comes sometimes?' And there are smiles and shouts of recognition. As we arrive at the end of the path of handprints, the newcomers are invited to add theirs to the blank section of the sheet: what was the future is now the present. You're asked what colour you would like your hand to be, and before you can decide a young woman nearby says 'purple!'.

To celebrate the start of the year, and as a prayer for the new housemates of the house, we sing and sign the Lord's Prayer, led by Hannah who gracefully and patiently shows us how to express the words with our hands. By the third repetition of the refrain you find you know what to do. A few people near the door slip away to the kitchen where it is quieter, finding the size of the group and the noise level overwhelming. Games and conversations resume.

I'm Bringing My Friend

'Catching Up' by Daisy Prior

'A friend may come – as a surprise – a grace.'[2]

The hospitality of the house is organised on a fortnightly rotating system, so that guests are invited according to a predictable pattern. This regularity is important for establishing the security of familiarity, and building up friendships in smaller groups. The unexpected breaking of this custom one autumn evening added something important to our idea of 'welcome'. One of the housemates recalls:

We had started to cook, and then the phone rang. 'It's Michael: he says he's bringing a friend!' 'Did you say it was OK?' 'Yes... I think we should explain to him he can't just do that, though, he should ask in advance.' 'Who is it?' 'He just said a friend.' That was how we first met Anthony, and he's been coming ever since.

This moment overturned an assumption that many of us fall into very easily: that 'more capable' people provide and decide, and 'less capable' people receive and are decided for. It was an immensely helpful reminder that, if I can decide to bring a friend to dinner, so can Michael. Anthony, the young man who was invited that day, remembers: 'I found out about Lyn's House through my friend Michael. He brought me here.' What do you like about it? 'I like coming because I can meet new people and make new friends. In the summer during the tea party we went outside and played croquet. That made me feel happy.'

One of the 'core friends', Hannah, has been involved from the beginning, six years ago, and her memory is like a non-visible version of the scroll that we use to tell the story, holding the details for the rest of us. She was present at the first meetings at which we discussed what we might do in practice to be a 'L'Arche-like' presence in Cambridge, and she met Jean Vanier: 'a man of faith, very kind.' Hannah remembers how the project began and exactly who was there at the start; the fact that it has rained every time except once whenever we've had a barbecue. She recalls with pleasure the stories that people have told her about their lives over dinner: 'when Sam told me about the Lego castle he got for his fourth birthday.' She remembers whose mother it was who made the patchwork blankets to brighten up the second-hand sofas in the studio, and all the singalong films we've watched together.

Hannah gently mocks the relative incompetence of some of the housemates who were less used to cooking for a group: 'It was Sam's turn to cook and he didn't know how to turn the oven on, and I noticed there was no light on and I said, Sam, you do know the oven isn't on, don't you?' The wonderfully international mix of housemates over the years means that we have all tried new kinds of food: 'Andrew cooked curry and I didn't know how hot it was going to be and then I felt a kick and he said are you all right?' Were you? 'No, I couldn't speak until I had drunk a lot of water!'

When asked what she appreciates about coming to the house, Hannah says, 'Cooking, helping to cook. I love the kitchen because it is welcoming. I love bringing things I have learnt to cook. And I love being able to cook there when I come: cheese scones and brownies straight from the oven.' What about the people? She says, simply, 'You guys mean a lot to me.' This is clearly expressed through her writing which is displayed on the wall of the prayer room: her personal 'guide for living a good life', and the meaning of the names of each of the housemates, which she looked up and copied out, as a loving gesture of personal recognition of each of them.

Sharing the Blessings

The hearth in the prayer room[3]

For Hannah, there is another dimension to coming to the house that is crucial. 'What Lyn's House means to me is a house of prayer; because whenever I go there I feel that God's presence is with me there.' Anthony also finds it an important part of what we share. 'I look forward to the meal and the prayer session before the meal, singing during the prayers and sharing the blessings.' Hannah says, 'I really like the prayer room because it is peaceful. I taught the Lord's Prayer dance which I led with Mum at the Diocesan Day.'

Prayer is a regular part of the evenings we spend together, and having a dedicated place, and using repeated, habitual actions, are important aspects of this. Luke, one of the first housemates, explains. 'Typically when there were guests in the evening we would go into the little lounge just off the kitchen that has become our prayer room, while dinner was cooking, and have a bit of Taizé singing, a simple Bible story, sometimes silence (of varying lengths, depending on the guests) and my favourite part – taking turns to pray out loud. To do this we would pass round a small cross – having something tactile proved popular – and the person holding it would pray out loud or hold silence and then pass it on to the next person.'

Praying with others can be a unique way of appreciating their individuality. Housemates and regular volunteers, including theological college students, have expressed a deep appreciation of the immediacy and depth of engagement in prayer of people who have a learning disability. There can be very earnest prayer, hearty singing and the holding of a cross, with prayer for peace in the world, and for family. One housemate recalled: 'Michael's prayers were also always something that stood out, since he seemed to be so concerned with disasters in the world, and would often pray for people suffering in wars, or natural disasters.' Shared prayer has also led to wider reflection. Another comment: 'Often a person with learning disabilities would use their time in prayer to speak of how they missed someone they loved who had died. Talking about lost loved ones was a topic which often came up in conversations and prayers and it made me wonder, how able are we at supporting those with disabilities cope with bereavement?'

Members of the community from different Christian traditions describe how shared prayer has deepened their own prayer life: 'One of my favourite experiences has been learning how to share space in the prayer room and engage with the different ways people understand being in the presence of God. It taught me a lot about my own prayer life.' 'I remember how this open praying helped me to speak plainly to God about my joys and struggles, a liberating contrast to how the prayers in the context of my theological college could sometimes get rather formal and serious.' Words like 'liberating', 'freedom' and 'surprise' recur in these reflections, qualities that have helped some of us to become more relaxed and honest in how we pray. 'I've had some of my most moving prayer experiences at Lyn's House. Each evening is never quite how you expect it to be. But whether it's singing the Taizé chant 'Bless the Lord my Soul', reading the Beatitudes, or drawing pictures together, I'm always struck by a sense of God's peace and wellbeing.'

With prayer, as with every other aspect of the project, there can be uncertainties, misunderstanding and frustration. Sometimes we can feel torn between allowing ourselves to be drawn into a different, more relaxed sense of time, and the constraints of cooking schedules and taxi arrivals. A housemate reflects: 'Samuel, for instance, always likes to choose and lead the music from his iPad. This could be difficult sometimes, for instance on an evening when I was a bit stressed and the dinner was already ready, and Samuel went to the wrong video, and then found a seven-minute version of the song he wanted to sing, so the prayer went on for well over twenty minutes.'

Many of the parents of young people with learning disabilities comment on how important the Christian ethos is for their son or daughter. 'He does feel more comfortable in a Christian environment. He's always believed in God and prayed independently.' 'Our daughter is a spiritual person, a person of faith.' 'Lyn's House and the church community are his main places. It is a solid safe place where he can come and feel completely accepted with his faith. He can talk freely about it without being told he is going on about it.' 'He likes the prayer part, to be able to pray especially for people in other countries – he doesn't have that opportunity anywhere else.' 'For years Lizzie went to Lourdes, she loved it, all aspects of it. It goes beyond words. Lyn's House has sort of replaced it.'

For some parents who are Christians, this matters to them as well: 'It is so important to us that it is a Christian foundation.' But in some cases, the parents may be agnostic or non-religious, while their son or daughter is an active member of a church. During the lifetime of the project two young people have been baptised, making an independent adult commitment. 'He's quite religious – he was baptised not long ago. He didn't even tell us – I'm not religious but I would have liked to have been there. Apparently he talked about it at Lyn's House: he appreciates being able to do that.'

A Place to Be

'An Advent Celebration' by Daisy Prior

It is early December and some of the regular non-resident members of the community are helping to decorate the house for the Christmas party. 'I'm Jewish, and I love Christmas!' says Rebecca, who has been coming to the house for three years. 'As a Jew (and not a particularly religious one, at that), I am not necessarily the most natural fit with such an explicitly Christian, theologically engaged group. But thanks to empathy and communication, I feel I am an equal member of the community, no less able to appreciate its richness than anybody else.' What is it about the community that helps her to feel that?

> From the very beginning, I loved how the community is not so much a place to do, but a place to be. Acceptance and inclusion at Lyn's House are multi-directional and encompassing. It is not difficult to imagine an organisation that exhibits compassion only to the community that it targets; Lyn's House is the opposite, rather seeking to engage and connect with each member – guest, volunteer, carer, housemate, or visitor – in their own individual ways.

Rebecca recalls her first visit to the house:

> Embarking on a fresh program in a different department in a new country – and a bit anxious about what the posh Brits would think of my unmistakably American accent – I was acutely aware that I was responsible for making the most of what was initially intended to be

a one-year opportunity, not only academically, but also socially and personally. Luckily enough, my new friend was already a part of the Lyn's House community and invited me to come along to the next event. That first tea party, I will admit, was not the easiest experience for me. The onslaught of new people, introductions, and repeated lines about my background and still under-formulated research question became a bit of a blur. By the end, I had taken refuge in the kitchen washing dishes, which is where I first met my now long-term partner. Yet despite my slightly overwhelming introduction to Lyn's House, I was struck by the warmth and camaraderie of the group, and that's what has kept me coming back for more than three years.

In setting up the house, we hoped to provide a meeting point for people of similar ages living very different lives in the same city, for mutual enrichment. Young people engaged in academic study at Cambridge often feel the strain and pressure of their studies and of social expectations. Lauren says: 'I have just begun a degree at Cambridge University and amidst all the craziness and pressure of study, this community has been a place of restoration, and friendship, and peace. It is the highlight of my week every time I get to come.' Heidi, a resident, comments: 'My time at Lyn's House teaches me so much. In the busyness of lectures and deadlines, it can be easy to lose touch with other aspects of people's lives.' Over time, for busy people in their twenties and early thirties who are working and studying in Cambridge, there can be a sense of rebalancing of life away from our own version of the 'cult of normalcy'.[4] Rebecca reflects on the contrast with other social spaces: 'Opposed to so many academically minded, ostensibly social gatherings where the emphasis may be on "demonstrating" or "collaborating" or "networking" or even "creating", Lyn's House is a place for existing honestly and presently.'

For Rebecca and other non-resident members of the community who have left a parental home but not yet set up a settled household for themselves the house has become 'home': 'Lyn's House has become a kind of second home for me not because I've ever lived there, but because of how the community accepts all of its members as we are. Like a home, Lyn's House is a place where it is safe for me to be exhausted or frustrated or down, as long as I live in the present and keep on trying. Like a home, Lyn's House has been a constant in my life despite Cambridge's constant churn of terms, students, fieldwork, holidays, and visitors. Like a home, the Lyn's House family cares less about what I am and more about who I am.'

I Had No Idea

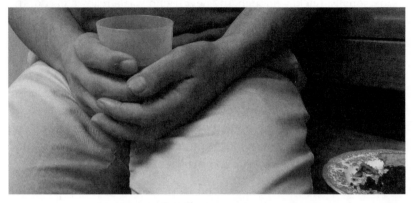

Sunday tea party

> *'Grace, for the Christian believer, is a transformation*
> *that depends in large part on knowing yourself to be*
> *seen in a certain way: as significant, as wanted.'*[5]

Friendship is not easily defined, but it has emerged as a major theme in this book. One of the deepest desires a parent has is that their child should find friends. For the parent of a child with a learning disability this can be an acute longing which continues as the son or daughter becomes an adult. The mother of a young man in his early twenties says, 'He values friendship greatly but is sensitive if he feels people don't immediately agree with him – he feels very rejected.' The parent of another says, 'Making friends is hard for him', adding, 'fortunately he likes his own company.'

The parents of young people with disabilities who are part of the Lyn's House community identify it as above all a place of friendship. Of the young man who 'likes his own company', his mother says, 'He's really enjoyed being able to make friends at Lyn's House.' Another parent tells me, 'Our daughter has lots of friends through Lyn's House. It is so precious to her.' Although the housemates are not the same from year to year, there is a continuous culture. 'What's important is the friendships she can have. Even though they come and go she still makes friends.' The diversity and variety of the community is appreciated: 'She has met with good differences – the cultural differences of the housemates, someone who is vegan.' Over time, these friendships can even build the sense of a 'second home': 'I can't think of anywhere else she'd rather go apart from being with her family. It's so important to her.'

These relationships are seen as significantly different from the relationships that people with a learning disability have with paid 'carers'. 'He's shut up in a flat on a new development on the edge of town – it's independent living with carers in each evening. He doesn't really have friends apart from through church.' 'It's so nice to know she is going somewhere she really likes, somewhere where she hasn't got carers and she hasn't got us, but she's with friends. She can just be Lizzie.' 'Our daughter says of one of the house members, 'She's my friend.' They keep up with each other through social media. The carers and staff she has for other things aren't friends in that way.' What qualities make up these relationships? 'The people at Lyn's House have the ability to be friendly, not patronising.' 'There's an acceptance of people.' 'There is a way of accepting and gently steering.' 'It is a tremendously loving and confidence-boosting place for a very diverse and different range of people and needs.' 'I think you've got it spot on. There's the ability to sit lightly and retain a free spirit.'

In a friendship, the expectation is that both parties feel cared about, rather than being an asymmetrical relationship in which one cares for the other, and there is mutual trust and mutual choosing.[6] 'People want to be there and have a relationship with him – it's not a job. It's something they've chosen. It's a subtle thing, isn't it?' 'Everywhere else there are sort of rules and expectations. The carers find it hard that she goes somewhere where she doesn't have carers or us. If they go somewhere with her they stick to her very closely. At Lyn's House she's free.' Some parents appreciate how the Christian commitment of the community alters the relational dynamic. 'Because it is faith based it is different from professional care. There is a big difference.' 'It makes a difference that it's Christian, absolutely. I'm sure she gets that. "Care plans" include spiritual/faith needs, in theory, but it depends on shifts and so on and they don't always get what it means. They treat it as just another option or activity.'

To live independently with disabilities is to risk hostility, mockery and more serious abuse. 'He's not disabled enough to have a bus pass, so he walks, but walking isn't easy for him and he doesn't walk in a normal way so people make fun of him. There are other times when he has said he has received verbal abuse.' For parents, knowing that their adult son or daughter is safe with other people relieves them of anxiety. 'It is safe for her.' 'It's nice he can go where I don't have to worry about him.' 'She can laugh or cry and that won't be abused.' 'It is a safe listening place for her.' On more than one occasion, young people with learning disabilities have talked to their friends at the house about abusive treatment, one from a taxi driver and another from a carer. 'She used Lyn's House to disclose something, a safeguarding incident with her carers that she hadn't told anyone else. She doesn't like to upset us.'

Although parents appreciate that 'it is open to us as well, and we know who is involved', Lyn's House is a setting in which young people with disabilities can also be independent of parents. 'Lizzie organises it herself – she just needs help with the details.' Occasionally parents have been almost pushed out of the door by their son or daughter when they drop them off for a social event. The independence is valued on both sides. 'We get to go for a walk together – we like being at Lyn's House too, and talking to people, but we don't want to stifle her.' 'I don't really know what goes on at Lyn's House; it's a place for him to be himself without his parents, and to let people see his talents.' 'It gives us a few hours together as parents. It's great that she also gets transport which adds to the time we have while she's there.' It is not always easy to balance safety with freedom, but 'at Lyn's House she's free. It's hard to say how much it means to her: it means so much.'

Our shared life overflows the physical 'house of hospitality' with its residential community. We have been invited to shows in which friends appear, and dinner at their houses; taken part together in a diocesan day of healing; been welcomed to a college chapel for Evensong and its dining hall for dinner; celebrated weddings and mourned the loss of a member of the community together at a funeral. Cambridge is a small city, and our paths regularly cross around the town, as in this chance encounter: 'Lyn's House is his only social outlet. He loves it, especially being with other people. We went out to lunch in town recently and he met someone from Lyn's House, and suddenly they were shaking hands, they were so friendly and having really interesting conversations. I thought, good heavens, is this my son? I had no idea.'

I Want to Tell You Something

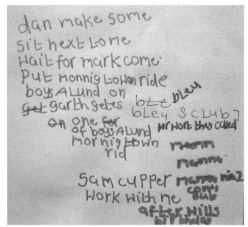

Pages from Amy's book

Cambridge is a university city and as is common in university environments there is a strongly verbal, logical culture, where the ability to express complex ideas quickly and eloquently is highly prized, and there is an accepted cultural 'etiquette' of conversation which easily excludes people.[7] For some of us our involvement with Lyn's House has meant finding ourselves at a loss as we struggle to find new ways of communicating and learn from each other. Sam says, 'It was often frustrating to see how easily volunteers and housemates could start up conversations around the table which just completely excluded our friends with disabilities.' We have not developed ways of communicating which are less verbal, less linear, or less competitive. Rather than at loggerheads, face to face, we have had to learn to communicate sideways or in a circular way, or via an activity around which we are gathered, such as cooking, felt-making, painting, making Christmas decorations or planting bulbs in the garden; playing games together such as Jenga; face-painting. Seeing how someone skilled in the art of creating with paint or cloth communicates has been a revelation to those of us who are narrowly verbal.

We have had to learn how to communicate where there is little or no spoken response. Amy doesn't speak, but communicates through drawing pictures and writing simple messages, and through gestures, expressions, touch; through participation in or withdrawal from activities. For one of the housemates Amy's presence has been a highlight of his time in the house: 'All the evenings with Amy, being invited by her quietness and slowness to just take things easy, to really pay attention to her and make sure she wasn't excluded. Similarly, Jennifer says, 'I developed a particularly strong friendship with one of our guests, Amy. Amy is unique in that she doesn't speak. This made her very vulnerable to being ignored, which I feared sometimes happened amongst the hubbub of the evening meals. However, her peacefulness was such a soothing presence, and when you gave her space to write down or sign her ideas, she had an amazing sense of humour. Being so steady and calm, Amy became a really helpful friend to me when I felt stressed because of things in my work and personal life.'

Singing and making music together have provided some of the deepest experiences of communication. Sam remembers how one friend at Lyn's House started playing the piano and he realised she was playing a song he always used to listen to when he was homesick. She was not aware of that connection. On another occasion there was only one house member and one friend for the dinner. They took turns singing songs to one another for an hour. 'Singing along together to well-known musical films such as *The Sound of Music* and *The Lion King* – one of the happiest things I've ever done and it took me back to being a child, in a way that was very healing.'

As in any circle of friends, born storytellers can delight us, or go on too long, or go off the rails. One man loves to improvise verbally on a theme or scenario during dinner, gleefully peopling his fantastic narrative with those present. Another begins with an everyday remembered incident that then morphs into a rollicking magical tale of adventure. Others have particular gifts of listening, attention, memory, acceptance. One friend, Christopher, has a musical memory that those who know him are aware of as being an astonishing gift, but appreciating it takes time and attention. His mother says: 'Our son is adopted, from when he was four days old. We weren't aware he had special needs. He has an amazing memory, for example the way he can conduct a whole symphony, his attention to detail.' She adds: 'He's very accepting of people – I wish everyone was more like him.' Another friend, Anthony, is known for his calm acceptance of everyone around him and his way of being is the antithesis of the competitive culture that some of us inhabit.

. Michael's mother comments, 'It's not easy for people like him to express an opinion.' But, she says, he and others have found that 'there's the freedom and space to say what he thinks' at Lyn's House.

How do you think that happens? 'People have antennae out to pick up non-verbal cues.' 'The patience I've witnessed in those at Lyn's House, keeping listening and conversation open and being interested enough to keep trying to understand and help him and others express themselves. He feels people don't listen for long enough and usually think they know what he's going to say. They help him feel he has something valuable to say and contribute and that matters. It is uplifting to see them respecting and listening to my son. It is an anchor for him. He has developed meaningful relationships.'

I'm Jesus

'An Impromptu Passion Play' by Daisy Prior

At the first tea party after Easter, Samuel directed us in an impromptu Passion Play. We were in the studio, chatting, eating cake and drinking tea as usual. Some people had been to see a Passion Play at a local church in Holy Week and were talking about it, and Samuel said something like, 'We'll do a play – I will be Jesus', pointing at himself.

Samuel was clear that we would start with the Last Supper. There was a low table – we gathered round it, sitting or crouching on the floor, as he directed, with Samuel sitting in the middle of one long side. A plastic cup of Coke and a piece of bread on a plate were found. Samuel prayed over them, holding them, and as he passed them round he told us that one of us would betray him. We spoke our lines – a shared story that we all knew: 'Is it I? Am I the one?' Owen spontaneously became Judas and slunk away to betray Jesus.

We became more absorbed, responding to his directions and his seriousness, but also laughing and excited as we grabbed props, cloths, dried flowers, brooms and furniture. Samuel held his two roles together like two natures, the suffering Jesus and the director of the drama. We moved to the garden of Gethsemane – a pot of dried flowers. I became Peter and Dennis, interpreter of John's Gospel, became John. Samuel fell to the ground and prayed – 'Take this cup away!' crying out in pain and fear, longing to understand. Guards seized him. As he was taken away for trial, the onlookers, pressed around the walls of the room, took roles, or sat engrossed. I crouched by an imaginary fire and was challenged to admit that I knew him. Did I know Samuel? Would I admit to knowing him in public? 'I don't know him,' I said, the words taking on new meaning.

Samuel lay on the floor with his arms stretched out on a garden broom as imaginary nails were driven in. Two others were crucified alongside him, on mops. Samuel stood with the broom across his shoulders, and concentrated on placing one foot over the other, as in paintings of the crucifixion, with a single nail through the feet – stumbling, trying, losing his balance, trying again. Women knelt at the foot of the cross, taking on the poses familiar from so many paintings of the crucifixion.

Samuel cried out to God, and then his head fell forwards. Someone sitting near the curtains pulled them apart. Hands reached out to help lay him down and carry him to the tomb, a sofa, and roll a round table on its side across to hide him. The mood was quiet – by now everyone in the room was absorbed in the drama, the serious playfulness of playing out the Passion, watching, speaking, saying the familiar words, improvising, suggesting what to use as props, deferring to Samuel who had it all clearly in his mind, simultaneously a lifeless body and director of the action.

Samuel showed the woman playing the role of Mary how he should sit on a low chair with her back to him, so that when he said her name she would turn round and see him. 'Mary,' he said, intensely and solemnly. 'Master,' said Mary. She ran joyfully to tell the others. Was that the end? we wondered. No, now the scene with Doubting Thomas.

And then did we finish? I don't remember. As often at Lyn's House, someone's taxi arrived and it was the beginning of the end of the party. Ordinary time resumed. We put away the props and thanked Samuel.

That was the day Samuel was Jesus. We are taught to see the face of Christ in the face of our neighbour and especially in the faces of those sometimes thought of as 'outcasts'. That day those words came to life.

I Don't Want to Go

Lizzie's hand

'Am I capable of love? ... I fail daily and fall out of the sky... I do not need to know the future.'

(From a poem by Luke, a house resident)

We have seen and experienced new kinds of pain, frustration and bewilderment through our shared life at Lyn's House. Sometimes, for those of us who are not living daily with learning disabilities, this has been a way of appreciating the experiences of others; sometimes we have learned to do things differently; often, we have to simply continue to live with the difficulty and puzzlement.

One evening, when Karen came to dinner, she wouldn't go home. She had recently moved, or rather been moved, to a care home, because of her increasing need for physical care, and 'home' was now an unfamiliar place full of strangers. 'It hurts,' she said. 'Where?' 'My leg,' said Karen, her face full of pain. The taxi came to collect her, and Karen couldn't move, and resisted the hands that tried to help her. The pain in her face made her friends reluctant to push or cajole. Eventually, someone went with her, hoping that would help her to sense the care that we all wanted to convey to her, but leaving her still felt like the cruel desertion of a friend. When Karen died, a few months later, the pain of her death recalled the pain of that evening.

When verbal communication is limited, touch becomes important, and when a friend depends on physical help, it is natural for someone stronger to offer it. What, though, if touching becomes a problem? Whose needs and vulnerability should come first, and how can everyone be made welcome and safe? How to express the equality of friendship, and at the same time protect vulnerable people from harm? The possibility of an intimate relationship with a partner, marriage, and the full expression of sexuality – these are aspects of life that are not equally open to many people with a learning disability. This is an area of painful difference, not difference of desire, but of unequal possibilities for expressing it.

We also, as a community, have to face and work within the finitude of our resources. Although contact and events continue all year round, the regular hospitality of the house is confined to term-times. 'It's hard when it's the holidays and the meals stop but we can understand why,' says a parent. Friendship and visits to a welcoming home can be a support but not take away apprehensions about the future. 'We're getting older... It means a lot to have people we know he can trust if he ever has a difficulty. He can be quite vulnerable.' 'He doesn't have much professional support – he's quite able in many ways, and we provide a lot of support, but we won't be around for ever. 'We're getting on, getting older and trying to plan provision for him but we don't know what to do. He'd be much better in a shared house.'

Time Stands Still

In the garden

'People don't have time these days – they're too
busy rushing on to the next thing. Lyn's House is
a place where time stands still for a bit.'

(Parent of one of the core friends)

It is a Sunday afternoon in July. A circle of garden chairs, benches, rugs and sofas in the garden; smoke from the barbecue on the patio; slicing and chopping of salad in the kitchen. Andrew, in trilby and apron, is in charge of barbecuing: he has lived in the house for three years and it is hard to imagine it without him. We're here to finish the year with farewells to the housemates who are leaving, but there are also visitors from a L'Arche community to welcome, and the fiancé of a house member who is getting married next month. We sit in a circle, and these important events are named, with cheers for the couple to be married, a welcome for the visitors, and then spontaneous speeches, with very openly expressed sadness, for those who are leaving: 'We will miss you very much.' 'To belong,' Swinton says, 'you need to be missed.'[8]

The age we live in has been characterised as one of 'lonely mindedness', in which many of us fall into a 'habit of isolation.'[9] The Lyn's House community is formed from a mixture of people who have experience of different kinds of loneliness. For some of us, the continued dependence of an adult son or daughter limits the time we have for deep companionship with our partner or friends. For others, our adult children have moved away, our homes are quiet, and we look back and forwards, reassessing what we value. Some of us are experiencing the anxious, striving and competitive culture of twenty-somethings who live alone while seeking intimacy. Some have been encouraged into a form of 'supported independent living' in which their main day-to-day contact is with paid carers. Busy graduate students and young people in their first adult job work long hours, while their closest friends live far away. For all of us, in different ways, hidden hurts and fears isolate us because we dread exposing them.

Both friendship and a form of shared life are therefore deep desires with which we are all familiar, despite our differences. Together, we have stumbled upon a way of overcoming isolation via shared hospitality. It is a very 'little way', to use the words of the Carmelite St Therese: one house, in one town; a few handfuls of people, some who stay while others move away; showing up regularly to eat and drink together, and being glad to be in each other's company, though sometimes puzzled or annoyed by one other; constantly encouraged by finding how much it means to us all. This 'smallness' is what Buber calls 'the tiny strictness and grace of the everyday': [10] 'strictness' in the sense of something that is detailed, up close, and drawn together, rather than something grand, or general, or at a distance. It is made up of this cup of tea that someone is making me now, this picture that I am drawing at the table with my friend, this song we're singing along to for the third or tenth time together this evening, this former stranger who is becoming a friend.

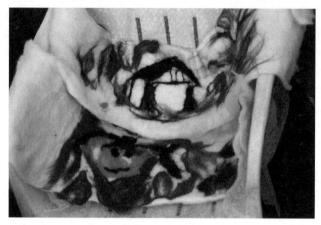

Artwork from the felting day

Endnotes

1 Jean Vanier, *Community and Growth* (revised edition) (London: Darton, Longman and Todd, 2007), pp.271, 265.
2 Janet M. Soskice, *The Kindness of God* (Oxford: Oxford University Press, 2007), p.176.
3 Jean Vanier uses the word 'foyer', meaning 'hearth', to refer to a L'Arche household.
4 Thomas Reynolds, *Vulnerable Communion: A Theology of Disability and Hospitality* (Grand Rapids, MI: Brazos Press, 2008), p.19.
5 Rowan Williams, 'The Body's Grace', in Eugene Rogers, Jr. (ed.), *Theology and Sexuality* (Oxford: Blackwell, 2002), p.311.
6 For more see R. Pockney, 'Friendship or Facilitation: People with Learning Disabilities and Their Paid Carers', *Sociological Research Online* 11, Issue 3 (2006), pp.1–9.
7 See John Swinton, 'From Inclusion to Belonging: A Practical Theology of Community, Disability and Humanness', *Journal of Religion, Disability & Health* 16, No. 2 (2012), pp.172–190.
8 Swinton, 'From Inclusion to Belonging: A Practical Theology of Community, Disability and Humanness', p.183.
9 Samuel Kimbriel, *Friendship as Sacred Knowing: Overcoming Isolation* (Oxford: Oxford University Press, 2014), p.1.
10 Martin Buber, *Between Man and Man*, trans. R.G. Smith (London: Kegan Paul, 1947), p.36.

CHAPTER 3

Living in Community that Embraces Others

E.S. Kempson

'Will you be my friend?' One little question, flickering with longing and love, sparked Jean Vanier to create L'Arche communities. As Deborah Hardy Ford recounts, his vision caught alight in her, blazed into the Lyn's House project, and continues to grow ever brighter even as it changes. Judith Gardom has taken this further in looking at the experiences of the core friends and others involved. In this chapter we will see especially the residential community's life and workings. My experience as a housemate in the community combined with wisdom from other housemates and the steering group inform this chapter.[1]

A Two-Sided Ethos

Our project has two distinctive traits: a residential Christian community and hosting people with intellectual disabilities. Linked with this, two elements have combined to create the distinctive character of Lyn's House. First, there are meals and social events that treasure and befriend people with intellectual disabilities ('core friends'), placing them at the heart of our activities. Second, there is a residential community ('housemates' or house members) committed to supporting these events, in friendship and love, and with the support of others (volunteers and a steering group). Together we do our best to form a community which creates a welcome for everyone who comes. Just as when hydrogen and oxygen combine, they make water, so whenever these two elements combine, there is a community that embraces others.

It is important to note that the community is *not* just the housemates. Everyone involved is a part of the community, from those who originally caught the vision, to the first core friend befriended, to the newest volunteer. This is why we name our members with intellectual disabilities 'core friends'; they are the very reason for existence, the *raison d'être*, of the entire project and community. They are not simply 'friends' (which would imply the other people involved are not friends) or simply 'guests' (which would imply they are optional additions to a pre-existing community). We build around our core friends, like the central beam of a house. They hold everything together. The community's foundation is the residential Christian community. They turn the house from a mere venue into a home. They are the main hosts who provide welcome. These two counter-cultural elements – centring the marginalised and a non-familial home-community – are the apex and foundation of all we build together, a house with many rooms.

It is readily apparent that our two-part ethos – fellowship with the intellectually disabled and a faith-grounded home-community – has a Christian foundation. Christ shared food with people society disregarded, and gave time to people with disabilities. Christ's followers are told to find and serve him in those who are in need. Jesus starkly asserts this radical alternative to typical family life when he denies his mother and brothers and says, 'Whoever does the will of God is my brother, and sister, and mother' (Mark 3:31–35; cf. Matt. 12:45–50). A new community forms itself, united by devotion to God.

Of course, many who are not Christians also value and ardently aid those with learning disabilities, offering love, hospitality and friendship. A number of individuals who are crucial to the creation and flourishing of Lyn's House have been of other faiths or none. Lyn's House is a product of Christian faith, but it does not require Christian faith from all its members – and even those who are Christians come from a variety of traditions. From these diverse belief systems, we have come to find the same treasure, such that we can be united in deeply meaningful work.

Deliberating on Life in Community

There have been five 'generations' of housemates thus far, each bringing personal histories, expectations, strengths, concerns and hopes. Loraine Gelsthorpe, as a steering group member, used an adapted concept of 'deliberative enquiry' over time, aiming to promote open discussion with Lyn's House members and listening to different perspectives.[2] This exercise recognised that with annual changes of housemates in Lyn's House there have been rapid changes in dynamics, with more challenges in some years than in others. But her enquiry showed that their 'Christian bonds and aspirations to be genuine friends to the "core friends", even if time-limited, have produced remarkable resilience, energy and creativity amongst the different groups'.

From the first, there has been an awareness of being involved in something new and exciting. One early resident member described joining the house, saying:

> Coming to Cambridge to study was a bit of a culture shock; being surrounded by driven people, reaching to be the best, I often felt like I was playing catch up. Somehow the invitation to be part of Lyn's House felt like an antidote. It was going to take time and energy but offered something of Jesus that I wasn't getting elsewhere. We were to develop a seed of an idea which was fragile and exciting. It led us to journey not individualistically but in community; not moving quickly but journeying alongside, at the pace of another – embracing those who might otherwise be left behind.

Another housemate gave voice to this hope for a different life:

> I pray that my time in 'Lyn's House' will continue to encourage me to live a slower paced life, accept my limitations, and to take pleasures in the little things of life.

Housemates have articulated different views of the same vision. One spoke of 'living out a moral obligation to strangers', while another most hoped for 'a loving community of diverse members', and another specifically highlighted 'the goal to provide hospitality to, and include in the centre of community life, people with learning disabilities'. Loraine Gelsthorpe noticed that, throughout, the language of 'journey' has come up.

> We've sort of learned how to be with friends together. You have to look and listen and be attentive and to learn where someone is coming from...and there have been struggles, but also companionship on the journey of discovery.

Another described the journey this way:

> We were all rather nervous to begin with, and rather daunted by the prospect of learning to live with a different group of people as well as making the commitment to meet with friends each week. It seemed rather a lot to take on. But we'd all been students at one point or another, however, and so took it in our stride. You gulp and get on with it.

If these reflections highlight aspects of community life, others deliberated on how shared meals with intellectually disabled friends illuminated their thinking.

One indicated:

> It has profoundly changed the way I think, act and define what 'normal' is... Sometimes after a long day at work the thought of hosting a meal can be quite daunting, yet I always end the evening feeling so energised and so nourished... It became clear to me very early on that the benefits flow in both directions.

Another resident described a special moment:

> We've been entrusted with a vision for the house. I've learned about patience and about being able to dwell in moments with people; there's no need to rush things. This is so refreshing. I spent ten minutes looking at a leaf with one friend. I learned so much from the experience of just being...emptying my mind of everything else just to be there with that person and to enjoy the moment.

Since the housemates are working adults, having a place to slow down, to be silly, to stop working or rushing and just be present, is an incredible gift. As people speak of the project, they touch upon how much being a housemate can change a person in relation to others.

> The experience of living in Lyn's House has been a blessing for me. I've grown emotionally, psychologically, and socially.
>
> I've surprised myself. I've surprised those who know me, my family and friends outside Lyn's House. There have been challenges, of course, but together we have overcome some of them.

Loraine Gelsthorpe observed that there have been mountains and cul de sacs in the journey for the housemates. Alongside the ordinary challenges of sorting out chores and feeling some were left doing more than others, there have been concerns that some were largely absent apart from their weekly commitments.

Living together has demanded continual effort to find a rhythm for daily life and hosting friends. It can be a lot for the housemates to take on: living in community, building a welcoming home, and doing the welcoming. It is easy to overlook most of what housemates accomplish because it is done in private. One description of this experience gives a hint of the interior changes.

> We are busy young people, us living in the house, and the little things (and practical things) are sometimes skipped over. Yet when we host others, we have to pay attention to both the state of the kitchen – which we've not remembered to tidy up for one another – and are constantly encouraged to slow down, to pause to let people form their thoughts and express their words, to gently guide someone from one room to the next, and to take time to put down the books and play snakes and ladders – switching off that part of my brain that says – 'Shouldn't you be working?'

Finally, a number of former housemates have found that their time there has shaped their sense of vocation and direction in life. More than one has been in theological training or started to pursue ordination. An early housemate says:

> The experience of living here has been wonderful. I think that it has helped me realise what I want to do in life or more the way I would like to be. I feel privileged to have been part of the adventure.

Personally, I had already found my vocation, to be a theologian. But I was looking for community when I came to Lyn's House. Living there was more of a home than any other arrangement in more than a decade since moving away from my parents. Being with friends always felt like a temporary measure, and it seemed the only stable homes were with romantic life partners. Lyn's House, however, changed my mind and heart. I would have been happy to stay years longer. When I did leave to marry my now husband, I was able to choose marriage from a place of freedom, not loneliness. My time at Lyn's House taught me that I could find a love in our community that would sustain me, that if romantic love had not happened into my life, I could still have a home shared with others, bonded through more than friendship – with a greater purpose that held true even when our feelings for each other faltered. This meant that as our own friendships grew, they reached into the deepest commitments and recesses of ourselves, usually only shared with God. I will always be thankful for this gift of home beyond family, a way of living differently and hopefully.

The Body and Its Members

There are many members that can make up the body of a community that embraces others. Much like describing the church as the body of Christ (1 Cor. 12:12–26), each of our different members is important for the health and life of the whole. As in First Corinthians, the parts of the body that seem weaker are actually indispensable and so are invested with greater honour. Thus, the core friends form the heart of our community. What follows are brief notes as to the role of each type of member at Lyn's House and my own thoughts on what form they might take in other similar communities.

Core Friends (Heart)

Core friends are individuals with intellectual disabilities who attend our weekly meals and special events. They are the heart of our community because they are its *raison d'être* and provide supporting friendships to those who come to know them.

Our core friends were originally found and invited through pre-existing friendships and church community connections. Subsequently, word of mouth (sometimes from one core friend to another) has expanded the group. Those without such connections could contact local churches or support networks and activity centres for people with intellectual disabilities, thereby spreading the word and finding interested individuals.

The House (Skeleton)

The house is where the core meals and most social events are hosted, as well as where the housemates live. This is the skeleton because it is the solid physical structure which literally supports the gatherings of the Lyn's House community.

Other like-minded individuals would need a large enough kitchen and dining room to host the core meals and space for the housemates' daily lives too. Ideally, there would be an area for prayer, though this could be done at the dining room table. A large garden or room for larger monthly gatherings is also desirable, though this could be held at a publicly available space if necessary (e.g. a church hall or park).

There are multiple ways to secure a domestic space: as with Lyn's House, a home-owner with a property could allot their house to the project; a group of housemates could decide to rent a property together with the express purpose of forming a community; a church could elect to use its residential property; or an individual could decide to open his/her own home to housemates for the purpose.

Housemates (Muscles)

Housemates are the members who live in our residential community together, shaped by prayer and hosting the majority of events. They are the muscles because they keep the project moving on a day-to-day and week-to-week basis.

At Lyn's House, housemates have been individuals without intellectual disabilities who are financially independent, whether in work or full-time study, and have paid a market rent for their rooms. Sometimes housemates are found through word of mouth and sometimes volunteers decide to become housemates. We have found at Lyn's House, however, that it is beneficial to advertise the opening positions when people move on. This has been done through church and academic connections, social circles and flat advertising sites.

Volunteers (Skin)

Our volunteers are adults without intellectual disabilities who attend the core meals, helping with the cooking and prayer, and forming friendships with the core friends and housemates. They are the skin of the body because they serve as sturdy helping hands and a loving touch.

Like the housemates, our volunteers have mostly been found through word of mouth, especially among the ordinands in training in Cambridge. Some have also come as a result of talks given to churches and colleges in the area.

Steering Group (Nervous System and Brain)

The steering group is perhaps the most stable member type, with the core friends a close second, as they are those who initiated the community and maintain its workings from year to year. Like a nervous system, their role may not be immediately apparent in the midst of daily action, but they are vital to connect logistical awareness among the members' different activities; likewise, they are the brain which holds the institutional memory, preserves the spirit of the community, and holds ultimate responsibility for the organisation. In this last instance, long-term organisational, personnel, and financial planning fall under their purview.

The steering group is most naturally composed out of those who gathered to create the community in the first place. They may double as members of other groups as well (e.g. housemates, core friends, volunteers etc.). If a Lyn's-House-type community becomes a registered charity, it would be natural to draw the board of trustees from the group. However, certain skill sets must be represented within a board of trustees, which may be an opportunity to draw members beyond those who have been involved so far.

Guests (Refreshing Water and New Blood)

A guest is anyone who has been invited to attend an event, or to assist in another capacity, but who has not taken on an additional role. At Lyn's House guests have included personal friends, co-workers, academics, priests, friars and people from other similar projects, such as L'Arche. They are like water because they may be with the body briefly, a refreshing presence like a bath, or they may become integrated into it more closely, like drinking water, becoming fresh blood to the whole system. Some of these guests give generous financial support to the community as well.

Guests are almost always found by word of mouth, but they have also emerged from expressions of interest in advertising or related social media, or active pursuit on the part of the steering group.

=※=

Theoretically, a Lyn's-House-type community could run with only the first three members: a place to meet, core friends to gather around, and a Christian community who gathers and hosts. In this case, the housemates would take on roles ascribed to the steering group and volunteers as well. Two other aspects remain, regardless of how many people are involved.

Legal and Safeguarding Elements (Antibodies)

The safeguarding of vulnerable adults is a significant responsibility. To that end, all people who regularly host or support our events, and so may end up alone with a core friend, have undergone a background check (DBS, which stands for Disclosure and Barring Service, in England and Wales – there are similar services in Northern Ireland and Scotland).

Likewise, the responsibility of providing housing and taking generous donations is taken seriously. It is prudent to have typical rental agreements that specify rent, length of tenancy, as well as good financial practice throughout. We have also found it beneficial to have clear allocations of responsibilities among housemates and the steering group regarding utilities, Council Tax and so forth.

These precautions are like the antibodies of a body. They go unnoticed until something goes wrong and then one is beyond thankful to have them – or else it could mean the end of the organisation entirely, not to mention the harm, personal and financial, that it could cause.

Finances (Food)

Finances give the body sustenance to continue. In the case of Lyn's House, this has literally been to put food on the table for events.

The other main expenditure is on taxis to take the core friends to and from events as needed. As I write, a decision has been made to hire an assistant to run the increasingly demanding email, logistics and public relations burden of the project (which so far has fallen on the housemates, leaving the muscles at times with an over-burdensome load).

Fundraising for small items often comes organically; a volunteer refuses to be reimbursed for their dinner groceries; a housemate buys a useful item that the house needs, etc. Larger amounts from local churches, academic and charitable organisations have also been indispensable.

Walking Together Day by Day

Body parts assembled together are merely a cadaver, unless they share an animating life. By the time I arrived at Lyn's House, a rhythm of life had developed. In a typical week, we would have regular times of *prayer* together as housemates, *core meals* with core friends and volunteers, and sometimes a *tea party* on Sunday afternoon with almost everyone: housemates, core friends, volunteers, the steering group and guests. From Monday to Friday, we housemates began our day together before God (and before caffeine!) with *morning prayer* in our small living room. On Monday evening we would also have *housemate dinner*, which was a time to socialise together and address house concerns as well as resolve any logistical details for the week's events. These times were crucial for us living in the house to keep a sense of connection and friendship with each other, even as we ran all the other events.

Core meals are the crucial *sine qua non* of the welcome offered by Lyn's House: two housemates and a few volunteers welcome a handful of core friends for the evening. I have fond memories of laughter over tea, sorrows and triumphs shared in prayer, stories and jokes with dinner and pudding. Each of the gatherings is different, and having a smaller sized group returning fortnightly gives the space and consistency needed for familiarity, security and real friendships to form. Then, at the monthly *tea parties*, everyone would be together, taking over the kitchen-dining room, studio, living room and garden. For a lazy two hours, everyone mingles and gets a chance to meet and know the people who don't attend their own *core meal*. At some point, semi-spontaneous song, storytelling or prayer brings everyone together at once.

Additional gatherings, inviting all the core friends, always seem to be appearing as one-off spin-offs of the core meals. Film nights, arts afternoons and even evensong with a formal hall in college have all punctuated our months. *Steering group meetings* are called bi-monthly to keep everything running smoothly, ensure safeguarding, and foster the inspiring vision, usually with housemates contributing too. An *induction day* has also been effective for getting a new configuration of housemates and volunteers off to a good start. Just as the *core meals* overflow into *additional gatherings*, the life of the house, committee and volunteers has overflown into *additional events*. At various times these have included: *training days*, offered to new volunteers or other people wishing to improve their relationship with intellectually disabled people; *theological discussion days* to reflect on the significance of the project or experiences for faith; and *outreach activities* that bring the gift of the community to those beyond its membership, including public talks (at churches, schools, colleges) and extending to our website, social media presence and newsletter.

There is an element of a bring-and-share lunch to all our events. A few basic ingredients are provided, but the events, relationships and community are built out of what each and every person brings, from the core friends to the most temporary guest. In this way, our community is not a service provider. There is not a product for consumers, or benefits presented to the needy. It is community built out of what each person is willing and able to give in the present day, week, month or year.

Even with our limitations and the little or large ways we fail ourselves and each other, an amazing amount of good has grown out of our community: from the steering group who began a community where there was none, from core friends looking for new friendships, from carers, and from us housemates whose faith joined us together in prayer just as we were joined in the work. Building relationship and community together is its own reward, one of the most important in life: to feel loved and cared for by others, to have people whom one can show love and care for, and to feel God's love as we are with each other through the good times and the bad life has to offer. Whatever else may take up our time and energy, community is knowing that this is a place where one can always be welcomed, as if it were your own home.

Forming and Sustaining a Community

Learning to make a home that embraces others is a bit like baking bread. Only three ingredients are essential: flour, water and heat (for bread) or housemates, a house and time in residence (for a home). But if you want to bake nutritious desirable bread, it is wise not to stop there. Procure the best flour and a reliable oven. Add in rich fats, lifting yeast and tasty seeds. Take care while kneading, give it time to rise, and don't forget to set the timer! Like bread, if you want community life to be fresh and wholesome instead of tough, stale and bland, there are key ingredients and certain practices to add in as well. At Lyn's House, we have been developing our own recipe for community for over five years. From the beginning it has been a treat, but some months our community 'bread' has been overworked, a bit wet, or burnt up. By learning from mistakes, mishaps and triumphs, the bread of 'home' has become more reliably sustaining and deliciously enjoyable. What follows is my list of key ingredients, incorporating advice from a list (contained in Appendix 2: 'Our Accumulated Wisdom for Welcome and Community') contributed by Matthew Harbage, a housemate in the first year of Lyn's House who was an ordinand at Westcott House, Cambridge, and went on to Anglican ministry. These are techniques for making a good home out of a Christian residential community, one bonded by a common intention rather than family ties.

The first key area is communication. To start off on the right foot and keep in step with each other as the weeks pass by, one needs clear open conversation and to revisit topics with care (care for each other). Second come questions of time and space. We've found relationships flourish when housemates spend three types of time together: project, prayer and spare time. As for space, it pays to segment private areas from public ones and to address issues in a spirit of service and patience. Coming to community beyond the housemates, invaluable support has been drawn from individual support networks, a house mentor and the wider Lyn's House community. Lastly, a few words from our struggles with being human, on handling limitations, forgiveness and difficulties when they arise. There are many ways to form community, and this advice is based on our collective experiences, rather than being a final word on the matter.

On Communication

Open caring communication is vital. These are some of the lessons learned. At the outset, discuss and agree on expectations for the community including: what times and activities the housemates expect to have together; how chores will be done; guests staying over; how money is handled; how to raise and address complaints or make changes; romantic relationships within the house; how long each housemate has committed; how someone might leave early if their circumstances change. These need to be agreed, but all decisions may be revised and changed. Starting with an open understanding means that when tasks are undone, people fall short, or someone wants a change (which are to be expected) they can be addressed openly as well. These opening discussions are also an opportunity to connect with each other, discuss different approaches to chores, previous experiences in living with others, preferred ways of dealing with differences, and so forth. Practice having these conversations and getting to know one another is the beginning of growing in knowledge and care as community.

Once there is a shared vision and understanding of community life, it takes attention to sustain it. When four or more live together, accidentally leaving someone out is easy. It's worth agreeing to a fixed time each week to talk about practical house concerns, any plans to travel or have guests, and plans to achieve the community's goals. Our housemate dinners on Monday served this purpose. When issues arise, turn towards each other, not away. Matthew reflected:

> Throughout your life as a community it can be really exciting to dream together about where you are going as a community. Remember forming a community and being a community is a journey. People's roles may change and goals shift over time. Be open to the Spirit leading you in new directions, but also hold on to your core reason for being together.

Reading, individually or together, can also catalyse communication and vision-forming, since there is a wealth of experience already available. Resources include books by and related to: Jean Vanier; the Taizé community (an ecumenical Christian fraternity); traditional monastic Rules of Life (e.g. the Rule of St Benedict, in use for over 1500 years); 'New Monasticism' (contemporary reinventions of monastic practice); and even contemporary relationship advice (e.g. works by John Gottmann or Gary Chapman).

On Time and Space

Project time, prayer time and spare time are each invaluable to community living for different reasons. Spending time together on a project beyond simply being a house community can be crucial. I have lived in flat-shares formed just to be a community of people living a Christian life. We ate and prayed together, and I gained a great deal, but when people fell out or become busy with life, there wasn't much to keep us together. I have found that you need something to help focus the community, put arguments behind you, and remind you why you came together as a group. Providing a welcome for people with intellectual disabilities has done this for us at Lyn's House. When the work comes out of our faith, it binds us with others who share the work, even when we are utterly annoyed or frustrated. It unites us in a way that does not rely on having personality traits or life experience in common. I ultimately found myself with solid friendships where I would have given up under other circumstances.

Praying together, gathering in the Spirit, puts all our effort, turmoil and triumphs into perspective and binds us together. The project 'work' would keep the house functioning, but shared 'work' needs a shared 'why', or else it could slide towards a tenancy agreement with a job attached. We found morning prayer helpful, because we shared our love for God as revealed in Jesus Christ and our commitment to love our neighbour as ourselves. When I was in the house, we came from varied Christian traditions, some in tension with each other. But if we respected each other's core faith as compatible in prayer together (however else our opinions differed) and no one became combative or aggressive on these issues (such behaviour being unacceptable for any reason), then our differences were a source of learning rather than division.

Project time and prayer time may keep a community together, but in order to live harmoniously and weather conflicts, spare time together is vital. These periods are idle, without a set task, talking about something substantial or nothing much. In my time, we reserved ten minutes after morning prayer for tea and coffee and ambient chat. Spare time can be for celebration too. As previous housemate Matthew said, 'Celebrate the little things, and the big things. God loves to bless His children and you will have much to be joyful for I'm sure as you serve him together!' These idle celebratory times are fun, but also necessary. This is when a sense of group-ness, of knowing each other personally, is developed. It is like cartilage between bones – there will be points of friction when complaints are brought up and changes made, but if those are the only time when housemates see each other outside prayer and the project, it will be blunt, painful and, in all likelihood, ineffective. The 'spare' time, idle time, you spend with each other is like the cartilage in the joint – it needs to be there ahead of time to cushion when friction arises. When relationships had become edgy and tense, the ten minutes over tea and coffee completely turned things around.

When it comes to space, everyone needs privacy, especially people who regularly host others in their own home. We found it useful to divide our house in half, into space for the housemates' private use and more public space for events. This way, housemates could come and go as they needed, regardless, and the broader Lyn's House community could be at home in their own familiar space without feeling invasive. For us, there was a side entrance to the house which facilitated this nicely, allowing frequent independent access to the kitchen-dining room, prayer-living room, studio and garden, while housemates had a space all their own: the front entrance and hall, the bedrooms and upstairs. Importantly, housemates were free to use the more public spaces as they saw fit outside events, and could always pop in to say hello or use the kitchen.

Regular household tasks are better approached as acts of care and loving service rather than as 'a chore' or points of pride. When dishes and hoovering are rota items, they tend to fall to the bottom of everyone's to-do list. Then it can become a question of who is the first to break down and do what needs doing. But chores need not be mere tasks when we live in community. They are an opportunity to show care – noticing, sharing and doing – for the other people we live with and those who we host too. Likewise, it is important to express discontent in a clear and collaborative manner, rather than taking umbrage or sulking, so that an approach that works for everyone can be found. Everyone has different standards, habits and views on cleaning practice, and it takes time, patience and compromise to collaboratively find a solution for all involved.

On Wider Community Support

Life from before Lyn's House continues, and so one naturally should continue one's individual support circle and old self-care habits or practices that are self-grounding. This includes personal prayer or worship life, because being in a praying community will not replace that. It is also important to keep in touch with your people outside the community: family, friends, church community, spiritual directors and mentors, even therapists. They can help to orient us when we're feeling low, lonely, or need help with direction. Vice versa, experiences and insight from living in community may contribute to some of them in their lives as well.

In Lyn's House, there has never been an official leader or head of house. With only four housemates, creating a house hierarchy has been unnecessary, but a need has been felt for mentorship, guidance and accountability. An older wiser Christian, experienced with community living, is an invaluable resource, and this year, for the first time, one has been appointed. It is best for this individual not to be a member of the steering group, so that the mentor can focus on the health and life of the housemates together, undistracted by concerns of running the project. Additionally, living together means sharing our personal lives with each other, something that the volunteers, core friends and steering group are not necessarily involved in. It means being trusted with other housemates' personal lives, confidences, vulnerabilities and hopes. It seems best for the mentor to be able to keep the whole house's confidence and to be the only one acting in this regard. Otherwise, the risk of broken confidences or favouritism could spoil the good of having a mentor and guide through Christian community living. In addition to a mentor, housemates of previous generations can be an invaluable source of wisdom too.

Times spent playing games with core friends, touching base with volunteers, and working with the steering group can all be a support to community living as well. Sometimes, stress among housemates comes from trying to do too much, so when the steering group members provide relief from tasks this can work wonders. Having a debrief with volunteers or chat over a drink grows the circle of friendship and wards off any sense of isolation. The core friends especially give everyone a chance to leave behind concerns of the day and simply be present. Providing hospitality becomes a two-way street of friendship, if we let ourselves receive and do not insist on always being the ones who give.

On Being Human

Accepting our limitations has been a theme from the beginning. As one of the first residents, Matthew, said of the housemates:

> We are all able-bodied people, with no immediately visible disabilities. Yet we have been learning, in many different ways, that we all have disabilities of one sort or another, and have been growing in our understanding of what it means to serve others out of our own limitations.

Remembering our limitations, being gentle with others and ourselves, includes being realistic when we set community goals and expectations. It is wise to balance time constraints within a structure that facilitates creativity instead of constraining it. For some, making time for rest and potentially space away from the community house has been restorative. I have grown wary of imbalances among the commitments of each housemate to the project, even if they appear voluntary. For, as Matthew observed, 'It's part of life that we often want to do far more than we have capacity to do. Somehow being 'limited' is part of what it means to be human, and we do ourselves harm when we try to pretend we aren't.'

Forgiveness is, in some ways, the currency of communities. Living with other people means our private lives overlap. We discover things we enjoy and find annoying about housemates, and probably find out what they like and don't like about us. Matthew again:

> If you are honest and caring with one another, you can learn a lot about yourself (both strengths and weaknesses). This is an amazing opportunity to love one another, and to bring yourself honestly before God when you pray, warts and all. It is an opportunity to love one another unconditionally – to show one another the love of God even when you don't think the person in front of you deserves very much. You will probably fail a lot at loving one another so forgiving one another is therefore an essential gift in community. Forgiving yourself for your faults, and others theirs, and forgiving one another when you fail to love each other as you should.

Living together can be healing, or it can bring discord, if people turn against each other. When people turn away from each other, stalemates, stonewalling and passive aggression can turn into a cold war. Caring and hopefully forgiveness involve turning *towards* each other, not away or against. Taking time alone to cool off and gain perspective is OK, as long as a return is made when the opportunity arises. Forgiveness does not mean pretending no wrongs have been committed or mistakes made. It means facing them together and searching for a collaborative way forward.

Difficulties are inevitable. Broadly speaking, there are two kinds of difficulties that emerge for a household, ones from within and ones from without. It is the nature of communities that there will be disagreements, communication mishaps and hurt feelings. What makes a healthy community is not the absence of such things, but how they are dealt with. For challenges within a community like Lyn's House, I would suggest a modified version of Matthew 18:15–17. When a difficulty arises with a housemate, this means speaking to her/him individually to see if the two involved can resolve it together. If that fails, then raise it among all the housemates together to see if a collaborative solution and reconciliation can be found. If that too is unsuccessful, the issue can be taken to the appointed mentor of the house, so that their guidance may show a way forward and their wisdom may judge the matter. If at this point the problem is irreconcilable, even with an 'agree to disagree' approach, then it is time to reconsider whether the combination of housemates is best for all involved.

Exterior difficulties arise as well. Occasionally, housemates have felt abandoned by the steering group, especially when tasked with dealing with behavioural challenges of individual core friends or having unreasonable expectations placed upon them. For such exterior difficulties, it seems best to begin by discussing the issue as housemates among ourselves. Then, turning to the steering group with a common mind, it is easier to see how the situation may be addressed. Often, difficulties between housemates are side-effects from challenges related to the project. When there has been frequent contact between the steering group and housemates, that is all the easier and to the good. I have found that when housemates spend 'spare time' with the steering group this also cushions interactions, benefiting the broader community. Depending upon the exterior difficulty, the need for a pool of volunteers, inclusion of the housemates in some of the steering group's decisions about the house, and additional training has been valuable.

Creating a Welcome

If making a home is like baking bread, then creating a welcome is breaking bread to share with others. Creating a genuine welcome – the positive atmosphere of true hospitality – requires more than good intentions or plentiful tea and cake. Without preparation, appropriate organisation and resources, what was meant to be 'welcoming' could be as appetising as a well-intentioned mess, a half-baked lopsided confection. From my first core meal, I have never had cause to doubt the profound and lasting positive impact of Lyn's House on core friends. Their joy is unmistakable, as should be apparent from the previous chapter. But at times, things are untidy and less than what they could be. This is not a matter to simply muddle through. Because we are dealing with vulnerable adults, the consequences of a well-intentioned mess could be incredibly negative or hurtful. It takes confidence to know how to provide hospitality, and confidence to be vulnerable to those you invite to dinner. For this reason, I and others have accumulated wisdom from half a decade of creating a home that embraces others, and compiled it into appendices at the end of this book. If the vision's spark alights among other people, may this help you build another roaring fire – warming hearts and bringing light to darkness.

Possible Directions

As I think of my time in Lyn's House, it inspires me to imagine ways its two-sided ethos could come to life in new forms. There are intriguing permutations and variations of the Lyn's House model, some edging outside of it. Clearly, a few determined individuals may decide to begin a community in their own area – a new house, with new housemates, and new core friends – finding themselves building relationships they'd never had before. At its most basic, all you really need are housemates, core friends and a house.

There can also be non-residential approaches. This would consist of gatherings hosted in pre-existing homes. The loss of an intentional community and a consistent space would be felt, because of the familiarity and continuity that it brings (especially for those with learning disabilities). Nevertheless, the hospitality of opening and sharing one's home is valuable.

Alternatively, some individuals could decide to create a non-familial Christian home, and then welcome a different marginalised or vulnerable group. Welcome and hospitality could be extended, for instance, to refugees, at-risk children or adolescents, foreign students, homeless individuals, the isolated elderly, single parents, or people suffering from mental illnesses. Another variation would be to have a different constitution of housemates than ours at Lyn's House. Instead of young adults, a home could be composed of single individuals in middle age or older retired individuals who wished for community.

Finally, if the housemates found that their faith called them to projects which were not amenable to hosting meals, one could form the residential community around a different sort of volunteer charitable work, such as campaigning for worthy causes, community service or ministry projects of one kind or another. This wouldn't properly be a community that embraces others any more, because welcoming other (usually marginalised) people into the home is a vital part of the project. But the home community would still have the crucial joining elements of project, prayer and spare time together.

It is marvellous how much can be overcome and accomplished simply from the goodness of people's hearts. Circumstances do not have to be ideal, and with some small blessings scores of meals, tea parties, happy memories and uplifting friendships are created for everyone involved. For many housemates of Lyn's House, living in a home where faith and work were joined has been a source of life. It held us together through times we otherwise would have fallen out. It gave us the structure to bear with and support one who was in pain until her/his healing came. It gave us people to come home to. We shared the little joys of every day and the deep power of a life lived with faith, when it unexpectedly pulled us one way or another. Most of all, we had the joy of welcoming others into the home we had made, and their delight in making it a home away from home.

Endnotes

1   Though I am an academic theologian, here I do not write as a scholarly expert, but as one community member compiling collective wisdom. I would especially like to thank Loraine Gelsthorpe for her interviews with former housemates and her analysis. She is a member of the steering group and is Professor of Criminology and Criminal Justice and Director of the Institute of Criminology in the University of Cambridge. I am also grateful to Matthew Harbage for his list of top tips for community life. I am also indebted to notes taken by Judith Gardom and Deborah Hardy Ford from a presentation by Patrick McKearney (before my time) on communication. Each has directly informed sections of this chapter.

2   In the adapted version she used, the questions emerged from initial discussions, which were then fed back to housemates with enquiry as to whether these were the 'right' questions, prompting further reflection from the outset, and always concluding with 'What questions were you hoping that I would ask?', and 'What questions should I have asked?' The first questions posed in this process of deliberative enquiry were about hopes, fears, possibilities and expectations; creative possibilities; and challenges. Further questions emerged during each year regarding changes since the previous discussion, new challenges, resolution of previous challenges and the changing shape of creative possibilities. It is from her valuable work that the quotations come.

PART 2

A Wisdom of Community

— CHAPTER 4 —

Building Community Beyond Us and Them

Daniel Smith

Just as the body is one and has many members, and all the members of the body, though many, are one body, so it is with Christ. For in the one Spirit we were all baptised into one body – Jews or Greeks, slaves or free – and we were all made to drink of one spirit...the members of the body that seem to be weaker are indispensable, and those members of the body that we think less honourable we clothe with greater honour, and our less respectable members are treated with greater respect... Now you are the body of Christ and individually members of it.

(1 Cor. 12:12–27)

There is no longer Jew or Greek, there is no longer slave or free, there is no longer male and female; for all of you are one in Christ Jesus.

(Gal. 3:28)

'Inclusion' is an important word in contemporary society. People on the news talk about it, musicians sing about it, and religious leaders preach about it. Yet our society and our churches are still defined by harmful divisions, barriers and value judgements which determine how we treat people we perceive as 'different' from ourselves. This is no truer than for people with intellectual disabilities and in 1 Cor. 12: 22–24 Paul's discussion of how we should treat the 'weaker' members of the body of Christ might seem an obvious place from which to criticise this. Shouldn't the weak, the poor and the marginalised be at the centre of the church? This is certainly true, but we must be careful with this language of 'weakness' and strength.

It may well be true, as Stanley Hauerwas points out, that the exclusion of the 'weak' is one of the clearest signs that something is going terribly wrong with society, with the church, and with our own way of understanding and living in the world.[1] But the way we use language of weak and strong to speak about people with and without intellectual disabilities often reveals more about our limited understanding of their lives than about who they are in themselves, more about our limits than their gifts, more about our labels and barriers than the people they cause us to reject. To use Paul's term from 1 Corinthians, the way we understand weakness is often part of a story we use to justify 'dishonouring' some people in favour of those whom we commonly 'honour', that is, people we perceive as 'strong', 'able' or 'intelligent'. If, then, the problem lies with how we label some people as 'weak' and 'strong' in the first place, recognising how 'indispensable' the 'weaker members' of the body are, and clothing with greater honour those we think of as less honourable, is impossible if we do not recognise and transform the divisions that shape our perception. Only this will enable us to build truly mutual relationships and community.

This problem seems to have been familiar to Paul. As he suggests in Galatians, Christian identity and community has nothing at all to do with labels of race, legal status or gender through which society at the time created hierarchies to divide people up from one another. Being Christian, Paul tells us, means living in unity with one another in Christ, a unity which accepts differences, as his description of the body of Christ makes clear in 1 Cor. 12:12–27, but which also recognises an equality beyond the labels which shape how we view and treat one another.

In this chapter I want to explore what it means to take Paul's words in Galatians seriously when it comes to people with intellectual disabilities. What might it mean to let go of the weak–strong dichotomy, or any kind of 'us and them' distinction that shapes how we view others? How can we overcome this without also denying difference? What might it mean to recognise that people with these life experiences can and should be as central and important to our communities and friendship groups as any other human beings? What might it mean for us, for our societies, and for people with intellectual disabilities themselves, if we were truly to acknowledge and treat them as human beings just as whole, gifted and valuable as anyone else? Drawing on disability studies, disability theology and personal experience, I want to address the issues such questions raise by examining some of the common attitudes and practices which often obstruct our perception of and relationships with people who have intellectual disabilities. For shedding light on these helps us to better understand some of the obstacles that we must overcome, invariably with the help of those with intellectual disabilities, in order to build relationships and communities of true mutuality and equality.

Understanding Intellectual Disability and the Dangers of Labelling

In this first section I want to consider what we mean when we use a term like 'intellectual disability'. This is a matter of much more than just finding the right definition for certain life experiences, for the labels we use to categorise and distinguish groups of human beings often say much more about the kinds of experiences and traits that the person doing the labelling focuses upon, than about the self-experiences of the people we are actually labelling. Considering what we mean by intellectual disability may therefore allow us to recognise some of the realities of this life experience, but it also draws our attention immediately to the 'us and them' logic with which our labels are often imbued.

To start off, let's take a standard definition from medicine, drawn from the *Diagnostic and Statistical Manual of Mental Disorders (DSM-5)*. Here 'intellectual disability' is an umbrella term for certain neuro-developmental disorders which affect around 1 per cent of the world's population.[2] Intellectual disabilities must be diagnosed before the age of eighteen according to two criteria. First, 'deficits in intellectual functioning, such as reasoning, problem solving, planning, abstract thinking, judgment, academic learning, and learning from experience'. Second, 'deficits in adaptive functioning that result in failure to meet developmental and sociocultural standards for personal independence and social responsibility' with the result that, 'without ongoing support, the adaptive deficits limit functioning in one or more activities of daily life, such as communication, social participation, and independent living.'[3] *DSM-5* also states that someone can have a mild, moderate, severe or profound intellectual disability. Someone with a mild intellectual disability may be able to have a job, to manage their own personal care and require support only for complex tasks which require a certain type and level of intellectual and adaptive functioning – like shopping, managing money or arranging transport – while someone with a profound intellectual disability may have little or no capacity for language use or other forms of symbolic communication and will depend on others for virtually all personal and practical daily activities, though they may be able to participate in these to some extent, depending partly on their level of physical ability.[4]

This way of defining 'intellectual disability' accords with what scholars in disability studies and disability theology call the medical or individual model of disability. This treats disability primarily as a 'problem' with someone's body or mind, focusing on the limitations and symptoms which individuals experience.[5] This is, of course, an important part of understanding the lives of the people we are talking about here, for they do experience real limitations that directly affect their daily lives and understanding these limitations is vital for determining and responding to their support needs. Does this person have the ability to learn to look after their own money? Can this person develop the necessary skills for personal care and hygiene? Will this person be safe if they travel alone on public transport? Such questions are important and help care professionals to provide the correct level of practical support, both to aid people with what they cannot do, and to enable them in developing new skills.

The problem with a medical model of intellectual disability is that, taken alone, it presents a picture of people's lives defined simply in terms of what they are not, what they cannot do and do not have. It takes a particular narrative of what constitutes a normal, able or functioning kind of life experience, and uses this as the benchmark against which to measure certain life experiences as abnormal, dysfunctional and disabled. Ability and disability thus appear as totally distinct kinds of life experience, the former 'normal', the latter 'abnormal'. The problem with this, as disability studies scholars have shown, is that this view of disability is also reflected in wider society, where the judgement of physical and mental differences as 'deviations' from a 'normal' way of being human is often taken as the justification or explanation for the enormous differences between people with and without intellectual disabilities in terms of social status and opportunities.[6] Put simply, we represent and understand the difference between 'us and them' in such a way that social inequalities are treated as a tragic but inevitable result of their disabilities, rather than as a problem with our attitudes and with the values of our society.

How this plays out in a western society like Britain is not difficult to imagine and many of us will have heard the story, perhaps we have even told it ourselves. When we understand people with intellectual disabilities exclusively in terms of what they seem to 'lack' as compared to other people, we end up with a narrative focused on their needs, but not on their gifts. These require support, funding and housing, but their capacity to 'contribute' or give anything back to other people or to society is widely assumed to be limited in direct proportion to the severity of their 'dysfunctions', 'deficits', 'ab-normalcy' (read 'disability').[7] Framed within this narrative, the danger is that people with intellectual disabilities are seen as valueless, rather than as people who can and should be a central and vital part of healthy societies, communities and even friendship groups. They do not appear to us as the kind of strong, talented, independent people we have learned to value. Instead, they are weak, needy and unskilled, with nothing to share with others apart from their needs and dependencies. Within such a narrative, it is a simple matter to explain our exclusion and rejection of them in society as a result of their limited ability to participate, rather than our limited ability or willingness to embrace and include. We end up replacing the complex reality of the person before us with a one-dimensional surrogate, defined by our assumptions about what they are not, and whom we then find it easier to mistreat, exclude or ignore.[8]

Perhaps the most insidious part of this narrative is not just the practical reality of marginalisation, but rather the effect that marginalisation has in the long term on the way we view what it means to be human. For the more successfully we put out of sight and mind those people whom our society teaches us not to value, the more we are also ignoring those who most expose the limitations and harmfulness of our values in the first place. In such a context building relationships and community with people who have intellectual disabilities is more than just a practical response to injustice. It means we come face to face with people who challenge our deeply ingrained assumptions by being themselves in ways that transcend the limits of our labels and expose the falsity in our profoundly harmful association of ability and disability with 'normalcy' and 'abnormalcy'.

In Lyn's House it is precisely because of our deepening relationships that the question of language has been a recurring and developing topic, especially when speaking about people with intellectual disabilities and when distinguishing them from other people in the community. Is 'friends' the best term? 'Guests'? 'Friends with learning disabilities'? Are others also 'friends'? 'Friends without learning disabilities'? 'Visitors'? 'Volunteers'? 'Hosts'? What do such distinctions mean and why do we make them? And should we even use a term like 'disability', which some of our friends at Lyn's House have expressed a specific dislike of? In light of the discussion above it's easy to understand why!

When we make the space and take the time to really come to know and value the person before us, it is easier to see the truth of Paul's message. Living in community means developing relationships that take us beyond the barriers and divisions our labels create, perpetuate and allow us to justify. In the end, the way we use a label like 'intellectual disability' may say as much if not more about our values and norms and how they affect the way we view and treat others than it says about the people we think we are describing. Most importantly of all, what those involved in Lyn's House are discovering – and what so many have learned in L'Arche – is that as we make the effort to build deep relationships with people with intellectual disabilities, they themselves reveal the shocking paucity and harmfulness of the labels we attach to them and, within these labels, of the assumptions we make about what it means to be human, and to really understand this, we must consider some of these assumptions in more detail.

Rethinking Limitations, Vulnerability and Dependence

To do this, it is helpful to draw on disability theology, which has seen a growing body of literature written by the family, friends and carers of people with intellectual disabilities.[9] These authors often speak openly about the various things they have discovered as obstructions to the relationships they often write about, but one concern which recurs repeatedly are the values and norms that shape a modern western concept of human normalcy and flourishing.[10] As Jean Vanier reflects, our society celebrates competition and individualism and this shapes how we understand what a 'successful' and 'worthwhile' life looks like.[11] We value status, power, wealth and material goods, but to gain these, or, as Thomas Reynolds puts it, to participate in the 'cult of normalcy' where such things are the currency of human exchange and worth, requires certain kinds and levels of physical and intellectual ability.[12] This competitiveness and individualism appears to be rooted in an idealisation of independence and autonomy, such that 'success' and 'flourishing' become all about taking control of our lives, becoming self-sufficient, having the perfect body, the brains, and the money, to do and achieve what we want.

In a society and amongst people who hold such values, it is fairly inevitable that people with intellectual disabilities are viewed as leading lives diminished in wholeness and worth. For their limitations and dependencies seem entirely juxtaposed to the independence and control we idolise. In *Suffering Presence*, Stanley Hauerwas examines how this plays out in terms of our perception of suffering. Suffering, he argues, is an experience defined by its relationship to our sense of identity and purpose. In some cases we suffer in ways that we can incorporate into our sense of who we are and such suffering can therefore be an experience of growth. Some suffering however is fundamentally disruptive to our life plans; it cannot be easily incorporated into our sense of 'what we have or wish to be' and so it seems to 'alienate us from ourselves'.[13] This kind of suffering, Hauerwas suggests, is viewed as unnecessary suffering, the kind of suffering we use medicine to prevent or alleviate, and it is this unnecessary kind of suffering which, Hauerwas argues, often shapes how we view intellectual disability. The reason for this, he suggests, is that we often view people with intellectual disabilities by imagining what it would be like for us to be them, meaning that their lives always appear to us primarily in terms of the loss of those abilities and thus expectations which shape our sense of who we are and the goals we define for ourselves in our lives and it is this way of thinking, Hauerwas points out, that often underlies the assumption that people with profound intellectual disabilities suffer so much from their disability 'that it would be better for them not to exist'.[14] Hauerwas's discussion of this was written in the 1980s, but the view he critiques is one still present today, not least in utilitarian approaches to medical ethics, where a certain level of intellectual ability is presumed to be the defining feature of human personhood, and the benchmark criterion for determining whose 'preferences' are more important when it comes to practical ethical decisions around abortion, euthanasia, or even allocation of resources.[15]

One problem then is the assumption that the way we define ourselves and the ideals we pursue in our lives are a meaningful lens through which to understand people whose experience of embodiment may be different from our own. And as Hauerwas points out, it is not always clear that these 'differences' are in fact a cause of suffering. Indeed, people with intellectual disabilities often seem to suffer far more from 'being in a world like ours',[16] where they receive inadequate support both for care and for development and where other people treat them constantly as if who they are is a tragedy, a life to pity or to prevent altogether, often simply because we cannot fit their experiences into the mould of what we consider important in our lives. A deeper problem, however, lies in the validity of those values and norms which shape our self-perception in the first place, and which shape our assumptions about what this 'difference' between people with and without disabilities actually consists of. For the way we judge the lives of people with intellectual disabilities seems to be rooted in the assumption that limitations, dependence, vulnerability, or weakness, are something to do with 'disability', and that, by contrast, a 'normal' or 'whole' human existence is defined by independence, control and self-sufficiency. People with and without disabilities do, of course, experience forms and degrees of dependency or limitation that many of us do not and which should neither be denied nor trivialised. But to treat these as a total aberration from a 'normal' human existence seems to result from a profound misunderstanding of what it actually means to be human in the first place.[17] For we are not radically independent, self-sufficient beings, but fundamentally limited and vulnerable creatures, who are constantly in need of one another.

Recognising this is an important part of shifting our assumptions about people with intellectual disabilities and it also provides new insight into why they are often marginalised in the first place. For if we are all limited, dependent and vulnerable creatures, yet some of us grasp at ideals which deny this, then our rejection of those people who seem plainly to reveal these realities of human existence appears (in part at least) to be one terrible effect of our fleeing from realities in our own lives. We turn away from the vulnerable because they remind us of what we do not want to accept about ourselves: that we are vulnerable, that our 'abilities' are contingent, and that the ideals of self-sufficiency and control which society promises us will give us what we need, are ultimately unattainable. It seems, as Hauerwas suggests, that we reject people with intellectual disabilities because they remind us of the 'insecurity hidden in our false sense of self-possession'.[18]

Of course, fearing and fleeing from these dimensions of our lives makes sense. The day-to-day realities of dependence and limitations can be enormously frustrating, difficult, and even terrifying. They are realities which we fear for a reason and this is as true for people with intellectual disabilities as for those without. As Jean Vanier often notes, the people with disabilities who join the L'Arche communities are often filled with inner pain, anger and fear. They know more than most people what it is to have their needs unfulfilled, their limitations unsupported, and their vulnerability taken advantage of.[19] But there is another side to this picture. For being dependent and vulnerable is not only a troublesome part of human existence. We are all limited relational creatures, who exist in a web of dependencies and inter-dependencies. Being human means being exposed or vulnerable before those who can give to us what we cannot give to ourselves, for it is only *with* others that we can exist, heal, grow and flourish at all.[20] Perhaps it is due to our woundedness and fears that we flee from these dimensions of our lives. But if all we do is flee from them, we risk turning away from the very exposedness before others without which we cannot be whole. As Hauerwas so aptly puts it, 'our neediness is also the source of our greatest strength, for our need requires the cooperation and love of others from which derives our ability not only to live but to flourish'.[21]

To bring this back to our discussion in the introduction then, it seems that one of the problems with the 'weak–strong' dichotomy is that the way we understand such terms is often rooted in a profound misunderstanding of what it means to be human and of where we stand in the scheme of things. If what it means to be human is to be vulnerable, limited and dependent, who are the weak and the strong? Is it we, in fact, who are weak: weak in our ability to accept others who differ from ourselves, weak in our willingness to risk engaging with those whose lives seem defined by what we fear? And who are the strong? Those who can, to some extent, believe that self-sufficiency and independence allow them to escape from vulnerability and limitations? Or those who, in the midst of their limitations and vulnerability, are still willing to reach out to others, to build relationships despite being rejected, to have hope in a world that turns away from them? Clearly a simple distinction of weakness and strength as a way of thinking about those of us with or without intellectual disabilities is a problematic way of thinking and one that comes easily to mirror the kinds of assumptions we've just explored.

When we let go of our dichotomised ways of thinking about each other and about being human, we will discover new ways of valuing people with intellectual disabilities and not just as vulnerable recipients of care, but also as gifted care-givers. As I have found at Lyn's House and at L'Arche, responding to particular practical needs may sometimes require particular intellectual and physical abilities, but responding to another person's vulnerability with acceptance and love does not.[22]

The Importance of Independence

Learning to value weakness, limitations, dependencies and vulnerability is a vital part of accepting what it means for all of us to be human. Through this we can recognise an equality between people with and without disabilities that goes beyond our oversimplified division of 'weak' and 'strong', or dependent and independent. But there also needs to be a balance. Overvaluing such experiences can lead us to ignore how challenging the reality of living with high levels of dependency and limitation can be. It can also leave us looking at people with intellectual disabilities in a way that focuses more on the ways their lives challenge the false assumptions we make about our own, than on who the people before us are in themselves.[23] Perhaps most importantly of all, we can end up so focused on trying to value realities like dependence, limitation or vulnerability, that we forget how vital independence, control, agency and self-sufficiency also are for people with intellectual disabilities and it is this that I want to consider here.

The problem with how we view something like independence, control or self-sufficiency is that we often hold to these ideals as a way of denying or trying to escape from dependence, limitation etc. Recognising both the unavoidability and importance of experiences like dependence helps us to understand the mistake in this way of viewing something like independence, but that does not mean that there is no such thing as independence within the context of our lives as limited, relational beings. In Lyn's House this is something which our friends make very clear to us. Some of our friends have, for instance, taken up roles leading music or prayer, when we gather to pray together before meals, and clearly value the opportunity to share and lead in this way. So also, coming to Lyn's House without any carers is often a big thing, since it's the first time some of them have ever been invited to a dinner outside of their immediate family, care, or college context. At other times, our friends have talked about their desire to have a job, and those that have jobs – whether it's working in a charity shop or in a hospital cafe – enjoy and take pride in what they are able to do.

Having independence and control over one's life is obviously not the same for people with different levels of disability, but even for people with profound intellectual disabilities, independence and control are still important even if they might not be valued and understood self-reflectively. Practical independence, for instance, is vital wherever possible. Frances Young describes how essential it has been for her son Arthur, who has profound intellectual and physical disabilities, to learn to sit in postures that support his body in order to reduce physical discomfort and prevent other problems developing.[24] She also talks about Arthur's tendency to be resistant when being supported to eat or get dressed. Young notes that this resistance to others is one way through which Arthur can have some kind of power and control, even if it can make supporting him difficult at times.[25] This is a particularly important point in the context of care, for when we ignore the presence and nature of power in such relationships, we can easily be inattentive to whose needs or expectations are really determining the way we support someone in their daily lives. Do we support someone in a way that is really attentive to their needs and what it means for them to flourish in their day, or do we support them in a way that most suits us?

The Social Construction of Limitations

Aside from needing to sustain a sense of the importance of independence, a further reason why we must be careful when thinking about life with an intellectual disability is that the limitations or dependencies we perceive people to have may be caused, to some extent, by the harmful and exclusionary ways in which they are treated and not as a pathological result of their disability. In 'Effects of Social Exclusion and Interpersonal Rejection,'[26] Roy Baumeister seems to suggest just this. Baumeister draws on his psychological studies with college students and reflects on their implications for how we might understand intellectual disability.[27] He argues that the experience of feeling rejected and excluded makes people more aggressive, causes physical and emotional numbness and reduces the willingness to build relationships, despite the fact that people who feel rejected seek acceptance. It also impairs intellectual performance in terms of IQ, logical reasoning, extrapolation and making inferences, affects self-control and self-regulation, increases impulsive and 'undisciplined' behaviours, reduces self-awareness and increases self-defeating or self-destructive behaviours.[28]

Baumeister concludes from this that we may have much to learn from people with disabilities in terms of how they 'minimise the negative impact' of social exclusion on their lives. Yet he also notes that many of the features we directly associate with intellectual disability might not be 'properties of the persons per se but rather secondary results of chronic rejection and exclusion'.[29] This points, again, to the limitations in a purely medical definition of intellectual disability such as that provided by *DSM-5*, where faculties and behaviours which mirror those Baumeister identifies as directly affected by social exclusion, are presented as defining features of having an intellectual disability. Of course, this does not mean arguing that every limitation people experience results from personal and social injustices. But it does mean recognising the risk of a profound misdiagnosis, where the limitations which we perceive people with intellectual disabilities to have in fact reveal a problem in our societies and in the relationships these people experience, rather than just in the minds and bodies of the people themselves.

How do we respond to this? And how do we address the often very strong attachments people with intellectual disabilities can frequently form, at least in part as a result of their experiences of rejection and lack of relationships with people outside of their immediate family or care context? This was a question I asked myself early on in my time at Lyn's House, wondering whether it was fair to build close relationships with people there, if I knew I was going to be leaving after only one or two years. It was an important moment for me when I realised, if people form strong attachments because they are often excluded or lack many relationships apart from with their families, the only answer to this is for them have more and deeper relationships. You cannot 'save' someone who forms strong attachments from the pain of absence and goodbyes by avoiding being their friend. That might save you from being confronted with the depth of their need, but it makes the absence of relationships into a permanent fixture of their lives and a source of a deeper kind of pain altogether. At the same time, the Lyn's House community is a place of change, of departures and goodbyes. Our friends with disabilities are, in fact, some of the most permanent members of the community and each year they, like everyone else, have been sad at partings, excited about seeing people again, and gracious in welcoming new members into the community.

Communication and Exchange

In our discussion so far we have seen how our understanding of life with an intellectual disability is often warped by a purely negative perception of dependence, limitation or weakness, we have considered why these are an unavoidable and even important part of being human, and we have also balanced this by stressing the value of independence and control. In this final section, I want to consider one final obstacle that can obstruct mutual relationships and community and which is, in fact, a direct result of the kind of limitations that having an intellectual disability involves: that is, the capacity to communicate with language.

Linguistic communication is obviously vital to how many of us engage with one another in our daily lives. Complex language use has the enormous advantage of allowing us to communicate ideas, needs, hopes and fears in considerable detail and in ways that others can understand. For many people with intellectual disabilities, however – even many of those who can understand and use language – *complex* language is often more a barrier than an aid to communication and for people with more severe disabilities, language may not be a primary means of communicating at all. This obviously represents a real limitation and one which can be frustrating for people with intellectual disabilities when others cannot understand them and when they cannot understand others. For this reason language can easily become something that makes people feel excluded, an important fact to remember around the dinner table in L'Arche and at Lyn's House, and something we can all relate to in some sense at least, if we have ever been at dinner with people who all speak a language we do not understand.

Due to the value we give to language in our relationships and our ways of communicating, it is also one of the most common areas where we quickly start to view and treat people with intellectual disabilities in terms of what they cannot do and this, in turn, has a negative effect on our ability to receive and communicate with them. This is something Henri Nouwen touches on in his book *Adam, God's Beloved*. Adam, whom Nouwen got to know at the L'Arche Daybreak community in Canada, had a profound intellectual disability. He could not use language and his physical disabilities meant that he was very dependent on practical support for his day-to-day activities. Nouwen admits that he initially gave in to the temptation 'to look only at Adam's disabilities'[30] and to support Adam through his daily routine 'without being conscious of his person'.[31] Gradually, however, rather than focusing on the absence of language, Nouwen learned to listen to Adam's body – something that was a particular challenge and struggle for Nouwen, whose life as an academic theologian had been built around words. Yet as he slowly learned to listen to what Adam communicated with his body, Nouwen discovered the importance of something Jean Vanier also describes as central to the L'Arche communities: that 'understanding, as well as truth, comes not only from the intellect but also from the body'.[32]

Learning to listen to people with intellectual disabilities is obviously a vital part of building mutual relationships with them and this means learning to listen in new ways. Rather than focusing on the absence of what we normally count as communication and exchange, we must learn to pay attention to the presence of different ways and means of communication, for instance by listening, as Nouwen had to, to what people's bodies are saying, by attending to gesture, touch, sound, and even silence, stillness or simply what someone shares through their presence.[33] Such forms of communication are often difficult for those of us accustomed to using language; we often want something clearer, or more verifiable and our tendency is to assume that the lack of this indicates a total impossibility of communication. Yet engaging with people with intellectual disabilities in this respect, as in many others, in fact simply means becoming open to forms of sharing and communicating that are, or can be, important in all our relationships where other (non-verbal) dimensions of communication are always at play, yet often overlooked and sometimes unnurtured in favour of language. Realising this may also show us another reason why encountering and listening to people with intellectual disabilities can be a challenge: it requires us to employ means of communicating which, in us, may be quite underdeveloped.

Apart from the question of language or communication itself, there is also the question of what and why we communicate, what we expect others to give to and receive from us and of how we value this exchange in our relationships. To show what I mean here it is easiest to speak from personal experience. At Lyn's House our friends with intellectual disabilities all understand and use language, though one person communicates through gestures and writing rather than speaking. With most of my friends at Lyn's House I cannot talk in detail about things like my PhD, my political views or my personal anxieties. The kind of language that a detailed discussion of these would require would be inaccessible for most of them. With these friends, I may also have conversations that are quite unlike those I have with others: conversations that turn repeatedly back to a particular movie, or where someone responds to a question by talking about something else entirely. I have conversations with people who seem not to understand or use the social cues I am used to and where people use certain phrases – 'I'm not sure', 'I don't know yet' – that seem like they have understood and are responding to something I have said when in fact they use these phrases as responses when they do not understand what I have said at all!

This raises an important point about our expectations in conversation and other forms of exchange, for the fact is, people with intellectual disabilities may not pay attention to, or even be able to understand, many of the things by which we usually define ourselves and the things which we want other people to know or think about us. Building relationships with them means learning to value things about yourself and others that are important for this relationship but to which you might not have paid so much attention in the past. As Nouwen makes abundantly clear in *Adam, God's Beloved*, Adam could not affirm him in his self-image as an intellectual, as a man of learning and words. What Nouwen valued in himself, and what others 'normally' valued in him, did not matter in his relationship with Adam. And yet he felt deeply accepted and heard by Adam and found that he learned a great deal about himself from spending time with him. This was my experience living in L'Arche, too. 'Peter', with whom I lived, was not interested in my recently earned degree, in my musical abilities, in whether or not I sounded clever when I talked, and he could not have cared less about my self-image, from leather boots to gelled hair (which sometimes became a source of direct teasing!). He was interested in spending time together: going for a coffee, going to church, visiting friends and, through all this, slowly learning to trust me and I him. I remember the important moment when I realised one day that, despite the fact that our relationship gave no affirmation to those things by which I had learned to define myself, I was still wholly myself with Peter and this meant that all those things I had learned to value did not actually define who I was.

At the same time, both in L'Arche and at Lyn's House, accepting this can be very difficult, for sometimes in the absence of things which are fundamental to how we commonly relate to others, both in terms of our self-definition and in terms of communication, you find yourself being impatient, lacking in generosity, and resorting again and again to ways of thinking which quickly blame difficult relational dynamics on their limitations, rather than reflecting on your own. This helps us to see one final obstruction to building relationships and community with people who have intellectual disabilities, for doing so confronts us often with the paucity of our own hearts and the hearts of our communities. It is far easier to leave the marginalised at the margins and pretend we are doing all that is required of us, than to face our own impoverished ways of viewing and relating to one another and take up the challenge to change and to grow. And yet, once again, people with intellectual disabilities are frequently excellent teachers, offering forgiveness and friendship with generosity and ease that turns upside down our assumptions about who is caring for and welcoming whom.

Living Beyond Labels

The message here is simple. People with intellectual disabilities have limitations which mean they cannot do some, or many, of the things that other people do. These are real differences we must not ignore, but they have no impact on the fact that these are people just as whole, valuable and gifted as anyone else. The 'problem' here isn't their limitations or disabilities, but ours: our judgements, expectations, values, norms, fears and illusions, all that stands – and creates the distance – between 'us' and 'them'. Overcoming this means, in part, learning to see how they are just like anyone else and, in part, learning to overcome our stigmatising assumptions about the ways in which they might not be. It also means being attentive to the falsity and harmfulness of any perspective that treats a person's limitations as an explanation and justification for practices, attitudes and social structures that exclude them.

Of course, this is a process of learning and transformation, one which I have just begun to experience in recent years in Lyn's House and in L'Arche, and which numerous others have experienced there too. It's a process which comes, not from finding the right theory, or theology, not from abstract reflection or reading the 'right' books, however inspiring they might be. It is a practical kind of learning that comes through building and nurturing relationships with individuals with intellectual disabilities. This is the 'upside-downness' of Lyn's House and of L'Arche, that the people we think we come to support, the people with limitations who need our 'help', often support us in unexpected ways and frequently teach us a great deal about our own limitations, especially when it comes to how we perceive and receive them.

In only a few years, the people with intellectual disabilities whom I have got to know at L'Arche and Lyn's House have taught me a great deal about my (and their) limits, about my values and norms, about friendship, about sharing, having fun, building trust and facing challenges. They have done all this by being who they are beyond the boundaries of the assumptions I make about them, by offering friendship to me in unexpected ways, and by being the complex, gifted and interesting people that a label like 'intellectual disability' utterly fails to acknowledge. Transforming attitudes and building relationships that are genuinely open to mutuality and reciprocity is difficult: it takes time and it takes commitment. As Vanier points out, relationships and community get more complicated as time goes on, not less so. Once we start to say 'yes' to others, we also start opening the door to all the vulnerabilities, hopes, needs, desires, insecurities and everything else that we normally keep hidden away for fear of rejection. Faced with this reality, there will always be difficulties and obstacles. But as we commit to and continue on this journey, as we all grow and change, we move to a point where the obstacles are no longer the barriers between 'us and them', between 'disabled' and 'abled', 'weak' and 'strong', Jew, Greek, slave or free. Instead, they will be the struggles of building and sustaining loving community and relationships on earth, the struggles of living as creatures who will always be mysterious to one another, made by God to be different and distinct, yet, just as truly, made to move towards that unity with each other that Paul calls the body of Christ.

Endnotes

1   Stanley Hauerwas, Jean Vanier and John Swinton, *Living Gently in a Violent World: The Prophetic Witness of Weakness* (Downer's Grove, IL: InterVarsity Press, 2008), p.56.
2   American Psychiatric Association, *Diagnostic and Statistic Manual of Mental Disorders: DSM-5*, 5th ed. (Arlington, VA: American Psychiatric Association Publishers, 2013), p.40.
3   Ibid., p. 33.
4   Ibid., pp.34–37.

5 For a discussion of the medical model and the social model developed to oppose it in disability studies see Tom Shakespeare and Nicholas Watson, 'The Social Model of Disability: An Outdated Ideology?' in *Exploring Theories and Expanding Methodologies: Where We Are and Where We Need to Go*, Vol. 2, Research in Social Science and Disability (Amsterdam; London: JAI Press, 2001), pp. 9–28. For a discussion of these different models in disability theology see Deborah Beth Creamer, *Disability and Christian Theology: Embodied Limits and Constructive Possibilities* (Oxford: Oxford University Press, 2009).

6 For a good, short discussion of this problem with the medical model see Brisenden, 'Independent Living and the Medical Model of Disability'. *Disability, Handicap, and Society* 1, No. 2 (1986): 173–8. For a more detailed academic work see Michael Oliver and Colin Barnes, *The New Politics of Disablement* (Hampshire: Palgrave Macmillan, 2012). Note, both of these works are focused primarily on the experiences and perspectives of people with physical disabilities. Their arguments certainly apply in many respects to people with intellectual disabilities too, but it is worth noting that disability studies has largely left discussion of intellectual disability to one side. For more on this issue see Hans Reinders, *Receiving the Gift of Friendship: Profound Disability, Theological Anthropology, and Ethics* (Grand Rapids/Cambridge: William B. Eerdmans Publishing Company, 2008), chaps. 1–2.

7 For more on the problem with this 'contributory notion' of human worth see David Pailin, *A Gentle Touch* (London: SPCK, 1992), chap. 5.

8 This pattern of behaviour in how we often view others has been studied extensively in disability studies in terms of 'stigma'. Much of this discussion has been influenced by Erving Goffman, *Stigma: Notes on the Management of Spoiled Identity* (New York: Simon and Schuster Inc., 1963). For more on stigma and Goffman in relation to disability see Lennard J. Davis (ed.), *The Disability Studies Reader*, 2nd ed. (London/New York: Routledge, 2006), pt. 3. Thomas Reynolds also explores this in detail in *Vulnerable Communion: A Theology of Disability and Hospitality* (Grand Rapids: Brazos Press, 2008). Here he examines what he calls the 'cult of normalcy', commenting on how as we 'assimilate' people into the cult, or reject them when their real or perceived differences too strongly contradict our beliefs about human normalcy. This rejection, he astutely notes, is as much about reinforcing and strengthening the norms by which we define ourselves, as it is about excluding those who do not fit into them. There is thus a deeply disturbing sense in which our sense of our own identity and worth is in fact constructed and sustained by marginalisation. For Reynolds' argument on this see ibid., chaps. 2–3.

9 See for instance Reynolds, *Vulnerable Communion: A Theology of Disability and Hospitality*; Amos Yong, *Theology and Down Syndrome: Reimagining Disability in Late Modernity* (Waco, TX: Baylor University Press, 2007); Jill Harshaw, *God Beyond Words: Christian Theology and the Spiritual Experiences of People with Profound Intellectual Disabilities* (London: Jessica Kingsley Publishers, 2016); Brian Brock, 'Praise: The Prophetic Public Presence of the Mentally Disabled', in *The Blackwell Companion to Christian Ethics*, ed. Stanley Hauerwas and Samuel Wells, 2nd ed. (Oxford: Wiley-Blackwell, 2011); Molly Haslam, *A Constructive Theology of Intellectual Disability: Human Being as Mutuality and Response* (New York: Fordham University Press, 2012); Jean Vanier, *Becoming Human* (Toronto: House of Anansi Press Inc., 2008).

10 For works where authors speak frankly about how their own limitations, values and assumptions have affected their relationships see Thomas Reynolds, 'Love Without Boundaries: Theological Reflections on Parenting a Child with Disabilities', *Theology Today* 62 (2005): 193–209; Frances Young, *Face to Face: A Narrative Essay in the Theology of Suffering* (Edinburgh: T&T Clark, 1990); Frances Young, *Arthur's Call* (London: SPCK, 2014); Henri Nouwen, *Adam, God's Beloved* (London: Darton, Longman and Todd Ltd., 1997).

11 Jean Vanier, *The Heart of L'Arche: A Spirituality for Every Day* (London: SPCK, 2013), p.26.

12 Reynolds, *Vulnerable Communion: A Theology of Disability and Hospitality*, chap. 2.

13 Stanley Hauerwas, 'Suffering the Retarded: Should We Prevent Retardation?' in *Suffering Presence: Theological Reflections on Medicine, the Mentally Handicapped, and the Church* (Notre Dame, IN: University of Notre Dame Press, 1986), pp.165–6.

14 Ibid., p.171.

15 Alberto Giubilini and Francesca Minerva, 'After-Birth Abortion: Why Should the Baby Live?' *Journal of Medical Ethics* 39 (2012): 261–3; Peter Singer, *Practical Ethics*, 3rd ed. (Cambridge: Cambridge University Press, 2011).

16 Hauerwas, *Suffering Presence*, p.172.

17 This is something Vanier stresses throughout his work, *Becoming Human*, and also in *Signs of the Times: Seven Paths of Hope for a Troubled World* (London: Darton, Longman and Todd, 2013). This is also the essence of Hauerwas' and Reynolds' arguments in Hauerwas, 'Suffering the Retarded: Should We Prevent Retardation?' p.169; Reynolds, *Vulnerable Communion: A Theology of Disability and Hospitality*, chap. 4.

18 Hauerwas, 'Suffering the Retarded: Should We Prevent Retardation?' p.169.

19 This is in fact what the UK care sector means when it calls them 'vulnerable adults': that they are statistically more at risk of harm and abuse from others due to their dependencies and limitations. For a clear but disturbing report on what forms this abuse can take see Carwyn Gravell, *Loneliness and Cruelty: People with Learning Disabilities and Their Experience of Harassment, Abuse and Related Crime in the Community* (London: Lemos&Crane, 2012).

20 For more on this see Thomas Reynolds' discussion of the dual sense of vulnerability in Thomas Reynolds, 'Theology and Disability: Changing the Conversation' in *Searching for Dignity: Conversations on Human Dignity, Theology, and Disability*, ed. Julie Claassens, Leslie Swartz and Len Hansen (Stellenbosch: SUN MeDIA, 2013), p.20.

21 Hauerwas, 'Suffering the Retarded: Should We Prevent Retardation?', p.169.

22 For some good personal examples of this in the literature, see Christopher de Vinck, *The Power of Powerlessness* (Grand Rapids: Zondervan Publishing House, 1988); Nouwen, *Adam, God's Beloved*; Vanier, *Becoming Human*, pp.20–31. For a detailed anthropological study, see Michael Hryniuk, *Theology, Disability and Spiritual Transformation: Learning from the Communities of L'Arche* (Amherst: Cambria Press, 2010).

23 Jill Harshaw has recently made a similar point, criticising a view of vulnerability which focuses on its 'instructive capacity' in Harshaw, *God Beyond Words: Christian Theology and the Spiritual Experiences of People with Profound Intellectual Disabilities*, pp.44–5.

24 Young, *Arthur's Call*, chap. 1.

25 Ibid., pp.7, 14.

26 Roy Baumeister, 'Effects of Social Exclusion and Interpersonal Rejection: An Overview with Implications for Human Disability', in *The Paradox of Disability*, ed. Hans Reinders (Cambridge: William B. Eerdmans Publishing Company, 2010), pp. 51–9.

27 Ibid., p.54.

28 Ibid., pp.54–8.

29 Ibid., p.58.

30 Nouwen, *Adam, God's Beloved*, p.26.

31 Ibid., p.34.

32 Vanier, *Becoming Human*, p.25.

33 For a powerful personal reflection on the place of 'presence' as part of how someone with a profound intellectual disability can communicate and share with others, see de Vinck, *The Power of Powerlessness*. For a longer discussion of this point, see Daniel G.W. Smith, 'Rituals of Knowing: Rejection and Relation in Disability Theology and Meister Eckhart', *International Journal of Philosophy and Theology* 79, no. 3 (2018): 279–94.

— CHAPTER 5 —

Wisdom's Call

Suzanna R. Millar

(1:20) Wisdom cries aloud in the street,
in the markets she raises her voice;

(9:3) She has sent out her young women to call
from the highest places in the town,

(4) 'Whoever is simple, let him turn in here!'

(From the Book of Proverbs)

Introduction

What does 'wisdom' mean?

When I think 'wise', I tend to think 'clever'. I think 'learning-abled', and automatically disqualify the 'disabled' from the category. I spend most of my life in the university, teaching and researching the Old Testament. My environment is thoroughly intellectual, and so, from my perspective, thoroughly 'wise'. But when I engage with the Bible, or with my friends at Lyn's House,[1] I rediscover again and again that this is not necessarily what 'wisdom' means. They turn the whole idea upside-down.

I have come to think that my friends with learning disabilities may be better placed than I (for all my proficiency in Hebrew grammar) to truly understand biblical wisdom. I am at times too easily seduced by the culture of cleverness. With that in mind, my aim here is to listen to the call of wisdom, as it echoes through the Bible, and through the presence of my friends. I will focus on a few specific biblical texts. Let me begin by introducing them.

The Texts

Scholars talk about a 'Wisdom Tradition' in the Bible. This refers to texts with a distinctive worldview and mode of expression. And, as the name suggests, an emphasis on 'wisdom'. I have selected four texts on which to focus, which show features of this tradition: Proverbs, Matthew, James, and 1 Corinthians.

The earliest 'Wisdom' book in the Bible is Proverbs. Proverbs contains a prologue (chs. 1–9), a central section (chs. 10–29), and an epilogue (chs. 30–31). In the prologue, we are introduced to 'Lady Wisdom' and 'Lady Folly'. Each of them behaves according to her name, and each issues a call to follow her (see the verses which begin this chapter). In the central section, we find collections of mainly single-verse proverbs, which often draw a sharp contrast between the wise man and the fool, and give examples of what wise behaviour looks like. The epilogue offers a fleshed-out example of a wise life, epitomised in the figure of an 'excellent wife'.

The Wisdom Tradition continues in the Old Testament books of Job and Ecclesiastes, and beyond that in Jewish texts like Ben Sira and the Wisdom of Solomon.[2] The tradition seems to have influenced the teaching of Jesus. This is brought out most fully in the gospel of Matthew,[3] my second main text. Matthew focuses on Jesus' discourses more than the other gospel writers, and his book is replete with proverbs and parables. Jesus is often depicted as a sage, teaching his disciples in wisdom.

Jesus' wisdom teachings seem to underlie much in the epistle of James too, which itself continues the Wisdom Tradition.[4] James is interested in wisdom itself (e.g. 1:5; 3:13–18), and in a number of conventional wisdom themes (e.g. control of the tongue, polarities of character type). He writes in an aphoristic/proverbial style, and sometimes quotes or echoes Proverbs or other 'Wisdom' texts.[5]

My final writer, Paul, is less clearly influenced by the Wisdom Tradition. But I will focus on a section where wisdom and folly are central: 1 Corinthians 1–4. The Corinthian community seems to have boasted of their worldly wisdom, but Paul here sets this in sharp distinction to the 'wise folly' of the cross.

The Call of Wisdom

These texts reveal a counter-cultural conception of wisdom, one that is often embodied by my friends at Lyn's House. And this wisdom calls me in – through the emphatic cries of Lady Wisdom in the market-place, through the gentle silence of some of my friends. In their call I have heard, firstly, a call to silence. Listening, rather than speaking. Away from the eloquent rhetoric that I might think so clever. Secondly, their voices call me to community. True wisdom learns from those around and shows itself in living for the other. Thirdly, I am invited to the wisdom of childlikeness, and to a delight in creation. They call me, fourthly, to humility. True wisdom recognises its limits, and does not think itself too wise. But these limits are no cause for despair. Rather, they are prompts to the final and most important call – to Christ, Wisdom made incarnate. He is where, despite our limitations, true wisdom can be found. In this chapter, I will turn my ear to listen to these calls.

1. Their Wisdom Calls Me to...Silence

My first theme may sound paradoxical: a call of silence. But it is sometimes in this silence that the truest wisdom is found. In my world, I have expressed wisdom through words. I have esteemed those who give lectures, write articles and engage in debates. But the Bible and my friends don't revere such 'wisdom'. They call us instead to a wisdom of silence. The Bible warns of the dangers of unrestrained speech, which can so easily destroy, seduce and exclude.

Restraining Our Speech

Speech is a major topic in the Book of Proverbs. But (perhaps counter expectations) the wise man does not gush forth with his profound soliloquies. Instead, he holds his tongue. Indeed, 'whoever restrains his words has knowledge' (17:27), and 'a man of understanding remains silent' (11:12). By contrast, the *fool* loves the sound of his own voice. He 'takes no pleasure in understanding, but only in expressing his own opinions' (18:2).

This in fact has been recognised by proverbs throughout the ages. Just think of our English examples: 'silence is golden', 'children should be seen and not heard', 'think before you speak'. Ancient Egyptian proverb collections laud the 'silent man', as do later Jewish and Hellenistic moral texts. The epistle of James picks up this tradition (3:1–12). But James goes further and laments human *inability* to remain silent. Indeed, 'no human being can tame the tongue' (3:8).

James seems to be addressing primarily the 'teachers' here (3:1). They have the most opportunity to speak and may be most allured by temptations to verbosity (I should take heed). They are adept at mastering many different areas of life. They can control horses (3:3) and ships (3:4), in fact, 'every kind of beast and bird, of reptile and sea creature' (3:7). But this outward display of control means very little when coupled with a raging tongue. By contrast, whether they will it or not, my friends at Lyn's House often display the opposite. The forces of the world may rage around them; their tongues lie silent.

Restraint is commended because speech can be destructive. In the ancient world, words were thought to have power, especially when associated with blessing and curse (see Jas. 3:10). They had a real, tangible effect on the world. And even today, we recognise their force. Once I've said it, it's out there, I can't take it back. The proverb is a lie which says, 'Sticks and stones may break my bones but words can never hurt me.'

The Book of Proverbs highlights several types of destructive speech: gossiping, whispering, lying, slandering, loquacity, thoughtless talk, false witness. Words can be like a bloody ambush (12:6), sword thrusts (12:18), a scorching fire (16:27). Again, James heightens the rhetoric: '(3:5) How great a forest is set ablaze by such a small fire! (3:6) And the tongue is a fire, a world of unrighteousness...set on fire by hell...it is a restless evil' (Jas. 3:5–6). The forest fire brings complete destruction and is a hotbed of immorality – 'unrighteousness', 'restless evil'. It is even given alarming comic dimensions – 'set on fire by hell'.

In light of this, wisdom restrains its speech. Now, I don't want to condemn chatter. Indeed, it has brought much joy around the Lyn's House table! But several of my friends are also examples of restraint. Some do not speak a word. I have sometimes tried to fill every silence, to subdue the world through my language. But Proverbs and James say that this is folly. And my friends welcome me to be with them in what can be wise silence.

Avoiding Seductive Speech

In our restraint, wisdom calls us to avoid seductive speech. This may have a wicked, malign power, only heightened by its pretence of being wise and benign. One example is deception. Proverbs finds this a particular danger, describing the lies encountered throughout life. In the market-place a buyer lies about an item's worth (20:14), and the sluggard fabricates tales to avoid work (22:13). Lies are particularly dangerous in the courtroom (e.g. 12:17; 14:5, 25), where the one who 'breathes out lies' perverts justice. They are more serious than simple propositional falsehoods. They are socially destructive and morally abhorrent, an 'abomination to the Lord' (12:22). They are the sign of folly *par excellence*. Indeed, 'like a madman who throws firebrands, arrows, and death is the man who deceives his neighbour and says "I was only joking"' (26:18–19).[6]

Well-executed deception requires an intellectual aptitude: contrivance of a counter-narrative, analysis of the other party, sustained manipulative energy. Most of us know the mental energies involved. Deceit may be very clever, but it is not wise. And my friends at Lyn's House, on the whole, do not deceive (pretending to be allergic to lentils to avoid a vegan shepherd's pie doesn't count!). I have often been struck by their honesty. They simply don't bother with foolish falsehoods.

But seductive speech may be subtler and more pernicious than outright deception. It may involve flattery, promised benefits, dangerous allures. And Proverbs knows how tempting it can be to succumb to the words you want to hear. 'The words of the whisperer are like delicious morsels' filling your belly (18:8; 26:22). A striking example comes in the speeches of Lady Folly. She is depicted as an adulteress, verbally offering the reader exquisite fragrances and furnishings to tantalise the senses, and the prospect of the thrill of love (Prov. 7:10–23). Her lips 'drip honey, and her speech is smoother than oil' (5:3). The book imagines a young, male audience, who is meant to find her rhetoric persuasive. But he is also meant to see beyond it. He must learn to distinguish seductive speech, and to flee from it.

In the New Testament, seductive speech (though of a different nature) seems to have been a problem for the church in Corinth. Apparently, they were being seduced by the eloquent rhetoric of the surrounding Greek culture. The arguments' polished and pleasing form was as important as their content, and philosophical debates between talented orators were in vogue. Paul may allude to these groups – 'the wise…the scribe…the debater of this age' (1:20) – and the Corinthians apparently saw him as another rhetorician, competing in the dialogue.

But Paul stresses that the wisdom he preaches will not participate in these games. He preaches without 'eloquent wisdom' (1:17), 'lofty speech' (2:1) or 'plausible words of wisdom' (2:4). His personal demeanour is not persuasive: 'I was with you in weakness and in fear and much trembling' (2:3). He does not want the Corinthians to be seduced by any words – his own or someone else's. He apparently used unimpressive rhetoric on purpose. Any resultant faith would then be true faith, based not on 'the wisdom of men', but on the power of God (2:4–5; cf. 1:17).

I must admit that I often side with the Corinthians. I can succumb to the temptation of eloquent speech: being seduced by it, trying to seduce through it. That's the university game, after all. But Proverbs, Paul and my friends aren't impressed. My friends do not indulge in seductive speech. They do not hide in impenetrable, verbose, polysyllabic talk. Through them, I have learned that I can throw out the rulebook of my rhetoric game. God is not deceived, and my friends are not deceived, into thinking that clever words are wise.

Avoiding Exclusive Speech

Dispensing with seductive eloquence, these texts suggest that wise speech is accessible to everyone, not just the educated few. Take Proverbs, for example. Its wisdom is not cast as eloquent philosophy, but as short proverbial sayings, of the type often spoken to children. This is speech accessible to all. Proverbs are pithy and memorable, using simple language. They often draw straightforward contrasts between the wise and foolish, and give simple principles to follow. They are oral texts, with exhortations to hear and take heed. Orality democratises the book: it cannot be the secret property of the literati. I find it telling that the biblical book with the clearest guidance about wisdom uses such a simple medium.

And, even more telling perhaps: Jesus adopted this form. He spoke in proverbs and parables, addressing everyday people, not primarily learned elites. He used concrete imagery, familiar scenarios and memorable pictures, accessible to everyone. Jesus himself learnt in the synagogue, and seems to have been able to read (e.g. Luke 4). But when he teaches, he uses a down-to-earth, interactional medium, appealing to all. That is where true wisdom resides.

But how often my own speech excludes! I can easily fall into patterns of language that set up barriers. I remember one dinner-time conversation at Lyn's House about sleep. Nothing wrong with that. But we garbed it in the language of circadian rhythms, melatonin levels and the activity of the hypothalamus. Had we instead spoken of when-you-feel-sleepy and when-you-feel awake, we would have included instead of excluded. And our speech would have been much wiser for it.

Listening to Wise Speech

In face of these dangerous types of speech, there is, however, a speech which is wise – a speech which is restrained, edifying, simple and inclusive. It is this type of speech which calls from the Bible and my friends. Proverbs knows of it, and its rarity. 'There is gold and abundance of costly stones, but the lips of knowledge are a precious jewel' (20:15). It emanates from the mouth of Lady Wisdom herself, as she calls us to her. When we encounter such words, Proverbs commands us to 'listen!'[7] Indeed 'If anyone gives an answer before he hears, it is his folly and his shame' (18:13), and similarly in James 'let every person be quick to hear, slow to speak' (Jas. 1:19). In the rest of this chapter, I hope that you will listen with me for the call of wisdom.

2. Their Wisdom Calls Me to...Community

Learning from One Another

The world of the Bible is a communal world, very different from the individualised modern West. This communal ethos is clear in Proverbs. As one scholar put it, it envisages 'a small tightly-knit community, in which each individual's behaviour has a great impact on the life of everyone else.'[8] The addressee is often advised on interpersonal relationships, and is offered the reward of social esteem.

Within this context, Proverbs continually stresses the need to learn from one another. It knows that group interactions can have a great impact on individuals. It galvanizes people to 'walk with the wise, and become wise' (13:20). My go-to method of learning – sitting on my own and studying – is alien. Rather, readers are commended to go to wise individuals, 'father'-figures for advice. This is something I have struggled with. Foolishly, I have wanted and expected to 'make it on my own'. By contrast, my friends are generally unafraid to ask for help. Learning from one another requires a base level of trust. You must trust that your teacher knows what she's talking about, and that she has your best interests at heart. My friends have often demonstrated this trust beautifully.

In Proverbs, the boundaries between 'teacher' and 'student' are sometimes blurred. Not only must the *simple* take advice from others, but the *wise* must too (1:5). In fact, a key characteristic of the wise is that they learn from others.[9] The teacher must be taught. And the student can teach. My friends at Lyn's House have been some of my best teachers.[10] I hope this chapter shows something of what I have learnt from them.

Here is an example of some wise proverbs from one of my friends at Lyn's House.

Don't be afraid to be amazing.

It's okay to feel nervous, because we all feel it too.

I know how we feel, because it's okay to share how emotional we feel.

You don't ask, you don't get.

We don't wait for help, but help will come to us.

Always encourage others when they need encouraging.

Loving One Another

The wisdom of Proverbs requires not just *learning from* one another, but *loving* one another. The wise build up the community, while 'every fool will be quarrelling' (20:3). Wise community is one of the central goals of Lyn's House, and my friends have engaged in it whole-heartedly. Such wisdom is not just intellectual, but moral. Proverbs 1:2–7 gives a purpose statement for the book. It is filled with 'intellect' words – wisdom, instruction, insight, wise dealing, prudence, knowledge, discretion, learning, guidance. But right at the heart, in pride of place, is a trio of ethical terms – 'righteousness, justice, and equity' (1:3). And throughout Proverbs, wisdom is closely correlated with these virtues.

In the Book of James too, wisdom must be translated into practice (3:13–18). It is both cognitive and behavioural, both proclaimed and performed. True wisdom results in community harmony, while false wisdom brings disintegration. The latter is characterised by 'jealousy' and 'selfish ambition' – concern for oneself above the other (3:14). The term 'selfish ambition' (*eritheia*) seems to designate unjust political status-seeking,[11] and it becomes a favourite term for Paul.[12] My friends do not often harbour such ambition (perhaps because positions of high status are simply barred from them), but I have sometimes nurtured it. James equates this with 'lying against the truth' (3:14). 'Truth', like 'wisdom', is not conceptual, but existential and moral. This 'lying' amounts to indulging in competition rather than co-operation, and ultimately leads to community breakdown.

By contrast, true wisdom manifests itself in 'good conduct' (3:13) – ethical behaviour conducive to community life. Such wisdom is 'pure, peaceable, gentle, open to reason, full of mercy and good fruits, impartial, and sincere' (3:17). Its outcome is 'peace' (3:18) – the highest ideal of community harmony.

Wisdom, then, calls us to peaceable community – to learning from and loving one another. My friends at Lyn's House, it's true, do not always display this wisdom. They are not always learning, not always loving. Our community has had its fractures. But I do suggest that they are often better placed than I to accept wisdom's community call. As recipients of 'care', their lives are necessarily communal. And our tea parties show how full-heartedly they participate in community life.

3. Their Wisdom Calls Me to...Childlikeness
Adopting the Position of the Child

Within wisdom's peaceable community, how do the wise behave? The answer may be counter-intuitive: as children. In Proverbs, I must adopt the position of a child learning from her parents if I am to receive wisdom. Particularly at the start (chs.1–9), the reader is addressed as 'my son'.[13] All, no matter how old and wise, must adopt this role. In the later chapters, the implied addressee possibly 'grows up'.[14] But the parent–child dynamic is never lost.[15] By the final chapter, the addressee is the king. Yet a king chastised by his mother: 'What are you doing, my son? What are you doing, son of my womb?' (31:2). Even those of the highest status must be as children.

The familial structure is much more central in the ancient world than in the modern West. And it is central to the lives of several of our friends too. Several live with their parents into adulthood, yet retain the position of the child in the household. They know how to adopt it, therefore, while I have strained to flee the family nest.

The gospel of Matthew, too, suggests that, for true wisdom, I must be like a child. Indeed, God has 'hidden these things from the wise and understanding, and revealed them to little children' (11:25). The terms 'wise and understanding' are ironic, perhaps referring to the religious 'experts' of the day. The 'little children' are the disciples (cf. 10:42), and any who would follow Jesus. 'Little children' cannot work things out for themselves, but are open to revelation. Jesus sets this saying in the context of his own father–son relationship with God (11:26–27), a relationship in which he himself is the child.

Though the word 'wise' does not occur after v.25, many scholars think that the 'wisdom' theme carries through the passage. In fact, in vv.26–30, Jesus might imply that he himself *is* Wisdom. Throughout the Wisdom Tradition, Wisdom is depicted as a child of God,[16] and the things said of the Son here (11:27) are said of Wisdom there. No one knows the Son/Wisdom but God and no one knows God but the Son/Wisdom.[17] The Son/Wisdom mediates between God and man, revealing Him to them.[18] If we want wisdom, therefore, we must come to the Wisdom-Son of God, ourselves as children, and accept his revelation.

In v.28, Jesus issues an invitation to 'come to me', just as Lady Wisdom invites hearers to herself (Prov. 1:20; 8:1; 9:4–6). The metaphor shifts from family to agricultural labour, a familiar trope in the Wisdom Tradition. The sage in Ben Sira advises: 'Bend your shoulder and carry her [*Wisdom*], and do not fret under her bonds. Come to her with all your soul... For at last you will find the rest she gives... Her yoke is a golden ornament, and her bonds a purple cord' (Sir 6:25–30). Similarly, in the final chapter of the book, the sage invites: 'Draw near to me, you who are uneducated... Put your neck under her [*Wisdom's*] yoke, and let your souls receive instruction... See with your own eyes that I have laboured but little and found for myself much serenity' (51:23–27). The similarity to Matthew 11:28–30 is striking. And once more, Jesus takes the role of Wisdom.

The imagery may have changed here, but the message of childlike learning stays the same. In Jesus' day, children were not exempt from responsibilities: they were expected to learn from their parents and make a contribution to the household. But their responsibilities were limited. They were only given an 'easy yoke', a 'light burden' (11:30). They were not weighed down by ultimate responsibility for house-hold upkeep.

This is the role we should take. As 'little children', we are invited to work with 'gentle and lowly' wisdom, alongside the Wisdom-Child of God. The result will be rest; the soul-rest of a wise child lightly burdened by the world (11:29). My friends at Lyn's House have often emulated this. They bear responsibilities – fruitfully labouring in charity shops and chaplaincies – but they know that ultimate outcomes are out of their control. They avoid the snaring sense of responsibilities, and can wisely receive a childlike rest.

Adopting the Vulnerability of the Child

There is, however, a more troubling aspect in wisdom's call to childlikeness: in the biblical world, the child is utterly vulnerable. So are we called to be. In Matthew, the first child we meet is Jesus himself, who is completely dependent upon his parents. He is subject to whims of rulers, the threat of death, the hardships of forced migration. But to this vulnerable child comes a group of 'wise men' (*magi*) from the East – the stereotypical location of the finest wisdom. They recognise the value in his vulnerability, and in all their wisdom submit in worship to him.

At this time, children were at the very bottom of the social order. They had no status, no self-determination, no control over the direction of their lives. Texts from the period in no way idealise children. Jesus, however, reverses expectations. When the disciples argue about 'who is the greatest?' (18:1), Jesus responds with commands to serve children (18:5), and to become like children themselves (18:3–4). These acts would have been humiliating in his culture. Like the child, the disciples must place themselves at the bottom of the social order, vulnerable, threatened, completely dependent. My friends know what this feels like. But this fragile place is where Jesus, in all his wisdom, has positioned himself too, and where the kingdom of heaven truly resides (18:3; cf. 19:14).

Adopting the Joy of the Child

But lest this sound like too hard a call, childlike wisdom does not end there. It also invites us to joy. Indeed, this is a characteristic of Wisdom herself. Prov. 8 describes how Wisdom was the first thing 'brought forth' (*ḥōlāl*, 8: 24,25) and 'created(?)'[19] (8:22; *qānāh*) by God. Both of these verbs can elsewhere refer to human birth,[20] suggesting that perhaps Wisdom was 'born', like a daughter to her father. With Wisdom growing up beside him, God then sculpts the whole of creation.

The climax comes in 8:30–31. Here, Wisdom describes herself as 'beside him [*God*], like an *ʾāmōn*'. The meaning of this word is disputed, and scholars have suggested three main possibilities.

It might mean 'architect, skilled worker' (ESV, NRSV), fitting in with the previous imagery of creating. Or 'constant, faithful one' (NIV), for she has always been with God. Or, it might mean 'child, one growing up' (KJV, JPS).[21] Recently, a number of commentators have adopted this last translation,[22] recognising the imagery of birth and childhood. In this role, Wisdom 'plays' (*śāḥaq*) and takes 'delight' (*ša'ašu'îm*) – terms which elsewhere refer to children's games.[23] At the end of this most grandiose display of God's wisdom, when he has established the magnificent cosmic order, Wisdom plays. A profoundly wise attitude is thus encapsulated in childlike joy.

This joy perhaps relates to sheer wonderment at creation.[24] To the child growing up, the world is an exciting playground of new discoveries. It has been crafted by Wisdom, and she invites us to play in it with her, for she delights precisely in 'the children of man', 'the inhabited world' (8:31). In the next verse, she invites us to share her wisdom too: 'And now, O sons, listen to men: blessed are those who keep my ways. Hear instruction and be wise' (8:32–33).

It has been our aim to make Lyn's House a place of joy. My friends have taught me the art of celebration: exuberant abandon to delight in the mundane – the game of Jenga, the Elvis song, the sixteenth repetition of That Curry Story. They have taught me more about how to rejoice with wonderment at the inhabited world. Many of our celebrations happen over food and drink. Here, we're adopting Lady Wisdom's own strategy: 'she has slaughtered her beasts; she has mixed her wine', and she invites everyone around to the party (9:1–6). Now, we can't offer beasts or wine, but curry and Coke provide a welcome invitation to the Lyn's House Wisdom feast.

Jesus too celebrates with his friends over meals, much to his opponents' consternation. He depicts them like petulant children sulking at his celebration: 'we sang a dirge and you did not mourn' (Matt. 11:17). Jesus explains further that he 'came eating and drinking, and they say, "Look at him! A glutton and a drunkard, a friend of tax collectors and sinners!"' (11:19). Like Lady Wisdom, Jesus celebrates with food and drink. And like she, who welcomes all around (Prov. 9:4), he invites all outcasts in society. This childlike and inclusive celebration, his opponents cannot abide.

But Jesus says that his actions are fully justified. In Luke's version of the story, Jesus pronounces that 'Wisdom is justified by all her children' (Luke 7:35). Jesus envisions himself as the child of Wisdom, in contrast to the surly Pharisaic children. His celebration embodies this filial identity. Matthew's version takes this further: Jesus says 'Wisdom is justified by her *deeds*' (Matt. 11:19).[25] The 'deeds' are Jesus' acts of celebration. He is no longer the child of wisdom, but himself *is* Wisdom, who invites us to the celebratory feast. I for one intend to go. And there I will celebrate as I have been taught by Wisdom and my friends.

4. Their Wisdom Calls Me to...Humility
Acknowledging the Limits of My Wisdom

Submitting to the good of the community, and adopting the position of a child, suggest my next theme – humility. True wisdom is humble, and recognises human folly. In Proverbs, no one is ever completely wise. Wisdom is not innate or granted at birth, but is a lifelong, developmental process. The wise can always 'become wiser still' (9:9). They sometimes need advice,[26] and even rebuke (17:10). They are never wholly righteous (20:9).

Even the very form of Proverbs may signal the limits of the wisdom quest. Each proverb is a shard of insight into a particular situation. It is not a universal promise for always and everywhere. Each is like a fragment from a deconstructed mosaic. We can discern common hues and tones and guess at the overall picture, but we cannot see it as a whole.

Proverbs affirms that the student *does* have powers of scrutiny and comprehension. But their limits are starkly confronted when the student confronts God. For God is inscrutable, beyond comprehension, even leading the sage to declare 'there is no wisdom, no understanding, no counsel before the Lord' (Prov. 21:30). As one scholar has commented on this verse, the 'vital art of mastering life is aware that it must halt at these frontiers – indeed, it even contrives to liquidate itself there'.[27]

A key example of limitations comes in the mismatch between plans (under human control); and reality (under God's). Proverbs declares that 'many are the plans in the heart of a man, but it is the counsel of the Lord that will stand' (19:21) and 'the heart of a man plans his way, but the Lord establishes his step' (16:9 cf. 16:1). What's more, we are unable, not only to *control* our lifepath, but even to *understand* it: 'from the Lord are a man's steps; as for a person, how can he understand his way?' (20:24). This brings the wisdom's limits to a very personal level. The ways of the world are barred from my comprehension (30:18–19), and so too even my own way.

A similar message is found in the epistle of James. In what could be a midrash on Prov. 27:1, he recognises the limits of human planning. He reasons with his readers: '(4:13) Come now, you who say, "Today or tomorrow we will go into such and such a town and spend a year there and trade and make a profit" — (4:14) yet you do not know what tomorrow will bring... (4:15) Instead you ought to say, "If the Lord wills, we will live and do this or that"' (Jas. 4:13–15). These traders imagine the world as susceptible to their manipulation. They try to control the where, the when, the what, the outcome. James disillusions them: the world is not controlled by their will, but by God's. Their presumption amounts to inexcusable arrogance, and James forcefully dials up his rhetoric: 'all such boasting is evil' (4:16).

Too often, I think, I'm a bit like those traders. I do not like acknowledging my limits. I find that I want to plan every moment of my life, and fall prey to the 'you can do it if you set your mind to it' culture. My friends at Lyn's House do not on the whole suffer this delusion of being masters of fate. In fact, many important decisions are taken from them. In many ways, of course, this denial of agency is terribly sad. But I have learnt from their attitude within it. I am in reality no more self-determined than they are, but am often less grace-filled about it!

Confronting the Paradox in Proverbs

Viewing wisdom this way, Proverbs confronts us with a paradox. Wisdom is both a basic capacity of humans, and a fundamental incapacity. It is both accessible and off-limits. Proverbs mediates this tension through a religiously grounded humility: I must trust in God's wisdom, and not my own (3:5). Only by recognising my wisdom's limits can true wisdom be birthed in me. Proverbs know this posture as 'fear of the Lord'. 'Fear' does not mean 'terror', but religious reverence, a humble recognition of smallness before God, and contrite submission to Him. Some of my friends at Lyn's House are very adept at this posture, often allowing themselves to be vulnerable before God, and many of our prayer times have involved tears.

Proverbs pronounces, at several key junctures,[28] that 'the fear of the Lord is the beginning of wisdom'. This might mean two different things, and we probably don't need to choose between them.[29] Firstly: fear of the Lord is an expression of wisdom. It is wisdom's *rēʾšît*, the 'beginning' of its produce, its 'firstfruits',[30] even its 'foremost, best part'. This is the impression of 2:1–5. If you seek wisdom like silver, then 'you will understand the fear of the Lord' – the most precious end of all. The direction of causality here is that *wisdom leads to fear of the Lord*. I find this attitude challenging. The most important thing to learn is not the doctrine of the Trinity, or the Hebrew verbal system, or Paul's understanding of 'justification', but contrite reverence. My friends at Lyn's House may be one step ahead of me in throwing off such unwise aspirations.

But the Hebrew of this verse also allows the opposite causality. Fear of the Lord is the 'beginning' of wisdom, its 'starting point', that is, *fear of the Lord leads to wisdom*. This is revolutionary epistemology. All wisdom is ultimately based on a rejection of human pretences, and a willing acceptance of God's unknowable ways. It is not acquired *despite* human limitations, but *through* acceptance of them. My friends cannot then be disqualified. They and I can both trust in the wisdom-giving, incomprehensible God.

Renouncing My Criteria for Wisdom

Forced to confront my limits, I may even question whether I have the wisdom to know what wisdom is. Proverbs is scathing of personal criteria. Being 'wise in your own eyes' is the ultimate folly.[31] Those adopting such personal standards are actively anti-wisdom, and more hope is offered to the fool (26:12). It is a wise decision then to recognise your folly.[32]

In a similar vein, Paul makes himself a 'fool for Christ's sake' (1 Cor. 4:10), and exhorts the Corinthians, 'If anyone among you thinks that he is wise in this age, let him become a fool that he may become wise' (3:18). Acknowledging our folly – that 'crafty' plans will be caught, that 'wise' thoughts are futile – offers a powerful remedy against boastfulness and wrong-headed criteria for wisdom (3:19–21).

Boastfulness seems to have been a particular problem for the Corinthians (3:18–23; 1:26–31). Paul acknowledges certain characteristics that they deem pride-worthy: being 'wise according to worldly standards', 'powerful' or 'of noble birth'. But 'not many' of the Corinthians can actually claim such a status (1:26)! More pressingly, these standards are not God's standards, so are no grounds for pride. In fact, God's wisdom makes little sense by human standards. It presents us with a paradox: wisdom begins at the place of utter folly – the cross.

Confronting the Paradox in Paul

Paul's whole epistemology in 1 Cor. 1–4 is constructed around this paradox. It utterly transforms his perspective on the world, on theology, and on the Christian life. The cross is not a better form of human wisdom, but something completely different from it – even a contradiction to it. The cross, from a human perspective, is the ultimate folly (1:18, 21–23). It signals shame, degradation and weakness. The very idea of crucified Messiah(/Christ) makes no human sense, for 'messiahship' is surely synonymous with kingship and glory.

But the 'foolishness' of the cross does not have human origin. It is 'the foolishness of God', which makes it true wisdom and power (1:25). God turns all human systems upside-down. On the cross, Jesus willingly made himself foolish, weak, low and despised. Accordingly, God's favour lies with the foolish, weak, low and despised of society – with whom my friends can relate, but whom I too often shun. In the divine ordering, He uses these 'fools' to 'put to shame' the worldly 'wise' (1:27), and to exhibit true wisdom.

This means that all human grounds for boasting are lost. But in the paradoxical logic of a crucified Christ, and a folly-shaped wisdom, there is a truly humble boast – a boast in God himself. The prophet Jeremiah once wrote: 'Let not the wise man boast in his wisdom, the mighty man in his might, the rich man in his riches, but let him who boasts boast in...the Lord, who practices steadfast love, justice and righteousness in the earth' (Jer. 9:23–24). Paul draws on Jeremiah to imply that the Lord fundamentally manifests this nature on the cross – precisely where no 'wisdom', 'might' or 'riches' reside (1:31). The place of folly is the place of true wisdom.

The world's view of wisdom and folly, then, is based on upside-down criteria. If the world deems my friends low and weak and foolish, my friends may in fact be all the more wise. I am learning to recognise wisdom with these fresh eyes, prepared for it to be unexpected and paradoxical, and to meet me in surprisingly 'foolish' places.

5. Their Wisdom Calls Me to...Christ

Receiving Christ's Teaching

If Paul's cruciform wisdom is accepted, it follows that wisdom-seekers must come to Christ. In his earthly ministry, wisdom infused all his teachings. In Matthew's gospel, pride of place must be given to the Sermon on the Mount. This sermon ends with a story about wisdom and folly (7:24–27), which many of us will know best from the song (a favourite with some of our friends) – *the wise man built his house upon the rock...and the rains came tumbling down...* Unfortunately inexplicit in the song is what this 'rock' is. But the parable suggests a referent: the words of Jesus (7:24). His teaching is the true foundation for wisdom, and can withstand whatever storms are thrown at it (7:25). By comparison, any other philosophies or systems will be swept away. The parable suggests that we are inevitably all building on *something*. The stark choice is offered: rock or sand.

Jesus' foundational wisdom is not simply cognitive, but ethical: the wise man 'hears these words of mine *and does them*' (7:24). The radical love of the Sermon on the Mount, which can be displayed by abled and disabled alike, is an important wisdom criterion. Notably, the parable does not mention the appearance or grandeur of the house itself.[33] The constructions of the wise and foolish may appear basically the same, or the latter may even be *more* impressive than the former. What constitutes true wisdom is not visible on the surface. Those who look like fools may actually have the wisest foundation of all – if they have built on Jesus. Several of my friends at Lyn's House, I think, fit into this category.

Receiving Christ's Revelation

Wisdom, then, is not discerned for ourselves. It comes from God as a gift, a revelation. This is apparent in the epistle of James. His solution to a lack of wisdom is not to work harder or study more, but to 'ask God' (Jas. 1:5). This had long been recognised in the Wisdom Tradition. In one text, King Solomon says, 'I perceived that I would not possess wisdom unless God gave her to me; and it was a mark of insight to know whose gift she was' (Wis. 8:21). Solomon then breaks into an eloquent prayer for wisdom. In James 'any of you' may pray this prayer (1:5). God's response does not depend on intellect or prowess, but on 'faith' (1:6) – a simple and single-minded trust in God (such as some of my friends amply demonstrate). To these, God gives wisdom generously, unequivocally and without reproach.

For James, true wisdom 'comes down from above' (3:15), and brims with godliness (3:17). By comparison, human contrivances at 'wisdom' are 'earthly, unspiritual, demonic' (3:15). In a cataclysmic downward spiral, their origins here are the world, the godless human, even the devil. Not revealed from God, they are no true wisdom.

For Paul too, true wisdom is a divine revelation. As we have seen, in 1 Cor. 1 he lays out his paradoxical cross-centred epistemology. But he knows that, if assessed by human reasoning, it will be dismissed. The human mind does not recognise the wisdom of the cross. But the human mind is not the only tool we have. Rather, God has granted us his Spirit (1 Cor. 2:6–16), through which cruciform wisdom is *revealed* and *understood*.

Paul indicates that we cannot discover God's wisdom for ourselves, for it is 'secret and hidden' (2:7), and must be '*revealed*' to us (2:10). God's plans cannot be humanly perceived, or even imagined (2:9). Paul works here from the Greek principle that 'like is known by like'. The human mind is very much *unlike* God's mind, so the former cannot perceive the latter. But the Spirit of God, bound up with God's being, fully 'comprehends the thoughts of God' (2:11) and can reveal them to us. Accordingly, we have access to 'the mind of Christ' (2:16) and can see the wisdom of the cross.

What's more, by the Spirit's enabling, we can *understand* this wisdom. Using human logic, the message of the cross is inevitably found to be 'folly' (2:14). 'Natural' minds cannot understand its logic, for it defies human categories. But the Spirit teaches a new mode of thought, 'interpreting spiritual truths' to us (2:13), helping us to understand that which is 'spiritually discerned' (2:15). The intellectually 'abled' have no advantage over the 'disabled' in spiritual wisdom. Its content and processes do not depend on mental acuity. And we are dealing here with mystery. I have no way of judging whether and how this mystery is shaping my friends, drawing them in, being revealed to them. It will shape their wisdom in ways I can't fully understand.

Receiving Christ

Finally, receiving wisdom means receiving, not just Christ's teaching or revelation, but Christ himself. In Christ, Wisdom is incarnate – a person who calls us near. As we have seen, Wisdom is personified throughout the Wisdom Tradition. 'Lady Wisdom' is intimately related to God, and mediates between divine and human realms. She calls people to her, and makes God's wisdom accessible to them.

In the New Testament, this role is taken by Jesus. This is most clearly expressed in the description of Jesus in John 1: 'In the beginning was the Word, and the Word was with God, and the Word was God' (John 1:1). The 'Word' (*logos*) here is closely related to Wisdom (*sophia*), and the ideas are very similar to Proverbs 8, where Wisdom is also with God from the beginning. John then describes the Word's agency in creation, again paralleling Wisdom's role (Prov. 8:22–31).

Such ideas are evident in Paul too: Jesus not only reveals wisdom, but *is* wisdom. Paul preaches 'Christ the power of God and the wisdom of God' (1:24), and encourages the Corinthians that they are 'in Christ Jesus, who became to us wisdom from God' (1:30). Matthew too bears nascent Wisdom Christology: 'wisdom [i.e. Jesus] is justified by her deeds' (11:19), and Jesus adopts wisdom's role in calling to the heavy-laden (11:25–30) (see discussion of these passages above).

Like Lady Wisdom, Jesus invites us to himself. Becoming wise involves coming to a person, not learning about a concept. And like Lady Wisdom's, his is an open and indiscriminate invitation to all those around him – abled or disabled, educated or uneducated. Wisdom is relational, and my friends are, I know, adept at relationship. When we spend time with others, we often become like them. So coming to Christ means beginning to bear the image of his upside-down wisdom. And in my friends, I see the wise face of the foolish Jesus.

Conclusion

I have found writing this chapter challenging. I have not enjoyed removing myself from my safe academic paradigm, where clever = wise. Through my experiences at Lyn's House and through writing this chapter, I have been made painfully aware of my own wisdom's limits.

Beginning with the Bible and my friends at Lyn's House, I set myself the task of listening for the voice of Wisdom. In Proverbs, she is depicted as a woman who calls out in the bustling market-place of worldly claims. I have not always found it easy to hear her voice, and I am sometimes seduced by other siren songs. But I am learning to pick out her tones. And what a sweet melody I find: the Wisdom melody of silence, community, childlikeness and humility. It is the song sung by Christ. And by his image-bearers, the world's 'fools', my friends.

Wisdom's call is tender and gracious, and it changes me as I listen for it. Recognising my areas of folly, I grow in God's wisdom. May I keep attentive to the melody, as the Bible and my friends sing it. May I even join in the song. And may I, with Paul, with my friends, and with Christ himself, become a 'fool' that I may become wise (1 Cor. 3:18).

Endnotes

1   In this chapter, where I refer to 'my friends' I mean my friends at Lyn's House.
2   These are included in the Catholic and Orthodox Apocrypha, but not in the Protestant canon.
3   For an interpretation of Matthew as 'wisdom', see especially Ben Witherington III, *Matthew*, Smyth & Helwys Commentary Series (Macon, GA: Smyth & Helwys, 2006).
4   See e.g. Dan G. McCartney, 'The Wisdom of James the Just', *Southern Baptist Journal of Theology* 4, No. 3, (2000), pp.52–64.
5   e.g. Jas. 4:6; 4:13–17; 5:20, cf. Prov. 3:34; 27:1; 10:12 respectively. Strong connections are also found with the book of Ben Sira.
6   Cf. also 4:24; 10:6,11; 12:19; 16:28; 17:20; 21:6; 24:28; 25:18; 26:24–26,28.
7   1:8; 4:1; 5:7; 7:24; 8:32,33; 19:20; 22:17; 23:19,22.
8   Tomáš Frydrych, *Living under the Sun: Examination of Proverbs and Qoheleth* (Leiden: Brill, 2002).
9   10:8; 12:15; 13:1,10; 15:5,12,31; 17:10; 19:25; 21:11.
10 I am reminded of Henri Nouwen's words about Adam, a profoundly disabled, dear friend of his: Nouwen talks about how Adam had become 'my friend, my teacher, my spiritual director, my counsellor, my minister' (Henri Nouwen, *Adam, God's Beloved* (London: Darton, Longman and Todd Ltd., 1997), p.40).
11 William F. Arndt and F. Wilbur Gingrich, *A Greek–English Lexicon of the New Testament*, 2d cd. (Chicago: University of Chicago Press, 1979), p.309.
12 Rom. 2:8; 2 Cor. 12:20; Gal. 5:20; Phil. 1:17; 2:3.
13 Prov. 1:8,10,15; 2:1; 3:1,11,21, etc. The Book of Proverbs seems to have been written for young men, so uses the term 'son' throughout. But its message is equally applicable to females.
14 See especially William P. Brown, 'The Pedagogy of Proverbs 10:1–31:9', in W.P. Brown (ed.) *Character and Scripture: Moral Formation, Community, and Biblical Interpretation* (Grand Rapids: Eerdmans, 2002), pp.150–82.
15 E.g. 'my son' in 19:27; 23:15,19,26; 24:13,21; 27:11.
16 See discussion of Prov. 8 below.
17 E.g. Job 28:12–13; Sir. 1:1-10; Bar. 3:31–32.
18 E.g. Prov. 8; Wis. 8:3–8; 9:4–11.
19 Translation disputed.
20 See Gen. 4:1 for *qānāh*; Job 15:7 and Ps. 51:7 for *ḥōlāl*.
21 ESV = English Standard Version; NRSV = New Revised Standard Version; NIV = New International Version; KJV = King James Version; JPS = Jewish Publication Society.
22 E.g. William P. Brown, 'Wisdom's Wonder: Proverbs, Paideia, and Play', *The Covenant Quarterly* (2010) pp.13–24, Michael V. Fox, "Amon Again", *JBL* (1996) pp. 699–702.
23 'Play' in Zech. 8:5; Gen. 21:9; 'delight' in Isa 11:8.
24 Brown, 'Wisdom's Wonder'.
25 A few manuscripts of Matthew differ, and contain the wording of Luke.

26 E.g. 9:9; 10:8; 12:15; 13:1; 15:5,31; 19:25; 21:11.
27 Gerhard von Rad, *Old Testament Theology*, Vol. 1. (Edinburgh: Oliver and Boyd, 1962), p.440.
28 Esp. 1:7, which caps the 'purpose statement' of the book (1:2–7); 9:10, which concludes the book's Prologue (1–9); and 15:33, which is central to the first proverb collection (10:1–22:16). Note also the reference to 'fear of the Lord' in 31:30, which concludes the whole book.
29 See Zoltán Schwáb, 'Is Fear of the Lord the Source of Wisdom or Vice Versa?', *VT* (2013) pp.652–662, for a discussion of this issue.
30 e.g. Ex. 23:19; 34:26; Ez. 44:30.
31 Prov. 3:7; 12:15; 26:5,12; 28:11.
32 See Zoltán Schwáb, 'I, the Fool: A "Canonical" Reading of Proverbs 26:4-5', *JTI* (2016) pp.31–50.
33 Contrast Lady Wisdom's impressively pillared abode in Prov. 9.

CHAPTER 6

The Spirit Speaks to the Church

SHABBAT WISDOM

Deborah Hardy Ford

As I began to explore various categories and 'ways in' to this chapter, it suddenly struck me that there is something very Jewish about what happens in Lyn's House. There is something about its quality of time, relationship, celebration and joy that is deeply 'Shabbat'.[1]

Welcoming a Mystery, Being More at Home

Despite the many wonderful meals, parties and celebrations of different Christian feasts and seasons I've hosted or been invited to over the years, there is still an extra 'something' about Shabbat: something that, in my experience at least, my own (Christian) tradition simply doesn't 'get'. Some years ago now, when I was fortunate enough to begin to make friends, read sacred texts and celebrate Shabbat with those of other faiths,[2] I started to have a wonderful recurrent dream:

I find myself in the midst of an animated Jewish gathering. I'm anxious as to whether they will accept and welcome me as a non-Jew (let alone as a Christian priest), but I'm longing to stay and spend more time with them. I know that they have the secret to something wonderful that I need to discover too. Sometimes I am with them for a long time – sometimes only fleetingly – and I always awaken from the dream with a sense of longing for more.

The dream began then, I guess, because – although I'm not sure quite how or why – the more I have listened and learned about life and about God through Jewish friends, the more I have discovered the depths of my Christian heritage and identity in God. And the process has been *great*: I have laughed more fully and more deeply during these moments than anywhere else.

Until Lyn's House...

There have been a number of what I would call 'profound moments' that stand out for me in the life of Lyn's House to date. Initially I thought they were simply rather 'random' moments, but they have kept happening: and made me think again...and begin to wonder whether, perhaps – for those who have ears to hear – our friends with intellectual disabilities might be in touch with and expressing something about a much deeper reality than most of us are attuned to.[3]

One was a birthday party: this was early on in the life of Lyn's House. It happened to be my birthday and I realised what I really wanted to do was share it with friends at Lyn's House. So we organised pizza, cake and a data projector...sent out invitations,[4] and a diverse crowd of us gathered and ate, watched and sang (word for word) our way through the film *The Sound of Music*. We shared tears of deep hope and joy, as well as those of fear, grief and pain. It was a rare and beautiful thing: it had an almost liturgical quality to it. During the break for the intermission, one of our core friends suddenly exited the room. She re-emerged a short time later, her face covered by a delicate lacy veil to signify being bedecked as a bride, full of longing and anticipation: ready to meet her bridegroom in the wedding scene we were about to witness in the film.

It's one of the ways to understand Shabbat: preparing oneself and one's home with great care, both physically and spiritually, in anticipation of welcoming in (in this case) the Sabbath Bride or Queen.[5] One of the opening refrains in the prayers to welcome Shabbat is:

> *Come my Beloved, to greet the bride;*
> *let us welcome the Sabbath...*
> To greet the Sabbath, let us go,
> for of blessing, she is the source.
> From the outset, as of old, ordained:
> Last in deed and first in thought.
>
> *Come, my Beloved, to greet the bride,*
> *Let us welcome the Sabbath.*[6]

It is about cultivating practices, patterns and rhythms that help to orient our deepest desire as human beings: to welcome and honour the Divine presence within and among us: 'You are great, Lord, and highly to be praised (Ps. 47:2): great is your power and your wisdom is immeasurable' (Ps. 146:5)...to praise you is our desire, a little piece of your creation. You stir us to take pleasure in praising you, because you have made us for yourself, and our heart is restless until it rests in you.'[7]

No matter how much we long to meet a soul mate or lover with whom to share this life, our deeper human longing is for even more. Like Shabbat, Lyn's House is about going deeper into that longing: together. It's about welcoming and receiving the Divine presence in one another: God's mutual indwelling and the mysterious 'to and fro' of being both host and guest, where those who (on the surface, at least) appear to be doing the 'hosting' (serving and giving) gradually discover that, somehow, in doing so, they are actually just as much 'guests', receiving.

In the (Jewish) Kabalistic tradition, Shabbat is often known as 'the face' (Hebrew *panim*): the place where the 'inside' or 'innermost' ('holy of holies') of someone is revealed, and Shabbat a time when: 'We welcome the *Shekinah* – the glory of the Divine[8]– and (as we do) welcome our own soul back home... It's a time and space to welcome God in our midst and to remember, to listen and to see afresh... Shabbat is an invitation...to come home and to greet the shining face of the Shekinah in all of those around us... In the glorious paradox of the spirit, by letting a lover enter, we ourselves are let in as well...the true lover lets us realise the Eden we are dwelling in every day. That is what it means to feel at home in your life.'[9]

I remember Jean Vanier once saying (as he held up a huge hand to make a tiny space between his thumb and finger), 'You know, we only ever see or know this much of a person, only God sees and knows the rest: their real beauty – they are *so* precious.' In Lyn's House, where (for many) language and words are often difficult, faces and other forms of communication take on new depths of meaning. And all those involved in the community of Lyn's House – in whatever ways or levels – speak of it being a place where they can (sometimes rather tentatively and gradually) be more and more 'at home'.

As a parent says of a daughter's experience of Lyn's House: 'It's somewhere she hasn't got carers and she hasn't got us: she can just be herself. Everywhere else – even at home with us – there are certain rules, expectations or contractual obligations. At Lyn's House she's free: she just goes in and treats it as if it were her home. It's hard to say how much it means to her because it means so much. I honestly can't think of anywhere else she'd rather go or be: except, perhaps, her sister's or brother's. It's very, very important to her. And part of it is because it's a place where she can be at home in faith.'

Although spiritual needs are meant to be taken into account as part of a comprehensive 'care package' for anyone with learning disabilities, the reality is that this is difficult to ensure it is actually provided on the ground and is often very dependent on of any particular care-giver/provider's own stance and priorities. One parent described how her daughter had been in tears when her carer had presented her with an impossible choice: "'Would you like to go to church, or would you rather go to the pub and have a curry?" – both things she loved and wanted to do.'

Or another, who said about her daughter: 'She loves coming and the attention she gets at Lyn's House. We're quite a large family and she easily gets "lost" in a crowd because she's quite reserved. I don't really know what happens when she's there, because she doesn't talk, but she loves it! If I ever had to say she wasn't going to be able to go (if we were in the middle of a snow-storm and couldn't physically get there, for example), she'd be devastated. She *has to*: she loves it. And she certainly wouldn't go if she didn't want to: she'd make that very clear.'

Again and again people speak about what they encounter at Lyn's House as being mysteriously profound. As a resident member has put it: 'It's been very challenging at times, but it's been deeply meaningful and life-changing. I can honestly say it's been one of the most significant things I've ever done in my life.' There is something deeply transformational about it. And it is not unrelated to God.

Someone else describes Lyn's House as 'a place where time stands still...' It's another way to understand Shabbat: as an 'architecture of holiness' or a 'cathedral' in time. Here are some of the ways in which A.J. Heschel has spoken of Shabbat: 'It's a kingdom for all. It is not a date but an atmosphere...when the Sabbath is entering the world, man is touched by a moment of actual redemption; as if for a moment the spirit of the Messiah moved over the face of the earth... The meaning of the Sabbath is to celebrate time rather than space. Six days a week we live under the tyranny of things of space; on the Sabbath we try to become attuned to holiness in time. It is a day on which we are called upon to share in what is eternal in time, to turn from the results of creation to the mystery of creation; from the world of creation to the creation of the world.'[10] There is a call to create a special quality of space in time to welcome and honour God's presence in our midst; and to place ourselves and our lives within the 'bigger picture' of the Divine cosmos and drama. It's a time when we humbly open ourselves to the mystery of God; and to the mystery of one another and all that is yet to come: a time when heaven and earth meet: 'Where the modern and mundane open up to yield glimpses of something else.'[11] There are no 'blueprints', but it's not something that simply 'happens on its own'. At the same time, careful preparations play an important part.

Being Reshaped

As soon as one celebration of Shabbat is over, preparations for the next one begin. Part of heading back into the week of work is about anticipating its coming again: it's about cultivating a mood of longing and, as before any wedding feast, eyes are kept open for special food and little 'extras' that will help to heighten and add that special 'something' and enhance the quality of celebration on the day itself.

Although it's not about keeping kosher, Lyn's House has plenty of dietary restrictions and other details that need to be kept in mind when planning food for meals and celebrations, too. And it's not only about the practicalities: prayer is an integral rhythm and part of getting ready to welcome and receive the fullness of the spirit of Shabbat when it comes:

> Beloved of the soul, Father of compassion,
> draw Your servant close to your will.
> Like a deer will Your servant run
> and fall prostrate before your beauty,
> To him Your love is sweeter
> than honey from the comb, than any taste.
>
> Glorious, beautiful, radiance of the world,
> my soul is sick with love for You.
> Please, God, heal her now
> by showing Your tender radiance.
> Then she will recover her strength and be healed,
> and have everlasting joy...

Reveal Yourself, my beloved, and spread over me
    the tabernacle of your peace,
let the earth shine with Your glory,
    let us be overjoyed and rejoice in You.
Hurry, beloved, for the appointed time has come,
    and be gracious to us as in the times of old.[12]

Both Shabbat and Lyn's House have a place for prayer; candle-lighting; reading scripture; breaking bread; eating; talking; listening; singing; dancing; playing games; and enjoying quality time and attention together. Both are fundamentally about receiving what and who have been given:

> I love to change the world, but I rarely appreciate things as they are.
> I know how to give, but I don't always know how to receive.
> I know how to keep busy, but I don't always know how to be still.
> I talk, but I don't often listen. I look, but I don't often see.
> I yearn to succeed, but I often forget what is truly important.
> Teach me, God, to slow down. May my resting revive me.[13]

I have a friend who is a rabbi and in a conversation she described Shabbat in this way: 'It's a stepping back day: it's a day of humility and gratitude...with lots of talking, attention and listening...'[14]

One of the things that comes up again and again in Lyn's House is how hard it is when time together comes to an end and it's time to leave. We have yet to incorporate the wisdom of the little ceremony 'Havdalah' (meaning 'separation') marking the end of Shabbat and easing the transition back into the rest of the day, week and wider world ('holy' to 'secular' time). According to Rabbinic tradition, its deeper meaning relates to the story of Adam and Eve, sentenced to exile from the Garden of Eden on the sixth day of creation, when they sinned. But 'God granted them stay of sentence, allowing them to spend one day, Shabbat itself, in the garden. During that day, say the Sages, the sun did not set. Havdalah recalls the moment at the end of Shabbat, when darkness falls and Adam and Eve have to leave paradise for the first time and enter the world outside, with its darkness and dangers. As a gift, God showed them how to make light. Hence the light of *Havdalah.*' Prayers include: 'I call to you, Lord: save me. Make known to me the path of life... Behold, God is my salvation. I will trust and not be afraid. The Lord, the Lord is my strength and my song. He has become my salvation. With joy you will draw water from the springs of salvation. Your people is Your blessing, Selah. The Lord of hosts is with us, the God of Jacob our stronghold, Selah...' [15]

The discipline, wisdom and rhythms of Shabbat are about a radical reordering and rebalancing of everything: whole chapters of time (not just weeks, but months, years and the whole of life within the perspective of eternity); of ecology and relationships (with God; with creation; with oneself and with one another); of economy and power – from 'human' ones, based on scarcity, competition, dominance and exchange to those based on a Divine economy of abundance, mercy, blessing and plenty for all – and of where, and in whom, we place our deepest trust and hope.

Shabbat sets us free from ourselves and from our own compulsions – from all the things that define and confine us 'conventionally': 'To set apart one day a week for freedom, a day on which we do not use the instruments which have been so easily turned into weapons of destruction; a day for being with ourselves; a day of detachment from the vulgar; of independence from external obligations; a day on which we stop worshipping the idols of technical civilisation; a day on which we use no money; a day of armistice in the economic struggle with our fellow men and the forces of nature. Is there any institution that holds out greater hope for human progress than the Sabbath?'[16]

One of the particular gifts of most (if not all) of my friends with learning disabilities, is that they are not in the slightest bit interested or taken in by the things that so often seduce and define us: status, image, power, success, material wealth, etc. In a place like Cambridge, where those things are often highly valued, it is a deeply liberating, if somewhat disconcerting, thing: they are seen right through. Our core friends have the ability to see much deeper: right to the heart of who you are and what you really value.

Time L'Shma[17]

Like Shabbat, Lyn's House is about 'resetting our clocks' and finding our balance again. It's about refinding our rhythms and 'coming home': being reconciled to God, to ourselves, to one another, and to all creation. That's what happened at the *Sound of Music* birthday party. That's why it's so hard to leave when it all comes to an end – even when there is already a next time on its way. It's based on God's fourth Commandment for wise living: 'Remember the Sabbath Day, to keep it holy'– just as God rested on the seventh day of Creation:

'And on the seventh day God finished the work that he had done, and he rested on the seventh day from all the work that he had done... So God blessed the seventh day and hallowed it, because on it God rested from all the work that he had done in creation' (Genesis 2:2–3).[18]

The fulfilment of creation is when God *sanctifies*[19] (or 'blesses' or 'hallows') it: it is not simply a matter of 'resting' from work: the two are interwoven – like the logic of praise: praise somehow 'perfecting perfection'.[20] Making and having the opportunity to recognise and celebrate the joy and wonder of someone or something together (and it's something those with learning disabilities are very good at) makes it even better. It's the dynamic or 'crown' of creation that fulfils something even deeper: and there's a deep and innate longing for it in us all. Sharing joy. Jean Vanier describes it in the film documentary *Summer in the Forest* as 'wasting time together to become who we really are'.[21] It is part of becoming fully human.

Last year I was lucky enough to be in Trosly-Breuil (home of the first L'Arche community in France) when *Summer in the Forest,* which had been filmed there and featured a number of those living (and present) there, was being shown. Although the whole community in Trosly (which has now expanded considerably) had clearly 'lived' with the film and crew for several years during its making, this was the first time they were seeing it.

They watched and listened attentively as they appeared before themselves, bursting out and beaming with laughter as they recognised one another and their story/stories. The quality of their delighted innocence and joy was a rare and beautiful thing: there was no 'edge' to it at all. There was that 'primal' or childlike innocence and joy Jean Vanier sometimes describes: the childlike 'second naivety'[22] we are all invited to discover: 'Beyond the desert of criticism (critical and rational thinking), we need to be called again...to the discovery of a "second naiveté", which is a return to the joy of our first naiveté, but now totally new, inclusive and mature thinking.'[23]

It's what the quality of joyful trust and innocence at the heart of Shabbat and Lyn's House are about. It is not 'Utopia', but it is not an illusory fantasy (some sort of 'wish fulfillment') either. But the irony is, that even when something so good is on offer, it is not easy to receive. It's against the grain in more ways than one and takes real effort to help it happen. And it takes lots of encouragement and solidarity in commitment. Over the years in Lyn's House, I have heard more than one person say in a variety of ways: 'To be honest, it was the last thing

I felt like doing: I'd had a non-stop day at work; still had masses to do, and all I really wanted to do was go home for the evening, but I knew the others were all relying on me being there. And by the end of the evening, I have to say, I was also completely re-energised.'

It is not that the reality of life isn't often very difficult: living face to face is sometimes being honest about some of the very painful things that are going on for (and between) people, too. Being 'at home' means it's a safe enough place to gradually be honest and open about some of the less beautiful things and parts of ourselves, and the world we inhabit, too. Living with difference at any depth means having to hold the tension and discomfort between things we sometimes disagree vehemently about, and to keep on talking, listening and trying to understand each other in that.

But the paradox is that putting Lyn's House and its 'upside-down' values first pays off. The very keeping of the discipline or 'laws' of Shabbat (or their equivalent in Lyn's House) is what creates the space for being genuinely free and open to being surprised by something new. It is something the Jews are very good at: simply 'doing' and 'getting on with it' – whether you feel like it or not: and *trusting* the doing it – letting yourself live into it.[24]

One of the disciplines of Shabbat 'table talk' is to focus on celebrating the *good* things: simply for the sake of it.[25] Just as God does again and again at each stage of creation ('and God saw that it was *good*' – and at the end of the sixth day, on the eve of Shabbat, it was '*very good*'[26]). It is certainly not a denial of the terrible things happening in the world around – Shabbat includes serious prayers for the suffering in the world as it is – but it is about celebrating the fact that God is good and God's redemptive love goes even deeper *whatever.* The balance is tipped: that is why we can rest and celebrate in deep gratitude, relief and joy.

It is a moment of 'realised eschatology' – a glimpse of heaven – the spirit of the prayer Jesus encourages his disciples to pray: 'Our Father in heaven. Hallowed be thy name. Thy kingdom come, thy will be done, on earth as it is in heaven...'[27] – or as Jonathan Sacks describes it, a 'foretaste' of the day when all God's promises will be fulfilled in the ultimate wedding feast: 'Shabbat is not merely a day of rest, it is a rehearsal within time, for the age beyond time, when humanity, guided by the call of God, moves beyond strife, evil and oppression, to create a world of harmony, respecting the integrity of creation as God's work, and the human person as God's image. At that time people looking back at history will see that though evil flourished "like grass", it was short-lived, while the righteous grow slowly but stand tall "like the cedar of Lebanon". Because our time perspective is short, we seem to inhabit a world in which evil prevails. Were we able to see history as a whole, we would know that good wins the final victory; in the long run justice prevails.'[28]

On this day and in Shabbat time, the party has already begun: 'When Shabbat preparations are finally over, the week has been "washed off" (with a shower), special food has been set on a special table, the candles have been lit, and God's presence and love prayed and welcomed in, those gathered greet one another with the words, "*Shabbat shalom!*[29] May you dwell in completeness on this seventh day!"' And at that moment there is a new sense of time: something new has begun – like the moment in a marriage when the celebrant declares, 'I now pronounce that they are husband and wife.' A new dawn has come.

It's the spirit and focus of the film *Summer in the Forest*, too. After I first saw the film in Cambridge, I spoke briefly with its director Randall Wright about why he had chosen not to show more of the tensions or difficulties involved in the life of the community. He turned to me and said, 'People keep asking me that! I've made lots of films about suffering and tragedy – and so have lots of others: there's no shortage of films about all the bad things going on in the world. But anyone can make those. What I wanted to capture instead was the quality of laughter, joy and peace I found in L'Arche: that's a much rarer thing.'[30]

He had chosen to do what Denise Levertov captures in her poem 'Making Peace':

A voice from the dark called out,
　　'The poets must give us
imagination of peace, to oust the intense, familiar
imagination of disaster: Peace, not only
the absence of war.'
　　But peace, like a poem,
is not there ahead of itself,
can't be imagined before it is made,
can't be known except
in the words of its making,
grammar of justice,
syntax of mutual aid.

A feeling towards it,
dimly sensing a rhythm, is all we have
until we begin to utter its metaphors,
learning them as we speak.
    A line of peace might appear
if we restructured the sentence our lives are making,
revoked its affirmation of profit and power,
questioned our needs, allowed
long pauses…
    A cadence of peace might balance its weight
on that different fulcrum; peace, a presence;
an energy field more intense than war,
might pulse then,
stanza by stanza into the world,
each act of living
one of its words, each word
a vibration of light – facets
of the forming crystal.[31]

That's what Shabbat is about and that's what Lyn's House is about: creating *an energy field more intense than war* – or anything else that threatens to undermine or get in the way of it.

Invitation to the Church

A few months ago, I contacted the PA (personal assistant) of one of the 'the great and good' in the Church: someone who has been a good friend and supporter of Lyn's House over the years but is very busy and whom we hadn't seen for several years. So I emailed his PA to see if he would like to come for a meal at Lyn's House. The answer was 'yes, please' and we liaised about the details (date, time, address, etc.). The correspondence then went like this:

PA: Dear Debbie, Many thanks for this and I assume he just needs to turn up so that will be fine, thank you.

Me: Dear [PA], Yes, turning up is all that's required: simply 'wasting time' together for its own sake!

PA: I'm sure it's not and that you all get a lot from it. It is in the diary now.

Sadly, in the event, due to extenuating (all very good) circumstances, he was unable to come. It felt a bit like the parable where Jesus describes the Kingdom of Heaven as a Wedding Banquet held by the king for his son:[32] the preparations are all finished, everything is ready, the excitement and anticipation high. But at the last minute, those invited are caught up in other things and unable to come. They miss the moment.

Surely Jesus' teaching and reminder that 'the sabbath was made for humankind, not humankind for the sabbath'[33] is about exactly this – and a corrective to the whole range of ways we human beings distort things – *whatever* our faith, creed or philosophy of life. And his words are intentionally (and sometimes hyperbolically) sharp about the consequences if we don't, because it matters! God is *longing* for us to share in his delight with him. If we do not do it, we lose something of our humanity: we are less than who we are and can be: both as individuals and as a whole.

We *need* to be interrupted and to be freed from ourselves and from all the systems, structures, pressures, vanities and agendas we get caught up in (and will always get caught up in, however good or 'worthy' they might be), so that we mirror God, rather than the values of the society in which we live.[34] Shabbat certainly has an invitation for us all in doing that – and part of it is cultivating an ability to laugh at our*selves*. The poet Patrick Kavanagh describes the resurrection as a laugh set free for ever and ever:

> Christ was lately dead, Men were afraid
> with a new fear, the fear
> of love. There was a laugh freed
> for ever and ever. The Apostles' Creed
> was a fireside poem, the talk of the town...
> They remember a man who has seen Christ in his thorny crown.[35]

Shabbat also invites us to rediscover and celebrate God in the home, which Jonathan Sacks describes as 'the matrix' of Judaism – a time when strangers and the marginalised are made central, too: 'The prophets compared the relationship between God and Israel with the covenantal faith between husband and wife and parent and child, which is born and sustained within the home. Our relationship to GOD and to those closest to us are both covenantal – a mutual pledge of loyalty and love. Through the family and the quality of its relationships, Divine blessings flow into the world. Before the Friday evening meal, we enact sequentially the values on which the home is built…'[36]

When so many are too busy for the wedding feast, Jesus says, 'So invite the poor, the lonely, the disabled instead!'[37] He knows they won't miss their chance: they see and know what really matters and they know how to receive. Dietrich Bonhoeffer says: 'Every Christian community must realise that not only do the weak need the strong, but also that the strong cannot exist without the weak. The elimination of the weak is the death of fellowship… The exclusion of the weak and insignificant, the seemingly useless people, from everyday Christian life in community may actually mean the exclusion of Christ; for in the poor sister or brother, Christ is knocking at the door.'[38] Christian Salenson comments: 'The good health of a community is shown in its capacity to celebrate and feast: it's distance from the daily…and there are an infinite variety of ways and forms – both religious and not (but who is to judge that?). Every celebration worthy of the names is festive. The loss of the festive character (as one sees in certain liturgies) is the death of celebration. Celebration reveals the hidden meaning of a community and the "beyond" that keeps it alive, its mystery.'[39]

This is the mystery of *'an energy field more intense than war'*.[40] Shabbat and Lyn's House are close to its heart, inviting us in. What are we waiting for?

'The Spirit and the bride, say *'Come!'*[41]

Endnotes

1   The Jewish day of rest: the seventh day of the week.

2   The practice of 'Scriptural Reasoning' – see www.scripturalreasoning.org.

3   Through his experience communicating and working with those suffering with schizophrenia, Harold Searles suggests that his patients are deeply in touch with a reality that most of us find too much to bear. See H.F. Searles, *Collected Papers on Schizophrenia and Related Subjects* (London: Karnac Books, 1965).

4   The parent of one of the core friends told me how it was the first time in her life that her daughter had received a personal invitation to a birthday party and just how much it had meant.

5   See A.J. Heschel, *The Sabbath: Its Meaning for Modern Man* (New York: Farrar, Straus and Giroux, 2005).

6   *Authorised Daily Prayer Book* of the United Hebrew Congregations of the Commonwealth (with New Translation and Commentary by Chief Rabbi Sir Jonathan Sacks (London: Collins, 2006), p.267.

7   Saint Augustine (Translation and notes by Henry Chadwick), *Confessions* (Oxford: Oxford University Press, 1992), p.4.

8   The feminine or 'maternal' aspect of the Divine.

9   Naom Sachs Zion and Shawn Fields-Meyer, *A Day Apart: Shabbat at Home* (Shalom Hartman Institute, 2004), p.11.

10 From Heschel, *The Sabbath* (2005).

11 Judith Shulevitz: *The Sabbath World: Glimpses of a Different Order of Time* (New York: Random House Inc, 2011), p.20.

12 Yedid Nefesh (a song sung before the Welcoming Shabbat Service), in *Authorised Daily Prayer Book*, p.257. Kiddush prayers mark the transition from holy to secular time.

13 See Naomi Levy, 'To Begin Again' (a prayer of preparation for Shabbat) in *A Day Apart*, p.22.

14 In conversation.

15 Jonathan Sacks, Commentary, in *Authorised Daily Prayer Book*, pp. 578, 608. And one refrain sung to the last of the four prayers blessing God and one another is: 'A good week, a week of peace, may gladness reign and joy increase.'

16 Heschel quoted in *A Day Apart*, p.1.

17 The Jewish prayer 'Hear O Israel, the Lord our God is One'– prayed 'for the sake of the name' – giving thanks and praise to God for God's goodness, not for anything to be gained or received by it.

18 See the biblical narrative in Exodus 19, where, following their deliverance from Egypt, God speaks the words of his Covenant to Moses for his children on Mount Sinai: guidelines for living fully and well together.

19 Jonathan Sacks, Commentary, in *Authorised Daily Prayer Book*: 'Sanctifies' is 'the key word of the betrothal declaration under the bridal canopy in a [Jewish] wedding', p.287.

20 D.W. Hardy and D.F. Ford, *Jubilate: Theology in Praise* (London: Darton, Longman and Todd Ltd, 1984).

21 Jean Vanier. See www.summerintheforest.com.

22 Paul Ricoeur, quoted by Richard Rohr: see 'A Second Simplicity' at https://thevalueofsparrows.com/2014/04/22/simplicity-a-second-simplicity-by-richard-rohr.

23 In conversation.

24 Letting ourselves/wills be 'bent' to the gentle will of God's love: in the prayer 'The Blessing of Light', Evening Prayer – Form 2 – Monday and daily in Pentecost in *Common Worship: Daily Prayer* (London: Church House Publishing, 2011).

25 As in *L'Shma* – the Jewish prayer 'Hear O Israel, the Lord our God is One'– prayed 'for the sake of the name' – giving thanks and praise to God for God's goodness, not for anything to be gained or received by it.

26 Genesis, Chapter 1.

27 The Lord's Prayer – Matthew 6: 9–13, *Holy Bible, New Revised Standard Version* (London: SPCK, 2011).

28 Jonathan Sacks, Commentary, in *Authorised Daily Prayer Book*.

29 Or a variation on it, depending on the Jewish line of descent.

30 In conversation.

31 Paul A. Lacey and Anne Dewey (eds), *The Collected Poems of Denise Levertov* (New York: New Directions Publishing, 2013).

32 Luke 14:4–24; Matthew 22:1–14.

33 Mark 2:27.

34 Cf. Bonhoeffer's distinction between a 'spiritual community', which serves God, and a 'human' one, which ends up serving itself. Dietrich Bonhoeffer, *Life Together and Prayerbook of the Bible: Works, Volume 5* (Minneapolis: Fortress Press, 1996), pp.34–47.

35 Patrick Kavanagh, *Lough Derg – A Poem* (London: Martin Brian and O'Keeffe, 1978), p.12.

36 Jonathan Sacks, Commentary, in *Authorised Daily Prayer Book*, pp. 308–309.

37 Matthew 22:21.

38 Dietrich Bonhoeffer, *Life Together and Prayerbook of the Bible*, p.46.

39 Christian Salenson, *Boulversant Fragilite: L'Arche a l'Epreuve du Handicap* (Nouvelle Cite, Bruyeres-le-Chatel, 2016), pp.130–131.

40 Levertov, op. cit.; emphasis added.

41 Revelation 22:17 (NRSV).

— PART 3 —

Discerning Community Today

CHAPTER 7

Community as a Sign of Hope

Philip S. Powell and Ian Randall

In his book, *Signs of the Times: Seven Paths of Hope for a Troubled World* (2013), Jean Vanier talks about seven movements which he sees as crucial. In his introduction he speaks about the 'spirituality of L'Arche' as resting on 'the profound value of each individual, whatever their culture, religion, way of life, ability or disability'.[1] In the present chapter of this book there is an invitation to consider how this spirituality has been and can be embodied in various forms of community life. Three themes from Jean Vanier (each a chapter in his *Signs*) which offer hope are especially woven throughout this chapter: 'from exclusion to encounter'; 'from isolation to community'; and 'from strength to vulnerability'.[2] Jean Vanier's *Community and Growth* is also utilised here as a basic resource. There he writes: 'The difference between community and a group of friends is that in community we verbalise our mutual belonging and bonding. We announce the goals and the spirit that unites us'; and he goes on to say: 'Communities are truly communities when they are open to others, when they remain vulnerable and humble; when the members are growing in love, in compassion and humility'.[3] The chapter gives a brief historical account of communal initiatives in relation to those with learning disabilities and then offers personal reflections on possibilities.

Experiences in the Past: Exclusion to Encounter

A considerable amount has been done by Christian communities in the past to share life with those with learning disabilities. A late eighteenth-century communal initiative was the York Retreat, founded in 1896 by Quakers who were deeply concerned about conditions in the York Lunatic Asylum.[4] One influential nineteenth-century pioneer in southern England was Andrew Reed, minister of a large Congregational church in London. He was involved in many significant areas of social outreach as part of his ministry. In the 1840s he became especially concerned about those with learning disabilities (although that expression was not used then and words like 'lunatic', 'idiot' and 'insane' were common), who were often in workhouses or were chained up along with prisoners, and if they were seen in public were often the subjects of taunting. Theologically, Reed insisted that God's image is stamped upon all people, and practically, he decided to explore what could be done.[5] Reed was determined to learn from others and he sought out the views of Dr Jean Itard in Paris, Dr Saegert in Berlin and the French physician Édouard Séguin, who had established a school for people with learning disabilities. Reed was subsequently able to travel to see some of what was being done across Europe and he was impressed by, for example, the work of Dr Johann Jakob Guggenbühl, who created the Abendberg centre on a mountain in Switzerland above Interlaken.[6]

In London, Reed worked closely with Dr John Connolly, who was regarded as England's leading expert in this area. Reed also had a personal encounter through his congregation: Mrs Ann Plumbe, a member of his church, had a son Andrew (Andrew Reed Plumbe) who had severe learning disabilities. Ann came to Reed for advice, and Reed decided he needed to move from thought to action.[7] As a result of his research and connections he made, Reed gradually gained the backing of influential Victorian philanthropists, including those known especially for their Christian convictions, as well as political leaders such as Lord Palmerston and wealthy backers such as Baron Rothschild. As a result, in 1848, Park House, a community in Highgate Hill, was opened, and seventeen young people were admitted. After a year Reed could speak of 'a household of fifty persons'. The idea of this being a 'household', a 'community', was significant.[8] Medical staff were appointed. There was an emphasis on communal well-being, education, learning skills and recreation, which Reed sought to continue to embody in the much larger Earlswood Asylum, in Surrey, opened in 1855. In this venture Reed was able to have the support of Queen Victoria's husband, Prince Albert, and he spoke to the Prince of the hope that the community would be a place filled with laughter.[9] However, serious problems of management became apparent. These were addressed through the appointment of Dr John Langdon Down, who became the resident medical superintendent in the community in 1858. It was while there that he described the condition now known as Down's Syndrome.[10]

Andrew Reed was by no means alone in his concerns about the exclusion of those with learning disabilities, although in his ground-breaking work he operated on a larger scale than others of his time.[11] As another nineteenth-century example of a communal enterprise linked with education, in 1846 Charlotte and Harriett White, two sisters who were then in their twenties, set up a small school in Bath for children with learning disabilities. They were helped by local donations and by charging some fees, and they supported around twenty children. However, in spite of the efforts that were made by a few individuals and groups to show a better way, in 1881, twenty years after Reed's death, out of about 30,000 'idiots' – as they were still often called, without any regard for wide variations of conditions – living in England, it has been estimated that fewer than 1000 were receiving care that was appropriate.[12] Very large institutions, often with inadequate attention being given to individuals, remained the norm. Smaller communities were rare.

There were no significant changes in Britain in the early twentieth century. Indeed, the Mental Deficiency Act of 1913 reinforced the practice of people with learning disabilities being forced to live in asylums, with many never returning to their families. One of those who opposed prevailing attitudes (which were to some extent influenced by eugenics) and criticised the treatment of 'idiots' and 'imbeciles' in this period was the Christian thinker, G.K. Chesterton.[13] By the 1950s, as a result of the implementation of the 1913 Act, at least 50,000 people were in (mainly large) institutions.[14] Changes in policy came after World War II, due in significant measure to Judy Fryd, who, along with a group of fellow parents, formed the Association of Parents of Backward Children. Judy Fryd was initially concerned for her own daughter, Felicity, especially when she experienced lack of understanding from society and from professionals who were supposed to support her. The Association evolved to become Mencap. Although the Mental Health Act of 1959 stipulated that more community care be provided, the number of people in 'mental hospitals' continued to rise. Often hospital staff were among those calling for change.[15] Voluntary agencies, including churches, were pointing to new possibilities.[16] A book published by the Baptist Union spoke hopefully of the move from hospitals to care within community settings, while accepting the challenges of this change.[17]

L'Arche and Other Initiatives

From the 1960s there were varied initiatives aimed at enabling community life for those with learning disabilities. Of the responses in the 1960s arising out of Christian thinking, the most influential was the work of Jean Vanier and the L'Arche communities. In 1971 Vanier also co-founded, with Marie-Hélène Mathieu, 'Faith and Light', now in over eighty countries.[18] With the implementation of 'Care in the Community', as Jan Walmsley outlines in his analysis of developments in Britain from 1971, local communities were encouraged to be welcoming. He suggests that there was 'special emphasis on churches as a nodal point for community inclusion'.[19] The first L'Arche community in Britain was founded in 1973, through the efforts of Jean Vanier's sister, Thérèse Vanier. An example of a Christian group in the 1970s in Britain inspired by L'Arche but not part of L'Arche or Faith and Light was a group in Morningside Baptist Church in Edinburgh. A woman associated with the church who had learning disabilities found herself homeless after her mother died. She came to the church, and the minister, Peter Bowes, and members of the congregation, were moved to action when they heard her say: 'You're Christians. DO something.' A group from the church were encouraged by the work of L'Arche and in 1977 the Ark Housing Association Ltd was set up. Within seven years, the Association had ten houses in Scotland, with 100 residents. Growth has continued.[20]

A few other initiatives were taken by churches and individual Christians in Britain in the 1970s. One example was Byways, in Odiham, Hampshire, which was founded by a Christian young woman, Elsie Fountain, who adopted a child with learning disabilities. She took in others in the 1960s, and by the 1970s had a Christian home in which twenty-one women with learning disabilities were living. This example helped to motivate David Potter, a Baptist minister, to write an article in 1973 in the newspaper *Evangelical Times*, entitled 'A Cause for Concern', asking what could be done by churches. Potter had no contact at that stage with L'Arche. His article produced a significant response, with many people writing to talk about their pain at lack of support, misunderstandings and even ostracism they had encountered in local churches. In 1976 David Potter set up a charity, 'Christian Concern for the Mentally Handicapped', and under the auspices of the charity, led by David Potter and his wife Madeleine (and later called PROSPECTS), several community houses were purchased. The work grew until there were connections with over forty local authorities in Britain. Causeway Prospects was a further development, working with churches and Christian organisations to enable full congregational inclusion and personal spiritual development for people with learning disabilities.[21]

A major mainstream denominational step was the formation of the Baptist Union's pioneering initiative with people with learning disabilities, BUild, which began in 1983. It was the result of the work of a group, formed at first largely of lay Christians – which included health and education professionals, parents, and church workers, all contributing from their perspectives. The Baptist Union supported this endeavour. Faith Bowers, who with her husband Brian was a member of Bloomsbury Baptist Church, London, played a central role in the initiative. She later wrote that there was no attempt to 'tell churches what they ought to do, but rather [we] tried to prompt a sharing of experiences, good and bad, between churches – that seems the right way for Baptist Christians to help one another grow in a delicate area of ministry'.[22] Contacts were made with other denominations. It seemed then that only Roman Catholics were doing much about special church education, and they shared their insights. Other denominations were ready to take steps. In the Church of England, initiatives began to be taken in various dioceses, and in 2009 a 68-page document, *Opening the Doors*, was produced. This combined experience with theology and offered resources for church life.[23]

In September 2016 a celebration was held to mark the end of BUild. This ending, after over thirty years, did not take place because of a lack of interest in disability in church communities. The move was for the opposite reason: because over these decades more and more churches had welcomed people with learning disabilities into fellowship and worship. An example, which has developed over the course of more than fifty years, is the Lifeway group in Stirling, which is an integral part of Stirling Baptist Church and has been led for much of its life by one of the church members, Eileen Bebbington. At a celebration of its fifty years, in 2016, Lifeway group members took a greater part of one of the main Sunday services in this large congregation.[24] Faith Bowers, writing in 2016 from the perspective of a participant-historian, surveyed the significantly changed scene since the 1980s: she wrote: 'Many churches are linked with Prospects, which is now merging with Livability, which in turn amalgamated the Shaftesbury Society and John Grooms – all of them Christian bodies concerned for those with disabilities. Other churches work with Faith and Light. Social Services may also help: in our early days they were often suspicious of Christians but many have come to respect and value churches' supportive friendship for those in local group homes.' Community embrace has been key.[25]

Community as a Gift of the Holy Spirit: Reflections by Ian Randall

In this second main section of the chapter I want to offer glimpses related to my experience of different ways in which community can be worked out, and how, within these different possibilities, those with learning disabilities are finding their own place. I look at experiences in church life, in areas connected with theological exploration and spirituality, and in a specific community, the Bruderhof. As well as reflecting my own experiences, this chapter is intended to link with the story of Lyn's House, suggesting that there is room for ongoing investigation of new patterns of upside-down living.

Church Experiences

Many of my own experiences of community have been in the context of church communities. In the 1970s my wife Janice and I were members of a church which fostered a strong spirit of communal belonging. At the same time, this church was an open community. Among the connections the congregation made were with those living locally who had disabilities, mainly through two local schools. One of these was a school for the deaf. The Principal of the school, Mary Corbishley, who was given an MBE for her pioneering work, was part of the church community and through her the church connected with those who were deaf.[26] There was also a nearby school for those with learning disabilities, and although the congregation did not have the same personal contact there, occasionally services were arranged in the church which were especially geared for those from the school. I have a vivid memory of leading one of those services. One of the friends in the congregation came up and hugged me while I was leading. This was a new experience for me – indeed it has never been repeated in the same way since! – and was one of the events that opened me to the contribution that those with learning disabilities can make to church communities.

Over the years since then I have been involved in churches in various settings and in different locations as I have moved around in my work, and it has almost always been the case that friends with learning disabilities have had an important place within the church community. Faith Bowers, who as noted above has been very active in encouraging churches to engage with disability, writes of her own experience when her son Richard was born with Down's Syndrome. She describes how she and her husband, both 'of academic inclination and prizing intelligence', were 'appalled at the prospect of intellectual impairment'. At the dedication service for Richard, thanksgiving was muted. Yet it was clear to Richard's parents that 'their church was taking this child to heart in a special way'. It was on the afternoon after his dedication that Richard produced his first real smiles. Slowly Richard made progress. Faith writes: 'Often he first achieved new things at church. With so many protective eyes on him, he was allowed more freedom in the church hall than in other spacious places and this seemed to liberate him to new efforts.' For Richard the 'atmosphere of the church has always been one of welcome and friendship'. At age sixteen Richard asked the minister of the church if she could 'take him in the water because he loved Jesus'. He was prepared for baptism, received into membership, and has been an active member, with a gift of welcoming and pastoral insights, known and valued in his own congregation and in the wider Baptist community of churches.[27]

Spirituality and Community

Henri Nouwen has commented on community in this way: 'Community does not require an organisation or institution; community is a way of living and relating: you gather around people with whom you want to proclaim the truth that we are the beloved sons and daughters of God.'[28] I first began to explore the writings of Henri Nouwen in the early 1990s, beginning with his book *The Road to Daybreak: A Spiritual Journey* (1988), which described his journey to a L'Arche community in Canada.[29] I had started as a lecturer at Spurgeon's College, London, teaching church history and spirituality. As well as Nouwen, I was using Richard Foster, and especially *Celebration of Discipline*, as a guide to spiritual growth.[30] I had been part of the charismatic movement since the later 1970s, and I was now exploring how that spiritual experience could be enriched by contemplative traditions. Community then found its place in a new way. Nouwen suggests that there can be a movement from individual prayer in solitude, to community life, and then to ministry in the world. He comments: 'If we do not know we are the beloved sons and daughters of God, we're going to expect someone in the community to make us feel special and worthy. Ultimately, they cannot.'[31] I found here insights which became increasingly significant.

It was in the late 1990s that I began to experience some international dimensions of Christian spiritual traditions through living on a college campus in Prague. I was seconded to work in Eastern Europe by Spurgeon's College, and for some years Janice and I worked in a college – the International Baptist Theological Seminary (IBTS) – which was a community of students, teachers and other staff who came from many countries. Part of the learning, alongside academic theological study, was to understand differences in culture and background. An important part of the shared life was also the desire to develop spiritually. Carol Woodfin notes how IBTS embraced Anabaptist thinking. Texts such as that by the sixteenth-century Anabaptist theologian, Balthasar Hubmaier, the 'Pledge of Love', were used during the weekly Holy Communion. The 'Pledge' calls on participants to honour God, be reconciled with and serve others, and love one's enemies. The final section invites those who wish to confirm this pledge to eat bread and drink wine together.[32]

The communal life at IBTS was also shaped by Dietrich Bonhoeffer's *Life Together*. Because of Bonhoeffer's focus on a seminary, this work was especially apposite. And for some who had an idealistic view of community life, Bonhoeffer has strong warnings about Christian community breaking down because it has sprung from 'a wish dream'. The point is reinforced: 'Every human wish dream that is injected into Christian community is a hindrance to genuine community.'[33] Community is fraught with difficulty. Although the Prague college community did not at that stage have members with learning disabilities, I began to integrate into my own thinking Jean Vanier's vision of community and the spirituality of communion, in which those with disabilities have a special place. 'It is through everyday life in community and the love that must be incarnate in his,' he writes, 'that handicapped people can begin to discover that they have a value, that they are loved and so are lovable.' He continues: 'Communion is based on some common inner experience of love; it is the recognition of being one body, one people, called by God to be a source of love and peace. Its fulfilment is more in silence than in words, more in celebration than in work. It is an experience of openness and trust that flows from what is innermost in a person; it is a gift of the Holy Spirit.'[34] Here I found signposts for life in community.

Community as Vocation

This concept of community as a 'gift of the Holy Spirit' leads me to the third major influence on me in this area: the Bruderhof (place of brothers) community. In 1920 Eberhard Arnold, a German theologian and evangelist, together with his wife Emmy, set up a Christian community shaped by a desire for communal life which – as Eberhard put it – would draw together 'reborn people who have accepted the life of the Sermon on the Mount.' These were to be people who 'radiate the spirit of Christ – people who witness for Christ with their entire being', and 'who give up everything to live simply and solely for love and for productive work'.[35] There were many struggles in Germany in the 1930s, and the Nazis ultimately forcibly dissolved the community. Then followed endeavours in England, where growth was significant but where hostility to Germans during World War II meant members emigrating to South America. Today the Bruderhof consists of men, women and children (families and single people) living in twenty-three intentional communities of differing sizes, most in Europe and North America. In 2012 they produced a document, *Foundations of Our Faith and Calling*, 'about the basis of our life together'.[36] Shortly after this I was approached by the Bruderhof and asked if I would consider writing about aspects of their life and their history.

After I had spent some time with the communities and after reading the history of life in Germany and England (both countries where the Bruderhof is again established), I produced *Church Community is a Gift of the Holy Spirit: The Spirituality of the Bruderhof Community* (2014).[37] In this I quoted the statement in *Foundations* about church community being precisely that: a gift of the Spirit. The emphasis in *Foundations* is on God's help. Without that, 'we human beings are selfish and divided, unfit for life together'. The words of Jesus are quoted, 'Apart from me you can do nothing'.[38] There are examples in history. The Anabaptist Hutterite tradition of the sixteenth century, with its practice of community of goods, has offered particular inspiration.[39] Also *Foundations* highlights varied communal spiritual movements: desert communities, the community around Augustine of Hippo, Celtic

Christians, Waldensians, Beguines and Beghards, followers of Francis of Assisi and Clare, early Quakers and the Moravians.[40] Ultimately *Foundations* points to 'the first church founded at Pentecost', when 'the Spirit worked with unique power, leading Christians to share all they had, to serve the city's poor, and to proclaim the gospel boldly'.[41]

The Bruderhof communities have taken a particular interest in those with disabilities. A Bruderhof enterprise, Rifton Equipment, designs and manufactures adaptive equipment for children and adults with disabilities, allowing children with severe cerebral palsy, for instance, to interact more freely with the world. Bruderhof members who work at Rifton Equipment, based in the USA, know that their work is profoundly changing the lives of disabled children. Rifton product designers are Bruderhof members who work closely with parents and therapists.[42] Maureen Swinger, an editor and community member, has written about her brother Duane, who was born apparently healthy but when three months old was attacked by his first grand-mal seizure, with countless to follow. He was diagnosed with Lennox-Gastaut syndrome, a rare form of epilepsy. Seizures were so brutal that doctors did not think he would live beyond a year. That one year turned into thirty-one and a half. Because of Duane's personality, people often told the family what a gift Duane was. For Maureen he was a gift, in incredibly complex packaging, but hearing 'gift' she was sometimes only just able to hold back a comment, 'Would you like to do the night shift with our gift?' Then at a Bruderhof meeting an essay by Eberhard Arnold was read about two goals: 'One goal is to seek the person of high position, the great person, the spiritual person, the clever person... The other goal is to seek the lowly people, the minorities, the disabled, the prisoners: the valleys of the lowly between the heights of the great... The first goal aims to exalt the individual, by virtue of his natural gifts, to a state approaching the divine. In the end he is made a god. The other goal seeks the wonder and mystery of God becoming man, God seeking the lowest place among us.' Out of this profound insight came new ministry for Duane, who although he never spoke became a teacher of others.[43]

For Bruderhof members, community is a vocation. I have been deeply impressed in spending time in the communities with this strong sense of calling, individually and corporately. At the same time there is a recognition that there are callings outside community life, and also that community exists for service. Bruderhof members have been and are involved in many outward directed ministries, in channelling resources, and in publishing books by a wide variety of authors. One of the publications, exemplifying breadth of vision, is *Called to Community* (2016). This addresses the question of why in an age of connectivity many people are isolated and fragmented, and offers an answer in following Christ in daily life, in a community that demonstrates the transforming love of God. The book contains fifty-two chapters relating to intentional community. It is significant, and perhaps not surprising, that there are chapters by Jean Vanier, on the themes of Communion, Beyond Self, Leadership, and Welcome, and that his work is drawn upon for the themes of God's Call, Deeds, Conflict, Dialogue and Celebration. The book features chapters by Bruderhof members, but Vanier's presence far outweighs either their contribution or that by anyone else. Among other authors are Bonhoeffer, Dorothy Day, a journalist and founder of the Catholic Worker movement who devoted her life to defending the downtrodden, Richard Foster, Thomas Merton, Nouwen and Chiara Lubich, founder and spiritual leader of the Focolare movement.[44]

Encounter, Community and Vulnerability: Reflections by Philip S. Powell

Over the past almost three years of my life, I have been a residential member of the Lyn's House community in Cambridge. This has not, however, been my first experience in community. For most of my adult life, for significant periods, I have enjoyed what I can describe as the blessing of living in community. Some of these communities have been large ones and others smaller ones, including experiences of encounter in different parts of the world. Although I speak of 'blessing', I have had both positive and negative experiences of living in community and there was a time when I said to myself, 'I will never again live in community'. But God had other plans for my life. When I moved into Lyn's House in 2015, I did so with an awareness of what it had meant and could mean for me to live in a Christian community. The following are some of my reflections on community experiences.

Because others in this book have addressed theological aspects that relate to the ministry of Lyn's House, I will not cover that ground. Rather I will look at the transformative effects of community. One key point I would like to make is that the Greek word *koinonia*, which is used over twenty times in the New Testament, refers to 'fellowship, sharing with others and communion' and goes to the very heart of what I understand to be meant by 'living in community'. The bar is set quite high by Paul in the New Testament to describe what living in Christian community should be like: 'If you have any encouragement from being united with Christ, if any comfort from his love, if any fellowship with the Spirit, if any tenderness and compassion, then make my joy complete by being like-minded, having the same love, being one in spirit and purpose.'[45]

So what does this 'fellowship' look like practically and on a daily basis, as experienced in Lyn's House, and what might that mean for those called to community? The primary purpose for which Lyn's House community exists is to create a place of welcome and hospitality, to build relationships with friends with learning disabilities, and to be a witness in Cambridge to a different way of being *human*. Jean Vanier writes of how day-to-day life in community can help people who are fragile 'to become more human, more open to themselves and others'. He describes a spirituality that 'is not cut off from humanity: it aspires to a growing love for others'.[46] But what happens in Lyn's House when the guests, the friends, are not around for the meals and it is only the residents in the house? I want to write about this and to offer reflections that I hope will be of help more widely.

Making a Commitment

One of the most important things I have learned about living in a Christian community – and this is noted by Jean Vanier in the quotation at the beginning of this chapter – is the *intentionality of will*. Vanier speaks of a 'covenant of love and mutual sharing'.[47] First and foremost, living in community is about a deliberate choice to be part of something that is bigger than myself. Without this sense of commitment on the part of each individual member who wants to join and belong to a community, there can be no authentic life together. So living in community is not about convenience or some pragmatic decision based on a cost–benefit analysis. It has to go beyond that to something deeper. It is about making a commitment to share life together with others. Now it is true that we all make decisions in life that include pragmatism and cost–benefit analysis and this is not necessarily a negative thing, but when it comes to living in community I consider that there has to be deeper commitment to be in fellowship with others who are different from me and who will sometimes behave in ways that go against my self-interest. There is also, I suggest, the need to reaffirm this commitment on an ongoing basis as we deal with the challenges of living together with others, since those 'others' in any community can be both a source of great joy and can also sometimes appear to be quite difficult to deal with.

In an initial meeting, as four new residents who had moved into Lyn's House in 2015, we shared during our discussion that what would go on between the four of us would become the reality into which we would be inviting others to come. If our relationships were in a difficult place, this was going to inevitably spill over and affect the ministry we were extending to others. Accepting this, we decided that we would commit to morning prayers in the house. This had been happening and has continued. The house residents come together every morning (unless there are reasons why that is not possible) for up to thirty minutes of Bible reading, liturgy, a time of silence and praying for one another. The commitment to pray together has made a huge difference to the way we relate to each other during the rest of the day. My perspective is that something was spiritually achieved at the prayer time that made living together in the house more enjoyable and more fulfilling. We have also had Monday evening community times for the four of us in the house: a time to share a meal together, deal with house business and catch up with each other. Life together in Lyn's House would not be possible without that commitment on the part of each individual member to live together and serve each other in love.

Embracing Difference

The second thing I have learned about living in community is that there will always be real differences between the members of a community. This might be seen as rather obvious and a given, since we are evidently all different, but there is something deeper going on when we live in a community with members who are very different. In 2015, when the four new members moved into Lyn's House, we were all strangers to each other, and very different in personality, nationality and lifestyle. I was from India and a bit older in age, there was Mel from Singapore, while Daniel and Suzie (both contributors to this volume) were English. There were all kinds of differences between us. Some of us liked eating meat and one was a vegan. Some liked to do sport and others had different hobbies like jewellery-making. Two were in relationships and two of us were single. These differences can challenge us but can also teach us a great deal. Only through living in community and dealing with the struggles do we learn how to really embrace difference. In our divided and broken world this is crucial.

Every single one of us has a *cultural lens* (or more than one) through which we look at the world and make sense of it. When people who are very different begin to live together in a community, sooner or later we encounter something another person is doing that we find rather stupid or bizarre. When we encounter strange things, there is a temptation to jump to conclusions – something is not right with this person. But living in community is about engaging in the difficult process of trying to understand another person in their difference, without judgement, and then even possibly embracing the difference. Nobody wants to be part of a community where they feel judged for who they are. We have a natural urge to resist and flee judgement. Equally true is the fact that we are drawn towards affirmation and praise. Living in community creates the opportunity for us to give affirmation to someone else in their difference, to show the other person love that transcends difference.

Living in various communities has taught me to make room in my heart to embrace others who are different from me. Certainly, this is true in Lyn's House with the friends, but also with those living in the house. The temptation to harden my heart when I encounter difference that challenges and/or threatens me is real, but through doing the opposite I believe I have become more of the person God has meant me to be. Jean Vanier relates the experience of Thérèse of Lisieux (in the nineteenth century), who used to find one of the other sisters in her community 'disagreeable in every way', and he points out the strength that is needed from God in such situations.[48] Without embracing difference there cannot be community. This is part of the call to communal life.

Difficulties and Division

Another lesson I have learned from living in community is that it is a demanding and costly undertaking. While community is certainly about enjoying the blessing of sharing life with others, it also includes dealing with conflicts. There will almost certainly be moments and even more extended times of struggle and of difficulties living in community. I remember hearing George Verwer, the founder of an international Christian movement called Operation Mobilisation, say many years ago: 'Where two or three of God's people gather together, soon there will be a mess.' Operation Mobilisation has had a great deal of experience of people sharing life together.[49] As a young Christian at the time, I found George Verwer's words jarring and rather depressing. But after years of living in community and being vulnerable I have come to realise how true his words are.

Here are a few apparently trivial examples. Actually, the consequences of what we think are trivial things might be significant. Sometimes a small misunderstanding can become a serious division within a community. Take for example, doing the dishes and keeping the kitchen clean. I have the habit of using the kitchen to cook my dinner and of leaving cleaning up for later. A few hours later I say to myself that it is already late at night and I will do the cleaning tomorrow morning. The next day I am running late and I am in rush to get to work, and I leave the dirty dishes on the kitchen counter all day. While I am not affected by this because I am out at work all day, another person living in the house and having to use the kitchen has to cope with the dirty dishes still lying around. This can lead to real difficulties and misunderstandings. One person feels entitled to a clean kitchen and another feels that there should be more flexibility in the house. Living in community is about engaging with and overcoming difficulties like these. It is about changing my own behaviour for the sake of another person's well-being. This does not come naturally to any of us but can make all the difference when living in community.

Also in every community there are always hidden power-dynamics between different members. It is probably the case that each of us knows ways to manipulate a situation to try to get the outcome we want. We may use passive-aggressive ways to influence what decisions are made and what ideas are rejected. In addition, cliques are sometimes formed between members in a community, and agreements are made even before there has been an open discussion about a subject. There will always be difficulties and the danger of division within communities. The risks are real, but so are the rewards when honest engagement with the difficulties leads towards deepening bonds of friendship.

Celebration

Another thing I have learned about living in community is that *heartfelt celebration* is a sign that life in community is working well. Among my happiest memories in life will always be the times I laughed really hard with my fellow housemates in Lyn's House. Humour and laughter make all the difference. In Lyn's House we have had a tradition of going out together for a meal to celebrate each other's birthdays. This is a way of saying to each other *you are special.* We have also made trips together into London and have played badminton on a Saturday morning. These activities bring us closer together. Celebrating together becomes more natural when we feel comfortable with each other. One person's success at work or another's positive meeting with a PhD supervisor become a reason to celebrate together. I have found that as a community we are in a good place when each one of us feels the freedom to be honest without false expectations or the need to pretend to be all right when things are difficult in our personal lives.

Let me mention two other issues regarding celebration in community. One is the need for trust between community members. The willingness to be vulnerable with people whom we are only beginning to get to know can be challenging. But the more I am willing to be open and not hide my brokenness, the more I create the context for trust to grow. We learn to become more sensitive to each other's needs. When the bonds of trust are strong, our celebration together as a community is richer and more beautiful. The second thing with regard to celebration is the role of forgiveness and reconciliation. The experience of saying sorry to another person in the community and receiving forgiveness becomes a reason to celebrate. As in the story of the Prodigal Son, the father called for a celebration because his son had returned home.[50] In Lyn's House there have been times of spontaneous celebration, when the four of us would sit around the dining table and drink and laugh together. Among the occasions when this happened were after times when there had been some kind of *putting things right* between us. Dealing with unresolved tensions in the house often moved us towards celebrating together. Celebrating together is a vital, life-giving aspect of community.

A Place of Healing

The final thing I want to mention about living in community is experiencing the gift of healing. Living in community can be a safe place and a risky place. In a profound way, it is both. Each one of us, through the ups and downs of life, has experienced judgement and rejection. There are times in our lives when the words and actions of others, especially if the person had a place of authority over us, have hurt us very deeply. Soon we learn to build protection mechanisms around ourselves to keep other people from getting too close to us, to hide our wounds and to cope with life. But the wounds are still there within us and affect the way we relate to other people.

When we move into living in a community, we have a choice either to learn to trust and be vulnerable, or to keep people in the community at a distance. We are afraid of the risk of getting hurt again. But at the same time, through living in community, when fellow members come alongside us, carry our burdens with us and manifest grace as we uncover what is hidden in our hearts, then we truly experience inner healing. Such healing is what happens when we begin to let go of the pain we have been carrying from the past and experience again the joy of being vulnerable with people who love us despite our shortcomings. In my own life, living with other members of Lyn's House has been a tremendous experience of healing.

Life in any community can sometimes be hard and it can be a place where we can get quite hurt by another person's words or actions. This is the risk of communal living. The community is a place of vulnerability. Life in community has a way of forcing us to go beyond relating to others at a skin-deep level. It has a way of displacing us out of our comfort zone. It has a way of bringing us face to face with the dark side of our own personality. Sharing real life together in community is also beautiful and rewarding. We have opportunities to learn, grow and change. We can become more fully human through living in community.

I conclude my reflections on living in community with some very realistic words, which are words of hope, from Henri Nouwen, who has had a significant influence on my thinking:

> Nothing is sweet or easy about community. Community is a fellowship of people who do not hide their joys and sorrows but make them visible to each other in a gesture of hope. In community we say, 'Life is full of gains and losses, joys and sorrows, ups and downs – but we do not have to live it alone. We want to drink our cup together and thus celebrate the truth that the wounds of our individual lives, which seem intolerable when lived alone, become sources of healing when we live them as part of a fellowship of mutual care.'[51]

Conclusion: Signs of Hope?

This chapter began with Jean Vanier's book, *Signs of the Times*, in which he outlines seven paths of hope for a troubled world. The suggestion here has been that spiritual life lived in community is a path of hope. The first section of the chapter outlined some historical developments in communal living in relation to those with learning disabilities. Community recognises difference. This may be the difference of friends with learning disabilities, which is the particular theme of this book as a whole, but the journey from exclusion to encounter in that area is part of a journey to which all are invited. After looking at historical examples, the second part of the chapter offered some experiences of the call from isolation to community in church life, in theological communities which have a focus on spirituality, and in the area of vocation. The third section recognises the difficulties of community, but at the same time the possibilities for celebration and healing. Henri Nouwen writes: 'For me, community has been most authentic in a Eucharistic faith community, and specifically for me this was L'Arche Daybreak. For you, community may be found in your local church or prayer group. However you define a faith community, it is your spiritual home.' In line with Jean Vanier's picture of movement 'from strength to vulnerability', Henri Nouwen makes clear that community is not easy, but that 'Jesus calls us to live together as a family of faith and commitment', learning in community to 'confess our weaknesses and to forgive each other', to 'let go of our self-will and to really live for others'. He concludes: 'Spiritual formation, therefore, always includes formation to life in community.'[52] This is an invitation to look at the possibilities of a life of faith and of hope.

Endnotes

1   Jean Vanier, *Signs of the Times: Seven Paths of Hope for a Troubled World* (London: Darton, Longman and Todd, 2013), p.7. He relates this to Vatican II, but the application can be ecumenical.

2   The other four chapters deal with 'from humiliation to humility', 'from conformity to conscience', 'from power to authority', and 'from secret to mystery'.

3   Jean Vanier, *Community and Growth* (London: Darton, Longman and Todd, 1989/2007), pp.18–19.

4   *Anne Digby, Madness, Morality and Medicine: A Study of the York Retreat, 1796–1914* (Cambridge: Cambridge University Press, 1985), p.15. Here the focus is on developments in Britain. For a volume with North American perspectives, see Michael Wehmeyer *et al.*, *The Story of Intellectual Disability* (Baltimore, MD: Paul H. Brookes Publishing, 2013).

5   A. Reed and C. Reed, *Memoirs of the Life and Philanthropic Labours of Andrew Reed, D.D., With Selections from His Journals* (London: Strahan and Co., 1863), p.384.

6   Ian J. Shaw, *The Greatest is Charity: The Life of Andrew Reed, Preacher and Philanthropist* (Darlington: Evangelical Press, 2005), pp.292–3; David Race, 'The Historical Context', in D.G. Race (ed.), *Learning Disability: A Social Approach* (London: Routledge, 2001), pp.26–7.

7   See David Wright, *Mental Disability in Victorian England* (Oxford: Oxford University Press, 2001), pp.20–32.

8   Shaw, *The Greatest is Charity*, pp. 294–8; Reed and Reed, *Memoirs*, p.394.

9   Reed and Reed, *Memoirs*, pp. 412–23.

10 For his life and work see Ward O'Conor, *Dr John Langdon Down and Normansfield* (The Langdon Down Centre Trust, 2009). Normansfield was a later development.

11 For further historical perspectives, see David Wright and Anne Digby (eds), *From Idiocy to Mental Deficiency: Historical Perspectives on People with Learning Disabilities* (London: Routledge, 1996).

12 K. Day and J. Jancar, 'Mental Handicap and the Royal Medico-Psychological Association: A Historical Association, 1841–1891', in G.E. Berrios and H. Freeman (eds), *150 Years of British Psychiatry, 1841–1991* (London: Gaskell/Royal College of Psychiatrists, 1991), p.270.

13 G.K. Chesterton, *Eugenics and Other Evils* (London: Cassel, 1922).

14 In 1951 a critique spoke of 50,000 people certified as mentally defective and having no legal safeguards. See Tim Stainton, 'Equal Citizens: The Discourse of Liberty and Rights in the History of Learning Disabilities', in L. Brigham, *et al.* (eds), *Crossing Boundaries: Change and Continuity in the History of Learning Disability* (Kidderminster, BILD Publications, 2000), pp.87–101, esp. pp.95–7.

15 See Race, 'The Historical Context', p.37; and for Mencap, pp.38–46. Also for Mencap, M. *Hilton*, N. Crowson, J. Mouhot and J. McKay, *A Historical Guide to NGOs in Britain: Charities, Civil Society and the Voluntary Sector since 1945* (Basingstoke: Palgrave Macmillan, 2012), pp.162–3.

16 See the discussion in Jan Walmsley, 'Straddling Boundaries: The Changing Role of Voluntary Organisations, 1913–1959', in L. Brigham *et al.* (eds), *Crossing Boundaries*, pp.103–22.

17 Faith Bowers (ed.), *Let Love be Genuine* (London: Baptist Times, 1985), pp.27–28.

18 Marie-Hélène Mathieu, *Never Again Alone! The Adventure of Faith and Light from 1971 until Today* (Bloomington, IN: WestBow Press, 2014).

19 Jan Walmsley, 'Ideology, Ideas and Care in the Community, 1971–2001', in John Welshman and Jan Walmsley (eds), *Community Care in Perspective* (Basingstoke: Palgrave Macmillan, 2006), p.44.

20 Bowers, *Let Love be Genuine*, p.37.

21 David Potter, *Through Changing Scenes* (Carlisle: Paternoster Press, 2001).

22 Faith Bowers, 'The Story of Build', *Baptist Ministers' Journal*, April 1993, p.8.

23 The Church of England report can be found at: https://www.carlislediocese.org.uk/uploads/2029/Opening_the_Doors_-_Ministry_with_people_with_learning_disabilities_and_people_on_the_autistic_spectrum.pdf.html.

24 Eileen Bebbington wrote in fascinating detail in 1983 about the group, which then numbered 25–30. See Bowers (ed.), *Let Love be Genuine*, pp.93–100. It has remained a vigorous group and won a local award.

25 See www.baptist.org.uk/Articles/471063/To_everything_a.aspx.

26 She told her story: Mary S. Corbishley, *Corby: Teacher of the Deaf for Fifty Years* (Rushden, Northants: Stanley L. Hunt, 1980). Mary Corbishley was known as Corby.

27 Faith Bowers, *When Weak, then Strong: Disability in the Life of the Church* (London: Bloomsbury Central Baptist Church, 2008), pp.91–4.

28 Henri Nouwen, with Michael J. Christensen and Rebecca J. Laird, *Spiritual Direction: Wisdom for the Long Walk of Faith* (London: SPCK, 2011), p.113. Here Matthew 18:20 is quoted by Nouwen: 'Where two or three are gathered in the name of Jesus, he is in the midst.'

29 Henri Nouwen, *The Road to Daybreak: A Spiritual Journey* (New York: Doubleday, 1988).

30 Richard Foster, *Celebration of Discipline: The Path to Spiritual Growth* (London: Hodder & Stoughton, 1980).

31 Nouwen, *Spiritual Direction*, pp.110–11, 114.

32 Carol Woodfin, *An Experiment in Christian Internationalism* (Macon, GA: Baptist History and Heritage Society, 2013), p.375.

33 Dietrich Bonhoeffer, *Life Together* (London: SCM, 1954), p.15.

34 Vanier, *Community and Growth*, pp.11, 25.

35 Markus Baum, *Against the Wind: Eberhard Arnold and the Bruderhof* (Rifton, NY, and Robertsbridge: Plough Publishing House, 1998), p.126.

36 *Foundations of Our Faith and Calling* (Rifton, NY, and Robertsbridge: Plough Publishing House, 2012), p.vii. The sections of *Foundations* are: basis of our faith; our calling; heritage; church order; church actions; and life in community.

37 Ian M. Randall, *'Church Community is a Gift of the Holy Spirit': The Spirituality of the Bruderhof Community* (Oxford: Centre for Baptist History and Heritage, 2014). I have continued to spend time with the Bruderhof and to undertake research on their community life. See Ian M. Randall, *A Christian Peace Experiment: The Bruderhof Community in Britain, 1933–1942* (Eugene, OR: Wipf and Stock, 2018).

38 *Foundations*, pp.7–8.

39 See Werner Packull, *Hutterite Beginnings: Communitarian Experiments during the Reformation* (Baltimore: The Johns Hopkins University Press, 1995).

40 *Foundations*, p.24.

41 *Foundations*, p.23.

42 www.bruderhof.com/en/life-in-community/working-together.

43 This was an article in *The Plough*, the Bruderhof quarterly publication. See www.plough.com/en/topics/life/parenting/special-needs-children/the-teacher-who-never-spoke.

44   Charles E. Moore (ed.), *Called to Community: The Life Jesus Wants for His People* (Rifton, NY, and Robertsbridge: Plough Publishing House, 2016).

45 Philippians 2:1–2. NIV.

46 Vanier, *Signs of the Times*, p.7.

47 Vanier, *Community and Growth*, p.18.

48 Vanier, *Signs of the Times*, p.99.

49 For the history of Operation Mobilisation (OM) see Ian Randall, *Spiritual Revolution: The Story of OM* (Milton Keynes: Authentic Media, 2008).

50 For reflections on this drawn from Rembrandt's painting in St Petersburg, see Henri Nouwen, *The Return of the Prodigal Son: A Story of Homecoming* (London: Darton, Longman and Todd, 1992).

51 Henri Nouwen, *Can You Drink the Cup?* (Notre Dame, IN: Ave Maria Press, 1996/2006), p.63.

52 Nouwen, *Spiritual Direction*, pp.113–15.

— CHAPTER 8 —

Experiments in Friendship

Patrick McKearney

It was a cold evening in January 2015 when Lizzie, the first of the guests, arrived for dinner early. In her thirties, Lizzie lives a few miles from Cambridge, in a Supported Living arrangement close to her parents, who had brought her regularly to Lyn's House at dinners, tea parties and movie nights since the beginning of its communal life. I showed her through to the warm and softly lit kitchen and was making her a hot chocolate when the doorbell rang again.

I shuffled back out in the chill of the corridor and opened the door to find the second of our guests that evening. He stood there, smiling a little nervously, holding a small carrier bag in his left hand, and holding out his right to shake. 'Hello,' he said. 'Samuel'. He and his mum stepped inside the corridor and she explained that this was his first time at a Lyn's House dinner and, having only recently turned eighteen, his first time at a dinner party altogether. They both looked a little apprehensive.

Samuel's mum said 'goodbye' and he and I headed into the kitchen. Soon the other volunteers, Peter and Rebecca, arrived as well. We prayed together, and then sat down for dinner. Lizzie was quiet, I suspect a little cautious in the face of a new person. Samuel was more animated, but was directing all his attention and enthusiasm to his phone, which he kept using to load YouTube videos throughout the time we were eating. It was an unpromising beginning to what turned out to be a remarkable few months.

The next time we were all together, a fortnight later, Peter asked us all to put our phones on the side during dinner time and explained to Samuel that this was so that we could talk to one another. With these kinds of explicit discussions, over the coming months, Samuel increasingly grasped the norms we were abiding by and started to relish the chances this gave him to be a lively and funny participant in conversations. Peter also worked closely with Samuel to come up with new ideas for what to do during prayer sessions, through which Samuel revealed himself to be a talented and powerful dramatist and performer.

Samuel would often lead Peter in dramatic renditions of biblical stories drawn from films he had watched countless times. And so Peter, Rebecca and I once surprised him by setting up the whole kitchen as a stage for him to enact his favourite scene from *The Prince of Egypt* of Moses and the burning bush. Peter had written down the transcript from the film for himself, and hid under the table to play the part of God, to which Samuel responded by taking on the part of Moses with alacrity and aplomb – following the transcript in his own head.

I noticed during this same period that Lyn's House was becoming an increasingly important place for Lizzie too. She would assiduously track, remember and repeat the dates she was next due to come. And in the intimate environment of the fortnightly dinners, she was also increasingly emerging from her shell. Sometimes this would involve telling all those sat round the table which character they were from *The Lion King* (cheekily calling Rebecca an elephant each and every time), singing over the top of any songs during prayer times the lyrics from whichever musical she was currently rehearsing, or arising after dinner to dance 'Gangnam style' in the middle of the kitchen. This kind of confident opening led to a deepening of her trust in others there as she opened up more and more about the things that really mattered to her.

What kind of space were we all creating and inhabiting those few months? What structures and activities made its existence possible? And what significance did it have in the lives of those with intellectual disabilities? Though I did not quite formulate it in these terms at the time, I think a great deal of what was so special about this period was that both Samuel and Lizzie were expanding into a social space they were not entirely familiar with. This was a space outside of care, outside of the family, outside of the home, and outside of an organisational setting; in which they could encounter the possibility of adult friendship with people who did not also have intellectual disabilities. In this chapter, I want to reflect on the place this social setting occupied and importantly continues to occupy in their lives – and how it relates to the social possibilities of people with intellectual disabilities in Britain more broadly.

Friendship in Britain

I want to begin by exploring the place of friendship as it is imagined and practised in British social life, and then go on to try to think about the role it plays in the lives of people with intellectual disabilities. 'Friendship', argues Brazilian anthropologist Claudia Rezende, is not a universal category, but rather is a locally variable set of phenomena that always build 'on culturally constructed notions of the person, gender, class, work, private versus public' and so on.[1] And a useful place to start thinking about the particular way that British friendship builds on some particular British social forms is Rezende's own analysis of sociality among twenty-something, white, middle-class friends in London in the early 1990s.

In an article entitled 'Gifts of Food' Rezende focuses on the, to her, curious fact that this tight-knit group of friends very rarely gave each other presents, even at birthdays. When asked, their explanations of this revolved around the fact that buying presents would cost a lot and that, as young professionals just beginning their careers, they did not have this sort of money. But Rezende looks beyond this explanation, towards the significant amounts of money (as well as effort and time) that these friends spent on buying drinks and cooking meals for one another regularly. They did, in fact, have money to spend on their friends, and spent it lavishly and generously: but they deliberately avoided spending this in the form of substantial individual presents, and instead spent it on shared perishable goods. Why was this? Rezende builds on a long anthropological tradition of work on gift-giving[2] to argue that the importance of this form of exchange, and its distinction from more obvious forms of present-giving, lies in its capacity to mark the difference between friendship and two other kinds of social relation.

The first of these is familial relations.[3] These young adults were all still heavily involved with their nuclear kin. They all went home at Christmas, and gave substantial and non-perishable objects to their kin. These presents were easy to keep track of and remember and thus built up layers of indebtedness and reciprocity between different members of the family. In doing so, these practices contributed to a broader British imagination of familial relationships as both intimate and obligatory. Relationships with kin, in other words, were seen to follow given patterns (often involving deference to parents) that leave little 'room for individual autonomy'.[4]

Rezende's argument is that the focus on food and drink among the young adults made their relationships and defined their connections in contrast to their familial relationships. This form of distribution makes contributions far harder to track, and thus debts far harder to accrue. This makes it possible for these gifts of food to be distinguished from those that, in the context of the family, might be given out of a sense of sentimental obligation. Instead, each and every round of drinks bought or meal cooked appears as an act of spontaneous, generous sharing with the group – an expression of choice, volition and desire rather than something constrained by expectation or custom. These practices thus contributed to marking friendships out as a space of a sharing distinct from the obligatory reciprocity of families,[5] and thus to imagining friendship as a relationship between free individuals based on nothing more than a 'wish to be together'.[6]

This emphasis on friendship as a realm of autonomy and choice distinguished it not only from familial relations but also from the relationships these young adults were involved in at work. These individuals were all several years into professional careers and understood their relations with colleagues and managers there to be, like their familial relations, obligatory. But this was a contractual, rather than sentimental, kind of obligation. For employment was also understood to be imbued with values like money, ambition and hard work that marked it out as part of the public, rather than the intimate, domain – and thus a space in which one could not be 'oneself'.

The exchanges of food and drink among friends, Rezende contends, take many of these professional values and transform them. Meals, just like work, involve significant amounts of time, effort and money. But, by applying these values to shared meals as opposed to individual accumulation, these young professionals were able to pursue a social rather than an individual end. At meals in people's private houses, these young adults said that they could open up more – disclosing something of their emotional life that they could not in public. These exchanges, in other words, 'stress the very opposite of market and work relations: self-revelation, trust and equality, against impersonality, formality and material interest'.[7] In this relational sphere, these young adults felt they were able to be 'themselves'.

Rezende's work gives us one idea about what British friendship might be: intimate in a way that work is not, and free in a way that neither employee nor familial relations are.[8] This, I think, gives us at least a working understanding of distinctions of central importance to the adult lives of British people that enables us to articulate how and why different kinds of relations are different from one another.

And it also gives us a way of sketching out some contours of what a certain kind of adulthood looks like in Britain: an engagement in the different spheres of family, profession and friendship.

I think Rezende's work also enables us to articulate these movements in spatial terms. It allows us, that is, to plot some of the locations in which these different kinds of relations take place, and how they are distinguished from one another along two axes: otherness and intimacy. Work is strictly confined to the public, and familial relations are restricted largely to the private – defining the distinction between homes and places 'outside' as that between public and intimate. By contrast, friendship involves a movement between both public and private as friends visit each other's houses but also meet in public spaces. And it also involves a movement along the axis of otherness: the interchanging of the roles of host and hosted distinguishes between one's own private residence and another's.

Again, this provides us not only with a typology of space but also a way of conceptualising adulthood in Britain: as a movement between public and private, professional and intimate, self and other. And it allows us also to see why friendship is such a central marker of this adulthood: for it involves a free movement between all of these spheres, signalling both autonomy outside of the family and authenticity outside of the workplace.[9] We might therefore conceivably describe adulthood in Britain as achieved by transcending the caring parental home and gaining the capacity independently to navigate between the public and the private – that is, to start 'a family of one's own', find a job, and form friendships.

Disability

People with intellectual disabilities stand in a problematic relationship to adulthood so conceived.[10] They have, over the past hundred years, found it recurrently difficult to transcend the care of their parents, to enter into professional life, and to form friendships outside of the very specific caring contexts in which they interact.[11] In this section, I want to look at the ways in which different regimes of care have responded to these 'predicaments',[12] and the effects this has had on the lives of people with intellectual disabilities. In what ways have different forms of care denied or facilitated their engagement in adult relationships and social spaces?

At the beginning of the twentieth century, people with intellectual disabilities typically lived either with their families or in large-scale institutions.[13] While families received little by way of support, they were nevertheless regulated by the government to make sure that they were controlling their intellectually disabled members – who were widely imagined as social menaces and threats to the gene pool.[14] The asylums that parents were often encouraged to place their children in were set up as 'total institutions' outside of urban centres similarly to prevent people with intellectual disabilities accessing and participating in the public sphere.

The, not exactly accidental, consequence of this regime of control was that many of those with intellectual disabilities acquired few of the markers of adulthood. Frequently confined either to their familial home, or to institutions existing outside the normal divisions between public and private they had, at best, thriving familial relations. Even then, the stigma of intellectual disability and their concomitant rejection from the public and confinement to the private sphere decisively hampered their ability to start a family of their own, to work and to form friendships.[15] For those who had no contact with family outside of the institutions, the main social relations they had were with professionals paid to support and control them, and with their peers with intellectual disabilities, relationships that were often marked by complicated power-dynamics as they vied for the scraps of power and freedom afforded them.

From the middle of the twentieth century onwards, reforms in policy, practice and attitudes led to drastic changes to this situation. New understandings of, and attitudes towards, intellectually disabled children – particularly through the creation of early-intervention programmes – led to a greater willingness and ability for parents to support their children at home.[16] And this coincided with a geographic shift in the support provided to adults as well, as the institutions were closed and the state moved to provide accommodation in ordinary residences in ordinary neighbourhoods. By the end of the twentieth century, these reforms aspired to reverse things entirely and make government-funded care for adults with intellectual disabilities a means through which these individuals could participate fully in British society.[17]

This aspiration is embodied in contemporary Britain most fully in a residential and care arrangement known as 'Supported Living'.[18] In Supported Living, a person with intellectual disabilities has full tenancy rights over the property in which they reside as well as control over what kind of care they receive within it. The carer is supposed to be simply a visitor, rather than any kind of authoritative presence, in order to make the domestic space as normal a private space as possible. The carer is there not to have authority over the person with disabilities, but rather to help them to do more on their own: be it household chores that will enable them to be self-sufficient, or forming friendships and finding work outside of the home. The hope is that those with intellectual disabilities can learn to live outside of care homes in their own smaller residences, to find and keep work in the public sphere, and to form a range of healthy relationships.

The introduction of this model, and of the wider policy reforms, has undoubtedly had profound effects on the adult lives of people with intellectual disabilities. It has opened up, for many of them, opportunities to escape constrictive regimes of care in order to work, form friendships and start families. But it is worth focusing as well on the problems that this model has encountered, for its own aspirations for people with intellectual disabilities are rarely realised fully. Only a few people with intellectual disabilities end up achieving, through this pedagogical programme, the kind of independence necessary to live alone or to find a job. And these individuals typically have very few friends in general, and fewer still without intellectual disabilities.[19] To put it bluntly: people with intellectual disabilities in Britain very rarely form significant intimate relationships with anyone outside of the caring contexts in which they spend their days.

Why is this? It is not implausible that their continuing dependence plays an important part in this. People with intellectual disabilities tend to continue to rely on relationships of domestic care with both their parents and professional support workers that sit awkwardly with dominant understandings of adulthood.[20] Their reliance, that is, upon paternalistic and mothering relations to facilitate their access to public and private, work and friendship, thus locates them as having not yet fully transcended childhood in one crucial respect.[21] And it may well be that their continuing association with the domestic sphere means they struggle to appear to both potential employers and potential friends as 'their own person'. The fact that they rely on other adults in order to engage in friendships may well mean that they seem to lack the kind of freedom, autonomy and authenticity deemed essential to intimate relationships. In this respect people with disabilities are often caught in a double bind: they rely on care to achieve what independence they can, but relying on care to achieve this renders their independence less convincing.[22]

But, while dependence is probably part of the answer, I suspect there is more going on here. The British emphasis on choice, preference and the 'wish to be together' as characteristic of friendship makes this kind of relationship very free but also very fragile.[23] It is hard for it to emerge spontaneously in public because its emergence seems to rely on both parties expressing their desire to be around each other – something that many aspects of British etiquette militate against. In this context, the close following of interactional norms takes on a particular significance as it enables people to establish trust with strangers so that, if they spend time with one another, friendships can develop.[24]

This is where, I suspect, the problems arise for people with intellectual disabilities. These individuals rarely share social spaces, such as workplaces, with the cognitively able for very long. And even on the fleeting occasions they do, people such as Lizzie and Samuel frequently diverge from widely followed social scripts through which British people establish relations with one another. I suspect, in other words, that when the cognitively able encounter people with intellectual disabilities, they find their atypical way of engaging in conversation and social interaction confusing at the very least, and deeply disconcerting at worst, and so struggle to know how to 'go on' interacting with them.[25] I suspect they intuitively see very little relational future with someone who appears to interact so differently from them. In this context, without either extended contact or interactional conformity, there is nothing to bring people with and without intellectual disabilities together. There is very little of what we might call natural 'relational space' between them – and thus no arena in which a relationship as fragile as friendship might slowly blossom.

So we might speculate that there is, at present, a certain lack of 'fit' between people with intellectual disabilities and British forms of sociality.[26] By this I do not mean that there is something inherently wrong with people with intellectual disabilities – but rather that their particular impairments and dependencies stand in a problematic *relationship* to the ways many British people construct, imagine and practise friendship. If this is the case, then it is clear why the Supported Living model of care continues to encounter problems. While founded upon a recognition that people with intellectual disabilities are unjustly excluded from social life, the focus of this model of care's attempt to change their place in such a social order focuses squarely upon changing the person with disabilities themselves. In other words, it attempts to find a better 'fit' between people with intellectual disabilities and society, by changing the former and not the latter.[27]

Put like this, though, it is hard to imagine a way out of the difficulties that Supported Living encounters. For if the problems people with intellectual disabilities encounter in finding friendships are, at least in part, generated by societal-wide practices of friendship then it is difficult to see how they might be changed. Even were anyone to launch a nation-wide education programme to tackle stigma against people with intellectual disabilities, it is not clear that this would have much effect. I suspect the reason people with disabilities rarely form intimate relationships of this sort is not just prejudice, but also their lack of fit with values so deeply held as to be unarticulated and interactional norms so naturalised as to be imagined immutable. It is not at all clear that how any government might reshape such ingrained patterns of British sociality without becoming authoritarian, bankrupt or both.

It is with this in mind that I turn now to look at organisations and communities that have inserted themselves into this ill-fitting gap between people with intellectual disabilities and the patterns of friendship they encounter.

Rewriting Friendship

For the past two hundred years at least, there have been a number of experimental initiatives – more often than not, religious in inflection – operating at the fringes of the dominant forms of care in Britain. Ignominious as their history soon became, many of the asylums were attempts to find new solutions for the care and rehabilitation of the intellectually disabled and mentally ill that operated neither solely at the level of the individual, nor at a scale as grand as the 'societal' or the 'national'. The Quaker-run York Retreat, founded in 1796, is probably the most illustrious, and most famously critiqued,[28] of these early ventures: aiming to explore the possibility of accommodating and treating the mentally ill without resorting to violence. In the twentieth century, similar ventures took shape in the margins of dominant patterns of care in the form of religious and secular therapeutic communities designed to create alternative social environments in which those with mental health and other problems might recover.[29]

I am interested, here, in a quite specific class of these initiatives: those that aim to create this kind of alternative social environment not simply as a way to provide an innovative form of care, but also a way to remodel, on a very small scale, patterns of social belonging so as to make them more accommodating of people with intellectual disabilities.[30] The earliest of this type of venture that I have been able to find evidence of is a nineteenth-century initiative by John Langdon Down, the controversial physician who gave his name to Down's Syndrome. Langdon Down took a number of children with Down's Syndrome into his own home and raised them, to the last sartorial detail, to be good Victorian children.[31] This constituted a difference not simply to the care these children received but also to the kinds of social relationships they were incorporated into – creating, as it did, a new form of adoptive and communal kinship specifically geared to include them.[32]

In 2013–14, I conducted fifteen months of fieldwork on a L'Arche community in the UK that works to adapt British patterns of friendship (rather than kinship) around those with intellectual disabilities.[33] The community I studied provides accommodation for people with intellectual disabilities not in a separate village or anything that looked like a 'commune', but rather in relatively typical suburban houses dispersed across a number of standard residential streets within about a mile of each other. In some of these houses, a number of (typically young) carers live with long-term residents with intellectual disabilities. Together, they host other carers, friends of the community, and visitors for dinners and communal celebrations. These shared houses in L'Arche are deliberately crafted to be unusual social spaces. They are neither wholly public nor wholly private, but are rather relatively porous forms of domestic, or what we might call semi-public, spaces.[34]

This unusual setting provides the essential backdrop for extended social contact that goes beyond wholly familial or professional relations of care. L'Arche encourages carers not to be constrained by their contractual obligations in these homes, but to open up to the possibility of forming mutual relationships with those they support – in which they, as carers, might receive as much as they give. Carers in L'Arche are trained, that is, to look at the ways in which they might not simply care for, but might also actively like and share interests with the people they support. These attempts are often successful, in no small part because carers tend, through their training and simply through extended intimacy, to develop the kind of understanding of people with intellectual disabilities that strangers in public rarely acquire, and so have the capacity to develop new kinds of interaction with them.

The result is that people with intellectual disabilities often form lasting and meaningful relationships with their carers that are based on mutual attraction: founded, that is, on the kind of 'wish to be together' that Rezende identified among the young adults she studied. These relations remain professional relationships in many respects, and bounded by the kind of obligations and publicity characteristic of contractual work. But they are also deliberately infused with the values of spontaneity, affection and freedom that earlier I identified as so crucial to British understandings of friendship. To put it differently, L'Arche intentionally cultivates a form of relationship that melds aspects of care and friendship together – to make it possible for people with intellectual disabilities to form intimate relationships without having to transcend their dependence upon others.

In this respect, L'Arche does something quite different to other mainstream care organisations in contemporary Britain. It changes, that is, not simply the capacities that people with intellectual disabilities have, but also the social patterns they are part of. Rather than aiming to get people with disabilities out into the local 'community', the organisation instead creates a new kind of community around these individuals. This enables it to cultivate a new form of relationship that sits in between the public and private, dependence and independence, care and friendship. This is a space that affords people with intellectual disabilities new opportunities for intimacy and social belonging that do not depend on them overcoming their reliance on care. This kind of belonging is found *within* the novel caring relationships that L'Arche fosters.[35]

We might even go so far as to say that L'Arche generates a new mode of adulthood for people with intellectual disabilities to inhabit: one that does not resemble the autonomy to navigate between public and private spheres, and between clearly distinguished relations of family, friendship and work. Instead, L'Arche creates a new pattern for what an adult life might look like by creating new spheres and modes of relationship that escape some of the dichotomies (between dependence and independence, obligation and freedom, public and private) that are typically central to British imaginations of adulthood and the relationships that constitute it. If there is a kind of cultural script that enables British people to identify and work towards adulthood, then L'Arche might be seen as a way to rewrite it: to constitute, that is, just the kind of relational improvisation that anthropologists Rayna Rapp and Faye Ginsburg argue so often arise out of the ruptures to the social fabric that intellectual disability frequently causes.[36]

Lyn's House

I want to argue that we could see Lyn's House as another such experiment. Samuel, Lizzie, Peter, Rebecca and I were similarly trying to innovate new social forms, during those dinner times, that might fit both those with intellectual disabilities and the cognitively able alike and thus find ways to connect them.

Lyn's House has, at present, a less settled model than many contemporary L'Arche communities in the UK (which, although they began in an improvisatory way, have clear parameters from the regulatory framework of care they must legally conform to). But I want to contend that the model Lyn's House is feeling its way towards is quite different from that traditionally pursued in L'Arche and thus opens up new possibilities that are obscured in contemporary L'Arche communities.

Earlier I described L'Arche residences as located between the public and the private. And I want to contend that the same is true of Lyn's House, but with a crucial difference. No people with intellectual disabilities live in Lyn's House. Shared L'Arche houses are an (often confusing) mixture of the person with disabilities' house, their carers' house for a certain time, and a public space. But Lyn's House is, in many ways, a more recognisable social space: the private property of those who live there, and thus the house of someone *other* than the people who visit. The residents are thus the ones who host both the cognitively typical and disabled people who visit. Several times a week the house opens up to people who (at least, at first) are often relative strangers and thus exhibits the same mixture of intimacy and commonality that earlier I describe as porosity. But the distinction should be clear: it is a place that sits not between people with disabilities' *own* private place and the public, but rather between *other* people's private place and the public sphere.

This draws our attention to the fact that, though Lyn's House may be a caring environment in one sense, it provides none of the specialist care necessary for people with intellectual disabilities to get by. It does nothing to replace the long-term caring relations with families and professional carers that the guests with intellectual disabilities depend upon. Families and (to a lesser extent) contracted carers do often participate in the life of Lyn's House, coming regularly to tea parties among other events. But, whatever Lyn's House is doing, it is not remoulding the way or the place in which care is provided in Britain. It is not refashioning the kind of existence people with intellectual disabilities have *within* their own households.

The distinction of Lyn's House from a space of care means that the dependencies and needs of people with intellectual disabilities, and the obligations these place on their carers, are not foregrounded in Lyn's House. The relationships people form there are not on the basis of any professional or familial duty towards one another – and particularly not on the basis of any obligation on the part of the cognitively able to 'look after' those who visit, for those needs are taken care of elsewhere. People with intellectual disabilities seem to come to Lyn's House primarily because of their independent desire to be there, just like the cognitively able. They do so because of a 'wish to be together'.

Lyn's House, like L'Arche, blurs the distinction between the public and the private. But it does not combine dependence and independence, obligation and freedom, care and choice, work and friendship in the way that L'Arche does. Instead, its model preserves these distinctions that can be found in British social patterns more widely. Lyn's House is not anyone's workplace, familial home, or place of care. And this quite clearly marks the relationships in it as occupying that third relational zone in British life: friendship. Relationships in Lyn's House operate largely within the ways in which friendship, as I described it earlier, is understood in Britain and they thus often bear many of its hallmarks: independence, spontaneity, intimacy, authenticity and freedom.

This might suggest that Lyn's House is simply preserving the problematic status quo that mainstream care can reproduce: a society in which friendship is understood in ways that are problematic for people with intellectual disabilities. But this is far from the case. For Lyn's House works with the cultural building blocks of friendship, as it is currently understood, in order to build an interactional environment that enables a better fit between the cognitively able and disabled. It is a kind of extended experiment in trying to use the distinction between family, work and friendship that so often excludes people with intellectual disabilities in new ways to see if something more constructive can be fashioned out of it. It takes features of British social life as given and seeks not to overhaul them with a systematic and totalising sociality, but rather to improvise upon them.

That is, at least, how I would describe what Peter, Rebecca and I were trying to do over those dinner times with Samuel and Lizzie. We were seeing how we might adapt the genre of inviting friends over for a meal around the particular ways in which Lizzie and Samuel needed and wanted to interact. With Lizzie and Samuel we were trying to find some kind of shared relational space, even though it was, at first, hard to locate or envision. Peter took Samuel's, at first seemingly somewhat out of place, interest in retelling biblical stories at random, and used it to create a kind of interaction that none of us would have imagined at first: performing a version of *The Prince of Egypt* in the kitchen. What emerged out of these kinds of encounters between our different ways of interacting were new modes of relating. We were creating spaces in which we might genuinely be friends – in which, that is, we might each be free, authentic and spontaneous and not simply resort to a certain kind of charitable or obligatory distance from one another.

Lyn's House therefore does something quite different from the typical form that L'Arche takes in the UK. While a residential L'Arche community requires remoulding a whole set of relationships between care and friendship, obligation and freedom, dependence and independence, Lyn's House works with widely held British patterns and norms. It simply reconfigures a small aspect of them: the particular spaces and ways in which friendship is conducted. It leaves intact the categories and values through which people with and without disabilities in Britain understand their social lives.

This does not always and inevitably result in the emergence of friendships. There are plenty of people who do not get on with each other, awkward moments, ways in which different ways of relating are not accommodated or made productive. I suspect this project will always entail complications for both the cognitively able and disabled participants in it, and that friendships in this space will often be partial and limited (just as they are, indeed, in other walks of life). But even in the midst of these complications the very pursuit of reconfiguring friendship has some clear consequences.

Lyn's House provides to those with disabilities a manageably ordered set of social relations that are neither wholly of their own making, nor wholly 'other' and distant from them. It does this, in part, by providing enough structure that the cognitively able do not run away from those with intellectual disabilities when they first encounter difficulties in interacting with them. Instead, the social setting holds in place the promise that friendships with such people are indeed possible, and suggests some routes by which the more and less cognitively able alike might develop the kind of interactional skills, habits and spaces necessary to make this possible.

Lyn's House provides the kind of relational space between people with and without intellectual disabilities that does not typically exist in mainstream British social life: an arena in which they might encounter each other over time, and in which interactional divergence and failure does not necessarily result in the foreclosure of relationship. It is, in other words, a space in which the pressure is taken off interactional conformity, enabling people to stay together long enough that the fragile relationship of friendship has a chance to emerge. We might call it, following anthropologist Cheryl Mattingly, a kind of 'moral laboratory':[37] a setting in which people can experiment with finding ways to work through relationships in a way they never normally have the opportunity to do.

Endnotes

1   Claudia Barcellos Rezende, 'Gifts of Food: Sociability and Friendship among English Middle Class People', *VIBRANT – Vibrant Virtual Brazilian Anthropology* 4, no. 2 (2007), pp.5–26.

2   See, for example, Marcel Mauss, *The Gift: The Form and Reason for Exchange in Archaic Societies* (London: Routledge Classics, 2002); James Laidlaw, 'A Free Gift Makes No Friends', *Journal of the Royal Anthropological Institute* 6, no. 4 (1 December 2000), pp.617–34.

3   Sandra Bell and Simon Coleman (eds), *The Anthropology of Friendship* (New York: Berg, 1999); Amit Desai and Evan Killick (eds), *The Ways Of Friendship: Anthropological Perspectives* (New York: Berghahn Books, 2013).

4   Rezende, 'Gifts of Food', p.23.

5   James Woodburn, 'Egalitarian Societies', *Man* 17, no. 3 (1982), pp.431–51.

6   Rezende, 'Gifts of Food', p.10.

7   Rezende, 'Gifts of Food'; see also Matthew Carey, *Mistrust: An Ethnographic Theory* (Chicago: Hau Books, 2017).

8   Rezende argues that this typology is, perhaps, only so clear because of the particular social location of these individuals. They were at a point in their lives, and part of a middle-class milieu, in which a clear distinction between family, work and the autonomous and intimate sphere of friendship was especially important to them. It would not be hard to think of relationships in Britain in which these boundaries are more blurred. Work on British working-class sociality, for instance, suggests there may indeed be more overlap between the categories of friend and kin in these settings at the very least. See, for instance, Jannette Edwards and Marilyn Strathern 'Including Our Own', in *Cultures of Relatedness: New Approaches to the Study of Kinship*, ed. Janet Carsten (Cambridge: Cambridge University

Press, 2000); Gerd Baumann, *Contesting Culture: Discourses of Identity in Multi-Ethnic London* (Cambridge: Cambridge University Press, 1996).

9   Carey, *Mistrust*.

10 See Gail Landsman, *Reconstructing Motherhood and Disability in the Age of Perfect Babies* (New York: Routledge, 2008).

11 Richard Jenkins, *Questions of Competence: Culture, Classification and Intellectual Disability* (Cambridge University Press, 1999).

12 Tom Shakespeare, *Disability Rights and Wrongs Revisited* (London: Routledge, 2013).

13 John Welshman and Jan Walmsley (eds), *Community Care in Perspective* (Basingstoke: Palgrave Macmillan, 2006); see also Peter Bartlett and David Wright, *Outside the Walls of the Asylum: The History of Care in the Community 1750–2000* (London: Athone Press, 1999).

14 Jenkins, *Questions of Competence*.

15 Robert B. Edgerton, *The Cloak of Competence* (Berkeley: University of California Press, 1993).

16 See Rayna Rapp and Faye D. Ginsburg, 'Enabling Disability: Rewriting Kinship, Reimagining Citizenship', *Public Culture* 13, no. 3 (2001), pp.533–56.

17 Welshman and Walmsley, *Community Care*.

18 John O'Brien, 'Supported Living: What's the Difference?' (1993), http://eric. ed.gov/?id=ED360801.

19 Carwyn Gravell, *Loneliness and Cruelty: People with Learning Disabilities and Their Experiences of Harassment, Abuse and Related Crime in the Community* (London: Lemos&Crane, 2012); Eric Emerson and Keith McVilly, 'Friendship Activities of Adults with Intellectual Disabilities in Supported Accommodation in Northern England', *Journal of Applied Research in Intellectual Disabilities* 17, no. 3 (1 September 2004), pp.191–7.

20 Landsman, *Reconstructing Motherhood and Disability in the Age of Perfect Babies*.

21 Jenkins, *Questions of Competence*.

22 Marcus Redley and Darin Weinberg, 'Learning Disability and the Limits of Liberal Citizenship: Interactional Impediments to Political Empowerment', *Sociology of Health & Illness* 29, no. 5 (July 2007), pp.767–86; Jenkins, *Questions of Competence*.

23 See also Barbara Bodenhorn, '"He Used to Be My Relative": Exploring the Bases of Relatedness among Inupiat of Northern Alaska', in *Cultures of Relatedness: New Approaches to the Study of Kinship*, ed. Janet Carsten (Cambridge: Cambridge University Press, 2000).

24 See Harold Garfinkel, 'Studies of the Routine Grounds of Everyday Activities', *Social Problems* 11, no. 3 (1 January 1964), pp.225–50; Alessandro Duranti, *The Anthropology of Intentions: Language in a World of Others*, 2015.

25 Ludwig Wittgenstein, *Philosophical Investigations: The German Text, with a Revised English Translation*, ed. Gertrude Elizabeth Margaret Anscombe (Wiley-Blackwell, 2001).

26 Rosemarie Garland-Thomson, 'Misfits: A Feminist Materialist Disability Concept', *Hypatia* 26, no. 3 (2011), pp.591–609; Jeannette Pols and Ingunn Moser, 'Cold Technologies versus Warm Care? On Affective and Social Relations with and through Care Technologies', *ALTER-European Journal of Disability Research/Revue Européenne de Recherche Sur Le Handicap* 3, no. 2 (2009), pp.159–78.

27 Patrick McKearney, 'L'Arche, Learning Disability, and Domestic Citizenship: Dependent Political Belonging in a Contemporary British City', *City & Society* 29, no. 2 (1 August 2017), pp.260–80.

28 Michel Foucault, Richard Howard and David Graham Cooper, *Madness and Civilization: A History of Insanity in the Age of Reason* (London; New York: Routledge, 2009).

29 Rex Haigh, *Therapeutic Communities: Past, Present and Future*, ed. Penelope Campling (London: Jessica Kingsley Publishers, 1999); Paul Gordon, *An Uneasy Dwelling* (PCCS Books, 2010).

30 Eric Emerson, 'Models of Service Delivery', in *Learning Disability: A Life Cycle Approach*, ed. Gordon Grant *et al.* (Maidenhead: Open University Press, 2010), pp.118–19.

31 Paul Williams, 'Residential and Day Services for Adults', in *Learning Disability: A Social Approach*, ed. David Race (London: Routledge, 2002).

32 See also Powell and Randall, Chapter 7, for more historical examples and for some contemporary parallels. For the Camphill communities see, e.g., Robin Jackson, *Discovering Camphill: New Perspectives, Research and Developments* (Floris Books, 2011).

33 See also earlier chapters of this volume for other work on L'Arche.

34 McKearney, 'L'Arche, Learning Disability, and Domestic Citizenship'.

35 McKearney. For a discussion of an analogous difference in the Netherlands see Jeannette Pols, 'Washing the Citizen: Washing, Cleanliness, and Citizenship in Mental Health Care', *Culture, Medicine and Psychiatry* 30, no. 1 (1 March 2006), pp.77–104, https://doi.org/10.1007/s11013-006-9009-z.

36 'Enabling Disability'; See also Cheryl Mattingly, *Moral Laboratories: Family Peril and the Struggle for a Good Life* (Berkeley: University of California Press, 2014).

37 Mattingly, *Moral Laboratories*.

— CHAPTER 9 —

Why L'Arche?
Why Lyn's House?
What Next?

Theresia L. Paquet and David F. Ford

'In L'Arche everything came out of friendship. This happened as a gift. Something so deep. We have received the mystery.'

'The advantage of L'Arche is fifty-four years of experience. An evolution has happened. It is evolving to something deeper.'

'It has to work!'

'I think of what is happening in Croatia. It is a community, not a residential house, a group of people bonded together with a mission to share life with people with learning disabilities.'

'All I know is there is a story of L'Arche that began: to follow Jesus to be with the poor. Where will it lead? I don't know. The whole vision needs to go further.'

'I believe there is a treasure of peacemaking. A vision where the weakest and the most excluded change us.'

'Trust in the Spirit!'

Those seven statements were made in October 2018 by Jean Vanier, who had had his ninetieth birthday the previous month. The setting was a week of conversations with a small international group in Trosly-Breuil, northern France, where L'Arche's mother community is. The writing of this chapter was also begun there during that week. Looking back on the earlier chapters, what Vanier said gathers together some of the key elements in the origins and shaping of Lyn's House.

There is *Jean Vanier* himself, who in 1992 challenged Deborah Hardy Ford to begin something in Cambridge. He continued to encourage what later was begun there, met with resident members of Lyn's House, with Lyn's House friends, and with steering group members, and helped in the ongoing discernment needed to develop the project. His writings continue to give basic learning materials and inspiration. And several members of the network of Jean's friends and collaborators, in Trosly and elsewhere, have been most helpful in the genesis and development of Lyn's House.

There is *L'Arche*, in which, as earlier chapters have shown, so many of us involved with Lyn's House have participated in various ways. It continues to inspire us as we and L'Arche both seek to evolve further to 'something deeper'. The two authors of this chapter have had distinct engagements with L'Arche.

Theresia L. Paquet (neé Bäumker) has an older brother, Charl, who has profound physical and learning disabilities, very similar to Adam whom Henri Nouwen encountered at the L'Arche Daybreak community in Canada and whose story he tells in the book by the same name. Theresia has grown up with, cared for and been inspired by Charl all her life. She first became involved with the L'Arche Kent community (the first community founded in the UK by Jean Vanier's sister, Thérèse, in 1974) in the hope of finding a place for her brother Charl there, as there had been a place for Adam at Daybreak.[1] Theresia sought to learn from L'Arche by becoming part of their community and as a deputy manager of one of their residential care homes for five people with learning disabilities. Since then, together with her brother Werner Bäumker, she has founded the care organisation Mannawell to take care of her brother Charl and other loved ones like him. Mannawell (see www.mannawell.uk) is now based in Cambridge, together with Lyn's House, with the vision of caring for people with learning disabilities in the spirit of L'Arche and Lyn's House. As Henri Nouwen did, Theresia hopes one day to write a book about her brother Charl's story. At the time of writing she is working part-time as the project manager of Lyn's House.

David F. Ford first came to Trosly-Breuil with a group of theologians committed to accompanying L'Arche, who eventually produced the book *Encounter with Mystery*.[2] He and his wife Deborah were later part of a smaller group, including Jean Vanier, Frances Young, and the then international co-ordinators of L'Arche, Christine McGrievy and Jean-Christophe Pascal, that met annually over many years to reflect on the development of L'Arche, on related strategic and theological issues, and much else. He and Deborah have had a range of other L'Arche relationships in the UK and around the world (including Liverpool, Bognor Regis, Ipswich, London, Canterbury, Chennai, Toronto and Atlanta) through friendships, visits, pilgrimages, retreats, consultations and international gatherings. From all this, and more, over half a century of L'Arche history and experience around the world have fed into the shaping of Lyn's House. At the time of writing he is a member of the Lyn's House steering group.

There is *friendship*. Friendships of many sorts have been as vital for Lyn's House as for L'Arche. Central are friendships with and between those with learning disabilities, who are the reason for both L'Arche and Lyn's House coming into being. There is a constantly expanding and deepening network of interwoven friendships at the heart of the Lyn's House community, including steering group, residents, volunteers, families, carers, past residents, and more. The chapters of this book testify to this in various ways, ranging from stories of transformative one-to-one relationships to a social anthropological account of how Lyn's House works in relation to the cultural norms of adult friendship in Britain today.

There is *gift*. The story of Lyn's House told in this book, like that of L'Arche, is full of gifts – of people, time and energy, inspirations and ideas, happenings, opportunities, a house and funding. The other side of that has been the uncertainty and vulnerability of depending on who and what is given, the risk of being committed to a venture that does depend on gifts of many sorts, some very costly to those who give them, and some vital but unpredictable, such as the recurrent searches for new residents in the house.

There is getting something to *work* in practice. This is an ongoing, never-ending concern, involving all sorts of meetings, discussions, discernments, decisions, negotiations, communications, vigilance and actions. The workload is often largely hidden, and inevitably has fallen more on some than others. There have been difficult relationships, painful misunderstandings and a need to learn from mistakes. All this is the stuff of getting any vision to work out on the ground, and it is continuing. The need has above all been for a combination of wisdom, of the sort Suzie Millar and other contributors describe, with a commitment to persevere.

There are *depth* and *mystery*. We have wanted to enter into and learn from the depths that have been sounded by Jean Vanier, Henri Nouwen and many others who have lived in and learned from L'Arche. We also try to go further, through the experience and reflection of those involved in Lyn's House. In this chapter those two concerns are summarised by responding to the questions: 'Why L'Arche?' and 'Why Lyn's House?' Central to both is the mystery Vanier speaks of, around which all the reflections spiral.

There is *what is happening in Croatia* and other improvisations on L'Arche in places such as New Zealand, the Czech Republic, Melbourne, Beauvais, Georgetown, Strasburg, Nottingham and Aberdeen. The challenge is to stay true to the heart of L'Arche as a community of transformative encounter and friendship centred on people with learning disabilities, while meeting the needs and taking the opportunities in diverse contexts. Lyn's House is one such small improvisation, an attempt both to be true to the L'Arche vision and to be responsive to Cambridge.

There is *Jesus*. The genesis and development of L'Arche is inseparable from Jesus. If *it is evolving to something deeper*, one thing that it must involve is going deeper into who Jesus is, into his life, death and resurrection, his example, his wisdom, his love and what he desires. Jean Vanier sought increasingly to do this as he grew older, above all through his meditative commentary, *Drawn into the Mystery of Jesus through the Gospel of John*,[3] and the retreats, videos, talks and other writings related to that. Those in the Lyn's House community also seek to go deeper into the life, wisdom and love of Jesus, as earlier chapters in this book show, and this chapter attempts to take that further. That includes facing the question of who Jesus is for multi-religious and 'multi-secular' settings, such as Cambridge and a great many other places today.

There is *peacemaking*. If peace is understood as good relationships across differences, leading to the flourishing of people in relation to God, each other and creation, L'Arche can be seen as a sign of peace. Jean Vanier's deepening engagement with Jesus was accompanied by a widening prophetic message to twenty-first century civilisation, culminating in *Signs of the Times: Seven Paths of Hope for a Troubled World*.[4] That is a call to transform our societies along paths from humiliation to humility, from conformity to conscience, from exclusion to encounter, from power to authority, from isolation to community, from strength to vulnerability, and from secret to mystery. Lyn's House is an attempt both to travel those paths and also to inspire reflection on them with a view to attracting others to join in travelling them.

And there is *trust in the Spirit*. In John's Gospel the Spirit is like a wind that 'blows where it chooses, and you hear the sound of it, but you do not know where it comes from or where it goes'; and the Spirit is given 'without measure' (3:8, 34). The first breathing of the Spirit of Jesus is from the cross, as he dies in humiliation: 'He gave up his Spirit/ spirit' [literally, 'he handed over the Spirit/spirit'] (19:30). No limit is set to this handing over. But he has just called those nearest to him, the disciple he loved and his mother, to form a new household (19:26–27). *So this Spirit springs from someone in the depths of suffering and humiliation, forms a community of love, and can be shared limitlessly.* The Spirit of Jesus encourages the creation of communities sharing life with those who suffer rejection and humiliation, and also opens them to welcoming signs of this Spirit blowing freely and 'without measure', far beyond their own community, and in many surprising people and places. Lyn's House seeks to live in this Spirit.

Why L'Arche?

There are many angles from which L'Arche can be approached, and Jean Vanier's statements, together with many others about L'Arche in earlier chapters, point to some of the most important. When L'Arche conducted a Federation-wide consultation on its identity and mission, the results were distilled under three headings: Relationships; Transformation; Sign.[5]

At the heart of the relationships is the experience of encounters that are transformative. One testimony after another of those involved with L'Arche, as also of those involved with Lyn's House in this book, tells of what happens in these relationships. Often they tell of surprising friendships; of the healing of wounds due to humiliation, rejection, trauma and brokenness of many sorts; of the recognition of the preciousness, beauty and love of those whom most people ignore, discount, marginalise or even fear; of the mutual recognition of vulnerability; of the mutual transformations that can happen; and of the joy and celebration that flows from these relationships. Through it all is the central importance for everyone, with or without learning disabilities, of being loved and of loving. Embracing it is a vision of common humanity, the treasuring of each person for his or her own sake, and our deep need to be loved and to love. Jesus too is vulnerable, loved and loving.

Why People with Learning Disabilities?

A fascinating question is: why have people with learning disabilities been found to be especially helpful in inspiring this vision and realising it in practice? It is, after all, a vision relevant to all people. L'Arche has in fact inspired a wide range of other valuable initiatives, in which the main emphasis has been on shared life centred on different groups, including the elderly with Alzheimer's, the homeless, disadvantaged children, prisoners and the mentally ill. So why those with learning disabilities?

Perhaps it is that they combine in themselves a number of elements.

The most important, of course, is that each is, as all of us are, infinitely precious, created in the image of God, a gift to be treasured, embodying and able to reveal the beauty and love of God. Each is, as all of us are, connected to every other creature through being created, loved and blessed by God, so that none of us is fulfilled without the others – and this interdependence is very obvious in those who require a great deal of assistance. The recognition of this reality, of our deepest identity being in relation to God and others, can come in many ways.

One of the other elements in L'Arche relationships between those with and without learning disabilities is the surprise factor. Outside families, there are few settings in most societies where such relationships can be formed and sustained, and within both families and most 'care relationships' there are complications that make anything like adult-to-adult friendships difficult. L'Arche's fundamental surprise, often spoken of by Jean Vanier and by assistants in L'Arche communities, is that an 'us caring for them relationship' is transformed into 'us in a mutual relationship together', in which, as in friendship, there is deep sharing that is not one-sided. The sign value of L'Arche owes a good deal to this reversal of expectation.

The sign value is also enhanced by its long-term character. The learning disabilities of those (often called 'core members'[6]) in L'Arche communities are generally permanent and lifelong, requiring long-term support of many sorts. One effect of this is the desirability of a long-term, stable community. Parents of those with such disabilities are often anguished at the prospect of their children being left without close relationships after they themselves die or are incapable of giving the necessary support, and their fears are well-grounded. L'Arche takes on, in relation to its core members, a permanent commitment to something more than professional care. It too faces great challenges regarding continuity, especially due to the turnover of assistants, but yet it usually does succeed, in one of its communities after another, in creating settings in which those surprisingly mutual relationships happen. This means that, if one revisits a range of such communities over many years, one learns to recognise a deeply moving quality of relationship, centred on intensive one-to-one engagement day after day. Testimonies to these transformative relationships are the core 'good news' of L'Arche.

Reflection on the content of the sign value of L'Arche for the wider society leads to a further element in the L'Arche combination: the challenge to so many of the things that are immensely important to our culture but which also give rise to a great many people feeling of little value, marginalised, excluded, inferior or even humiliated. Most L'Arche core members do not receive a mainstream education and qualifications, do not have a job or career or handle money independently, do not get married or have children, are not considered handsome, beautiful or fashionable, differ from the majority of people in their social and communicational capacities, cannot take part in most sport or leisure activities, do not take on institutional or organisational responsibilities, are not concerned with local, national or international public affairs, and are dependent on other people for many daily functions that most other people can cope with by themselves. In fact, of course, a huge number of other people experience one or more of those (and at the beginning and end of life most people experience all of them), but those with learning disabilities often experience them all together, year after year. One implication is that they may therefore represent in an especially vivid way what it means to be human without seeing any of those things as essential to each person.

A related implication is that they can be a sign of liberation from some widespread compulsions (though they can develop their own versions): educational achievement and qualifications; work, money and economic utility; sex and fashion; leisure and social media; politics, power and influence; and so on.

But more important than such negative implications is the positive one: to have a community centred on those who are so marginal to so many of the 'normal' aspects of society is an encouragement to everyone to realise their own human identity in liberating ways. Each of us is utterly precious, deeply in need of being loved and loving. If we find that it is possible to have a community of love, dignity, generosity and celebration centred on those who are usually on the margins, then this is a sign of hope for all. If the well-educated, those with successful careers, the entrepreneurs, the high earners, the glamorous, the sexually attractive, the famous, the healthy, the sports stars and the powerful are central to a society, then a great many people will be marginal in one respect or other. But if those with learning disabilities are central that need not happen. It becomes more possible to imagine what a community centred on mutual love and utter respect might look like.

L'Arche and Our Civilisation: Encounter, Presence, Commitment

Some of the broad, civilisation-wide implications of this were the subject of a rich reflection by the political philosopher Professor Ronan Sharkey in the October 2018 gathering during which this chapter had its origins. During the past thirty years, he first came from England and lived as an assistant in L'Arche's mother community in Trosly, and married Hoda, a fellow L'Arche assistant from Lebanon. When he became an academic they continued to live in Trosly and bring up their family in close relationship with L'Arche, and Hoda has worked within L'Arche.

Ronan spoke of the disclosive, revelatory quality of what happens through the sorts of encounters and sustained presence to each other that repeatedly happen in L'Arche communities. The following is my condensation of several hours in group discussion with him.

> People are deeply and lastingly moved. We feel we have entered deeper territory both between us and inside ourselves. So much of our civilisation is about the power to change the world. Our simple and complex skills are developed to affect the future. We think strategically, instrumentally, often bracketing out attention to people for their own sake, to our physical environment, to our bodies, to ourselves. This has always been so to some extent, but in the past few centuries modernity has intensified this instrumental, use-centred approach to reality and to people. It carries with it an evaluation of people according to their individual capacities and usefulness (often comparatively or competitively assessed), their 'skilful coping', their projects and their roles, and tends to confine their value as persons for their own sake to restricted spheres of intimacy and private life

– which are themselves often under great pressure from economic and other forces.

Deep down, many are very dissatisfied with this instrumentalising and individualising of human lives. L'Arche comes as a liberating alternative. It does not, of course, do away with 'skilful coping'; but by being centred on encounters and relationships with those whose coping is mostly 'unskilful' according to the dominant norms, it frees us to be present to each other in new ways, to be appreciated for our own sake, to celebrate the gift of each other to each other.

This combination of encounter and continuing presence to each other is fulfilled in long-term commitment. In this the relationship is the primary good, and our freedom is fulfilled and matured within it.

L'Arche and Our Civilisation: Impact on Society

That philosophical approach was strikingly supported by a remarkable piece of research, also presented to our gathering, by the economist, Professor Elena Lasida. She has spent five years leading a team on a research project covering all the L'Arche communities in France, enquiring into their impact on society. A great deal of the literature relating to L'Arche is about personal transformation; Elena's research concentrated on social transformation: how do L'Arche communities affect their wider social settings? Besides those in the surrounding social settings of communities, both assistants and core members were included in the research, partly through newly devised board games that elicited stories and insights which were recorded and analysed.

The conclusions are focused through three key concepts.

First is *'renversement'*, what the title of this book calls 'upside-downness', and is in line with Ronan Sharkey's account of the distinctiveness of L'Arche. People who come into contact with the communities are affected by the centrality of relationships which are not about status, achievement, practical usefulness, productivity or competition, but centred on presence, mutuality, generosity, meals and celebration. In particular, the research noted the importance of vulnerability, *fragilité*, as a key element in the quality of these relationships, in their transformative and creative potential, and in their message of interdependence.

Second is *'débordement'*, 'overflow' into other spheres of society. This was studied through the many areas with which L'Arche comes into engagement, from churches, social and medical services to hairdressers, bakers and cafes. There was a wide range of impacts, from values to governance, and conversations were set up between L'Arche people and those in the community. Perhaps the most striking thing to emerge was deep appreciation of the 'culture of joy' that was experienced.

Third is *'désarmement'*, 'disarming', the way L'Arche helps to enable relationships of peace, conversation and collaboration between people who are very different. There is a new sense of solidarity and unity together. This is also closely linked to vulnerability, *fragilité*, and includes facilitating the healing of divisions.

In the research, the process of engagement between L'Arche and their communities culminated in sharing the conclusions at a party.

A Christian Understanding

It is clear that trying to answer the question, 'Why L'Arche?', can lead into the deepest questions about humanity, society and civilisation. For Jean Vanier, Ronan Sharkey, Elena Lasada, those of us who began Lyn's House, and many others committed to L'Arche, the answers are inseparable from our Christian understanding, and that has already been reflected upon in some earlier chapters of this book. There is now a rich treasury of Christian thought inspired by L'Arche and the questions central to it, covering scripture, theology of various sorts, spirituality, ethics, politics and multi-disciplinary approaches.[7] It has been a privilege to take part in several of the projects that have produced some of those resources, now available in many media.

At the heart of all this is a 'virtuous circle' or spiral: L'Arche continually generates intensive wisdom-seeking conversations, which in turn help to generate fresh prayer, thought and action, including fresh improvisations on L'Arche. That week in Trosly in October 2018, during which this chapter was begun, is just one of many examples. It included a wide-ranging set of conversations, in which (besides those mentioned already – Jean Vanier, Ronan Sharkey and Elena Lasida) current L'Arche people, the head of Association Jean Vanier, a professor of disability studies from King's University College in London, Ontario, the head of La Ferme community of prayer (a vital part of L'Arche at Trosly), and a few others took part, aiming at setting up a centre that could help to develop Vanier's thought and practice further; and it coincided with a gathering of UK L'Arche leaders with

Christian leaders of several denominations that work with L'Arche, who were also seeking wisdom in engagement with L'Arche.

The contributors to this book have tried to take that L'Arche-related Christian thinking further, and one feature has been our diverse biblical inspiration. This has included the wisdom literature, the importance of the Sabbath, and key passages from the Synoptic Gospels (Matthew, Mark and Luke) and from St Paul. Jean Vanier himself drew on all those too, and his major religious writing was on the Gospel of John, which, of all the books of the Bible, has probably been the most influential theologically in Christian history. During one of the receptions surrounding the presentation to him of the Templeton Prize for 2015 he was asked about his current thinking on Chapter 19 of the Gospel of John. He replied in terms that have already been improvised upon above, in the opening section of this chapter on trusting in the Spirit:

> At the beginning of that chapter, Jesus is humiliated – he is flogged, a crown of thorns is pressed into his head, he is mocked, and slapped in the face.
>
> The people with learning disabilities in our communities have been humiliated too. They have been seen as of no worth, having no dignity. They have been marginal to what other people often value and centre their lives on: knowledge, education and work; sex, marriage, family life and friendship; health, sport and beauty; power, wealth and fame.
>
> Then Jesus is nailed to the cross, and what does he do from there? When he sees his mother and the disciple he loved at the foot of the cross, he says to his mother, 'Woman, here is your son', and to the disciple, 'Here is your mother.'[8] Then John says that the disciple took her into his home. *So, out of the depths of humiliation Jesus creates a community.* At the heart, the root, of this community is the humiliated one.

Given the range and depth of Christian thinking around L'Arche there should be little doubt that it rings true as something not only inspired by who Jesus is and by his message and continuing presence but also, inseparably, as a prophetic sign for our twenty-first century world. As with his mature thought on the Gospel of John, Vanier also, as mentioned in the opening section above, gave an example of prophetic wisdom through his reflections around the fiftieth anniversary of the

Second Vatican Council, *Signs of the Times*. Both his commentary on the Gospel of John and his updating of the message of Vatican II offer a challenge to others to take them further. One of the key elements in this is how a Christian understanding of L'Arche relates to other religions, beliefs and worldviews.

Into Multiple Depths

Within a few years of its Roman Catholic beginning in 1964, L'Arche met head-on two religion-related challenges: the Canterbury community was ecumenically Christian; and the first Indian community was interreligious. And throughout its history it has wrestled with issues raised by those who do not identify with any religion, and by secular understanding[9] and influences, not least in the attitudes and policies of governments, social and medical services, and cultures.

These developments raise a forest of questions, and L'Arche (both as an international federation and through its regional bodies), as well as the many collaborators, thinkers and others associated with it, have been tackling them in a variety of ways around the world. Here, we want to focus on one topic, a tension that has been the heart of the spiritual identity of L'Arche since it encountered those early ecumenical and interreligious challenges, and which has been important in the thinking that has shaped Lyn's House.

Christian Salenson, in his perceptive understanding of L'Arche, sees the tension that arose between Jean Vanier and Père Thomas Philippe (Vanier's spiritual mentor at the time of the founding of L'Arche, a Dominican priest who lived in Trosly-Breuil and played a key role in relation to Vanier and many of the early members of L'Arche) as one that is intrinsic to it.[10] It is the tension between being true to its Roman Catholic roots and being open to other traditions. Père Thomas wanted it to remain a Catholic organisation; Vanier wanted it to be ecumenical and interreligious; Vanier's way was followed, but there is an ongoing tension which, Salenson suggests, is healthy and requires continual attention.

One way of putting the question is: how can L'Arche be healthily plural? Its pluralism is now a fact, and any attempt to go back to being solely Catholic would probably lead to deep divisiveness in many regions of the international federation. In this it somewhat mirrors many formerly Catholic countries that are now religiously plural, and often in addition have many who identify with no religion. But for L'Arche to be healthily plural must mean that it continues to live from its Catholic roots, and if it succeeds in doing this, while at the same time embracing others who live from other roots, then it could be a sign of great importance for many societies – not only those considered Catholic in the past. Salenson (especially if his work on L'Arche is taken together with his work on interreligious engagement[11]) gives an example of a profound theological understanding of L'Arche from a post-Vatican II Catholic standpoint, combined with a richly Catholic theological approach to other religions, especially Islam. The implication is clear: L'Arche should seek both to be deeply Catholic and also to encourage others to understand and resource L'Arche from the depths of their own traditions.

This might be called a pluralism of multiple depths. The diversity of our societies often requires fairly superficial forms of relating across differences in order for life to go on. But, where there are deep, long-term differences (such as those involving religious and other core beliefs and commitments), to be superficial, or to fail in other ways to take seriously the character and extent of differences, is to court disaster. It means that the necessary conversations, debates, mutual encounters, learning and collaborations across differences and divisions do not take place. Therefore there is little basis for the sorts of negotiations, settlements and ways of living peacefully together that are needed to avoid divisions turning into conflicts and even violence. Our pluralist, divided and conflict-ridden world desperately needs signs of peace that enable the depth of engagement[12] across differences required to enable healthily diverse communities and societies.

In L'Arche it is especially important to deal with such differences, since it is constantly involved with questions that cry out for the depth of understanding and response that Jean Vanier and many others have opened up. So how might L'Arche be a place of multiple depths, between which there is conversation, learning and collaboration for the sake of healthy communities?

We have no overview of what is happening in L'Arche communities around the world, but in the UK we do see the increasing pressures that are making it difficult to sustain, resource and deepen its practice of Christian faith (in the UK L'Arche was ecumenically Christian from the beginning), to which it owes its existence, and at the same time to do justice to other faiths and non-religious beliefs and commitments. There are many hopeful initiatives, but they struggle with multiple pressures. The latter include the general attitudes of a society where much of the dominant ethos is secular and unsympathetic to any religious commitment; very heavy dependence on public funding (around 97% at present) which strictly limits expenditure to closely defined necessary 'care'; a mass of other regulations that control employment of staff and other aspects of the community; the difficulty of finding assistants and other staff who are open to the faith basis of the L'Arche ethos; the challenge of providing formation for the staff who are employed; and the overarching problem of how in current circumstances to shape the practices and spirituality of particular communities so as to be true to the core wisdom learned through half a century of living and thinking L'Arche. It is all too easy for the convergence of pressures to turn L'Arche into a 'care provider' meeting professional standards but not showing much of the distinctiveness and depth described above.

One result of such considerations has been a recognition among many in L'Arche that not only should the difficulties of the current communities be tackled (for example, by active fundraising to reduce dependence on public funding), but that new initiatives be explored, improvising on L'Arche in ways that try to meet the difficulties and renew it in fresh forms. Lyn's House is one such small initiative.

Why Lyn's House?

So, why Lyn's House?

The most obvious reason is the challenge by Jean Vanier to start something inspired by L'Arche in Cambridge, and the subsequent gathering of people with and without learning disabilities in order to meet Jean's charge. All that has been said above in answering the question 'Why L'Arche?' substantially applies to Lyn's House, and does not need to be repeated. But it is worth emphasising some elements that have emerged in this and previous chapters.

First, there are the features of the Cambridge context that made this sort of community seem appropriate. As Jean Vanier initially said to Deborah Hardy Ford, Cambridge is a place where there is a great concentration of people with learning abilities, and, in line with the experience of L'Arche, it is desirable for them to have relationships with people with learning disabilities. There is no L'Arche community nearby, and even the Faith and Light community for the support of people with learning disabilities and of their families had come to an end. Cambridge also has many young people at a formative stage in their lives, who go out into many spheres of society and parts of the world, so engagement with people with disabilities in the spirit of L'Arche is likely to have widespread impact. Further, Cambridge in many ways exemplifies a culture that has at its centre achievements, ambitions and abilities that are healthily decentred by L'Arche: intellectual, social, economic, technological, political, artistic, sporting and more.

Second, there is the immense difficulty in the UK of founding a L'Arche community along the lines of previous ones. The problems include all those facing L'Arche UK that have already been listed, together with policy developments that make it far less likely that those responsible for public funding will agree to support it. Yet the desirability of communities in which people with and without learning disabilities can experience the sorts of transformative relationships enabled by L'Arche is as great as ever. This is a strong incentive to experiment with other ways of embodying the L'Arche ethos.

Third, the key question about Lyn's House, therefore, is whether it really can embody the L'Arche ethos. Previous chapters of this book have given testimony, description and reflection (a good deal of it by people who know both L'Arche communities and Lyn's House) that suggest it can. There is also something hard to describe, let alone quantify: the sense of recognition, of 'family likeness' between the two.

But what is distinctive about Lyn's House?

The key difference from most L'Arche communities is that Lyn's House is not a professional service provider of care for people with learning disabilities. Rather, it makes L'Arche-like friendships central, set in an ecology of relationships that includes people with learning disabilities, a steering group, a residential Christian intentional community, long-term and short-term volunteers, families, professional carers, past residents, academic communities and more. This has been cumulative over six years, and is continuing to expand and deepen, most recently helped by the addition of a part-time project manager. The hope is that this complex community can exemplify in Cambridge, in an ongoing way, what is most important in L'Arche.

Why have an intentional Christian community living in Lyn's House as the place of gathering and hospitality? The rationale is in line with the desirability of both deep roots and radical openness, as discussed above. All those initiating Lyn's House, like all those who began L'Arche, were Christian. We wanted to continue the L'Arche tradition of deepening engagement with God and the Gospel, while also being open to all those God has created and loves. We knew that L'Arche UK was wrestling with how to be true to its Christian roots. We wanted to be a place where continual Christian prayer and living could happen in a community of hospitality and friendship, supported by a wider community of prayer, reflection and practical support. We see this as a potential contribution to the twenty-first century Christian development of the L'Arche vision and practice, and hope it can be of help to the whole L'Arche movement and beyond. We are also continually reminded of the difficulties, of the need for ongoing learning and relearning, and of our own fallibility and inadequacies.

In terms of a pluralism of multiple depths, this is a primary concentration on sounding Christian depth. Any rich tradition, we believe, needs such concentration and communal embodiment. We know that in L'Arche UK and L'Arche around the world there are examples of other traditions sounding their own depths in communities that experience transformative relationships and are signs of hope to the wider society. Already, for example, there are groups of Muslim scholars and L'Arche Muslim assistants seeking to make the connections between L'Arche and Islam; and in India there is a five-year process seeking to connect L'Arche to Hindu sources of wisdom. Lyn's House community is open to people of all religions and none, and is seeking to maintain that creative tension between particular roots and openness to all which Salenson identifies as essential to L'Arche. This book has been part of Lyn's House wisdom-seeking.

Two lines of reflection are particularly worth noting.

The first is on time, combining key points in two chapters of this book. Deborah Hardy Ford reflects on the 'Shabbat' wisdom of Lyn's House, its concentration on the sorts of things the sabbath is about: celebration, prayer, meals, music, time beyond work for relationships with people for their own sake, play, joy, 'wasting time together to become who we really are', an energy field of peace. This is 'time *l'shma*', quality time 'for the sake of the Name'. Patrick McKearney examines the social time of friendship among young adults, a time distinct from family time and work time, and connects that with Lyn's House. They converge in identifying Lyn's House as opening up a distinctive form of time for all involved, a time in which the differences among people are taken up into an energy field of freedom and celebration. As with Shabbat, it can take a good deal of hard work to enable it, but that is best seen as the effort of preparing for a special time, welcoming utterly dear ones.

The second is about commitment. The Jewish sabbath was not only the crown of creation but it was also the subject of one of the ten commandments, and so an essential part of the covenant of God with Israel. Covenantal commitment to God and to the L'Arche community was for many years part of L'Arche, and there is a fascinating body of reflection on it. For complex reasons, the practice of 'announcing the covenant' has not continued, but the role and form of commitment to L'Arche, especially by its long-term members (core members, assistants and leaders) remains an open issue.

A sharp way of formulating one aspect of this question in relation to the UK is: many pressures on L'Arche, from employment and other regulations, are towards contractual relations with those who work in it; yet traditionally L'Arche has encouraged a commitment better described as covenantal. The two need not be contradictory, but it is likely that L'Arche would not be L'Arche if all those employed in it regarded their commitment as purely contractual. Lyn's House is still exploring appropriate forms of commitment by those involved in various ways, with both contractual (for example, tenancy agreements for those living in the house) and covenantal dimensions. We hope that this exploration too can in time be of help to the wider L'Arche federation and beyond.

Overall, Lyn's House might be seen as one small improvisation on L'Arche with particular emphases on the potential of the Cambridge context, on shaping a new sort of complex community that still embodies the L'Arche vision, on combining a primary quest for Christian depth with engagement with the depths of other traditions, on creating special times and social spaces for friendships, and on exploring what sort of commitment all this requires.

Improvising Further: What Next?

What about further improvisations on L'Arche? We see these as needing to be about creating space and time for new sorts of community in line with the L'Arche ethos.

We offer four lines of thought as suggestions to stimulate others to further thinking, imagining and action.

First, there is the potential of other higher-education settings besides Cambridge to do things akin to Lyn's House. This is already happening in Aberdeen University, where the Professor of Pastoral Theology and Pastoral Care, John Swinton,[13] with full University support, under the auspices of its Centre for Spirituality, Health and Disability[14] in the School of Divinity, History and Philosophy, has founded Friendship House. Part of the project are three PhD students who are undertaking research in the area of disability, and offering hospitality in Friendship House. There has been fruitful exchange between Professor Swinton and those involved in Lyn's House. Both Professor Swinton and a member of Lyn's House steering group have also been in conversation with L'Arche-related groups in American universities that are seeking to develop similar settings. There seems to be no reason why the rationale for Lyn's House, that those in centres of learning ability need relationships with those with learning disabilities, should not lead to multiplication of such places around the world.

Second, L'Arche itself has several projects with some similarities to Lyn's House in various parts of the world. In the UK, for example, the L'Arche Nottingham Project began as a group of people praying for a L'Arche community around fifteen years ago. A number of parents of children with intellectual disabilities had heard of L'Arche (mostly through reading books and attending spiritual retreats), and felt that it was something that they wanted for their children and for Nottingham. The group expanded and explored the possibility of a residential community. Eventually, in 2014, they decided to meet every week for a meal, and now there are two core groups, RoseArk and Agape, that do this and also gather monthly together for community events. In 2016 the community became a formal project in L'Arche UK, and in 2019 both parties will decide whether it should have full L'Arche membership.[15] Members of L'Arche Nottingham have visited Lyn's House and the two have shared experiences and reflected on both their similarities (especially the emphasis on hospitality and friendship) and their differences (especially the residential dimension of Lyn's House, and its close ties to Cambridge University and other educational institutions).

Third, there is the possibility of having activities like those of Lyn's House – long-term hospitality and friendship centred on a residential community that does not provide professional care for those with learning disabilities – attached to a community that has been set up for other purposes. For example, there are colleges in Cambridge University or the Cambridge Theological Federation that might be open to adding this dimension to their life. Another possibility being explored is with Rose Castle in Cumbria. There, the Rose Castle Foundation is renovating Rose Castle to serve as a centre for reconciliation, interfaith engagement, religious literacy and conservation,[16] and many of those involved (including active local supporters) are keen to relate to those in the local community with learning disabilities.[17]

Finally, there is the possibility of a type of residential community for people with and without learning disabilities that combines elements of Lyn's House with elements of classic L'Arche communities.

The inspiring aspect of L'Arche is that people come together because they want to be together: they choose to join communities knowing what the values, behaviour and expectations of that community are. It is the mystery of a Christian community that is aware of being drawn together. The members become, as in the opening quotation of this chapter, a group of people bonded together with a vision to *share life together* with people with learning disabilities.

What if this sharing of the detail of everyday living, not just meals and social interactions as in Lyn's House, but day-to-day sharing of living space, is opened up to people who also have other missions and vocations in life?

Separating the residential element from the professional care element, in part or completely, opens up the possibility of having people with and without learning disabilities sharing life together (and living together) on a purely social rather than a professional basis. This would allow people who have other professional or spiritual missions and callings, or who are still studying (as are some in Lyn's House) or even retired, to choose to live together with people with learning disabilities. People from outside the home, on a professionally employed basis, would primarily meet the physical care and support needs of the people with learning disabilities. Would this encourage a return to a commitment by community members that is covenantal rather than contractual, as the part that needs to be contractual under current regulation (the personal care) would be separately provided?

This model of care delivery falls more easily within the current system of adult social care in the UK. There is a desire in the system to see a separation of professional and personal involvement between the 'professional' person employed to care and the person being cared for or supported. That makes the L'Arche message of interdependence – relationships that are centred on presence, mutuality and the importance of the vulnerability of *both* parties – difficult to encourage and celebrate openly in this system. It is also a way of working towards a solution of the problem mentioned previously: that it is all too easy for the convergence of pressures to turn L'Arche into a 'care provider' meeting professional standards but not showing much of the distinctiveness and depth described above.

The distinctiveness of the Christian roots of L'Arche could be fostered by accepting people to live in the house who deeply commit to the Christian ethos of the community (as modelled by Lyn's House), whilst ensuring that the community and home created is one radically open to welcoming any guests and volunteers. Asking house residents for a Christian commitment is easier to implement because it is the decision of the community of people living there, and not the decision of a care provider organisation regulated by other governing and regulatory bodies within a society where much of the dominant ethos is secular and unsympathetic to any religious commitment.

Nonetheless, the care provider that is chosen to deliver care to the community, could still specify that to be part of a Christian community is a desirable characteristic in the staff they recruit and ensure that their values align with the organisation's values. Value-based recruitment, as advocated in adult social care in the UK, is a value-based approach to the attraction and selection of staff, which enables organisations to assess whether an individual aligns with the values, culture and expectations of the organisation. For example, the mission of the care provider Mannawell is explicitly based on Jesus' message of loving your neighbour: *love is patient, love is kind...it always protects.*

As for people with learning disabilities living in such an intentional Christian community, personal experience has proven that many value the explicitly Christian ethos of L'Arche. There is a great loss for them when new assistants caring for them do not appreciate the importance of the spiritual dimension, and their Christian practices are then not upheld in their daily lives. For example, there can be lack of support to pray, to attend church, or arrange for time and space being created for spiritual reflection or singing in worship.

Moreover, the potential of this model is that social interactions are protected from taking place when people who provide care are exhausted from their caring responsibilities. This can easily happen when staff teams are stretched in a social care system that is severely and increasingly underfunded. By reducing the responsibilities and physical care tasks of the people living together, more time, more space and more freedom are created to engage with the people with learning disabilities as friends would engage. *Thus, the people with and without learning disabilities living in community can focus on investing in relationships that have the freedom to be mutual and interdependent.* This relates to the reflection on the *social time* of friendship, and the *'Shabbat' wisdom* of Lyn's House, and its concentration on celebration, prayer, meals, music and time beyond work for relationships with people for their own sake.

Thus, the possibility of a type of residential community for people with and without learning disabilities that combines elements of Lyn's House and L'Arche has this advantage: it takes care of the person with learning disabilities, meeting their basic need for physical care and support, whilst building community around them that can meet their social and spiritual desires.[18] The joy is that this opens up to them a circle of friendships and their own mission field of people whose lives they can touch with the message that *each is, as all of us are, infinitely precious, created in the image of God, a gift to be treasured, embodying and able to reveal the beauty and love of God.*

Conclusion: 'Yielding to a greater yes'

We have been especially concerned to show some of the ways in which the 'Why?' of L'Arche connects with the 'Why?' of Lyn's House, and how both open up a vision for further creativity in shaping new communities that are in line with the thought and practice of Jean Vanier and others. But through all this we have also tried to make wider connections with some of the profound questions and challenges of our time. In conclusion we expand the horizon of L'Arche and Lyn's House even further by returning to the source of the title of this book, the poet Micheal O'Siadhail.

In 2018 he published a remarkable major work, the result of a decade of writing: *The Five Quintets*.[19] It is five long poems on each of five themes, each moving from early modernity up to the twenty-first century. The themes are 'Making', engaging with the creative arts (including poetry, music, drama, painting and fiction); 'Dealing', on economists, money and the economy; 'Steering', on politicians, power and politics; 'Finding', on the sciences; and 'Meaning', on ways of making sense of reality, such as philosophy, theology and other forms of enquiry. It has strongly impressed a wide range of early reviewers, not least for its depth, scope and daring.

O'Siadhail even dares to follow Dante's *Paradiso* in attempting to imagine the conversation of heaven. This climaxes in the final canto of the final quintet, where the culminating conversation is between Dietrich Bonhoeffer, Hannah Arendt, Said Nursi and Jean Vanier.[20] This extract begins with Vanier's first contribution to the conversation:

Is that
Jean Vanier in love with all the least,

that tall and gentle presence laughing at
whatever Dietrich Bonhoeffer just said?
They're bubbling in an ease of trust and chat.

Jean Vanier joins in. 'I think I yearned
to soothe a human wound of loneliness
which each of us alone has slowly learned

'to heal in yielding to a greater yes
that bends to wash the bruised and unloved feet,
to tend with water and the towel's caress,

'to live by folly winning in defeat.
What if the weak become our first concern,
what if such love decides our balance sheet?

'And God so loved the world. We each in turn
knew wounds and gains we had to reconcile...'

Later, Vanier intervenes again, responding to the poet:

'Of course, there were the days of touch and go' –
It's Jean who laughs and turns to answer me –
'How could I live at L'Arche and never know

'such steel-grey moments of despondency?
But I rejoiced now even in the day
when nothing big or worthy seemed to be

'achieved and relished moods of come-what-may
which let the slow osmosis of all time
seep through the day's unplanned cantabile

'and made that habitat a paradigm
of how in healing others we are healed –
a catalyst, a beautiful enzyme

'thrown in to leaven now a world congealed
in grids of power and gain, a tiny rift
where wounded glory is again revealed.

'So little, you can say, so slight a shift
and yet enough to let the grapevine spread
a rumour of love's overfall as gift.'

We hope that Lyn's House, and this book, can play a little part in spreading that 'rumour of love's overfall as gift'. And, in that heavenly poetic conversation, Vanier goes on to speculate about future improvisations on L'Arche – perhaps not surprisingly, since O'Siadhail has in fact followed with great interest the founding and development of Lyn's House:

'I still can wonder where it all has led
or how it will expand or change its tack...'

We too wonder, and work for the further realisation of this vision.

Endnotes

1   This did not prove possible, one result of which is the vision for the sort of combination of L'Arche and Lyn's House that is laid out later in this chapter.

2   Frances M. Young (ed.), *Encounter with Mystery: Reflections on L'Arche and Living with Disability* (London: Darton, Longman and Todd, 1997). Long before this, in 1972–3, David F. Ford was a student of Henri Nouwen, taking his course 'Ministry as Hospitality' in Yale Divinity School. Nouwen, as other chapters in this book indicate, went on to live in L'Arche Daybreak in Toronto and became one of the leading writers on the personal and spiritual significance of L'Arche and the relationships it can enable.

3   London: Darton, Longman and Todd, 2004.

4   Jean Vanier, *Signs of the Times: Seven Paths of Hope for a Troubled World* (London: Darton, Longman and Todd, 2013). See above Chapter 7.

5   For an account of this consultation, and a much fuller discussion of L'Arche and the thought of Jean Vanier, together with reference to some key writings on L'Arche by Vanier and others, see 'An interpersonal wisdom: L'Arche, learning disability and the Gospel of John' in David F. Ford, *Christian Wisdom: Desiring God and Learning in Love* (Cambridge: Cambridge University Press 2007), pp.350–79.

6   'Core friends' in Lyn's House.

7   See, for example, the writings of Thérèse Vanier, Alain Saint-Macary, Henri Nouwen, Stanley Hauerwas, Frances Young, Gilles Le Cardinal, Hans Reinders, Christian Salenson, Anne Gibson, Pamela Cushing, Sue Mosteller, Hilary Wilson, Tim Kearney, Anne O'Sullivan, Ruth Patterson and John Swinton.

8   'When Jesus saw his mother and the disciple whom he loved standing beside her, he said to his mother, "Woman, here is your son." Then he said to the disciple, "Here is your mother." And from that hour the disciple took her into his own home.' (John 19:26–7).

9   A rich example of dialogue between Jean Vanier and someone who has been influential in secular thinking is: Julia Kristeva and Jean Vanier, *Leur regard perce nos ombres. Échange* (Paris: Fayard, 2011).

10   Christian Salenson, *Bouleversante Fragilité. L'Arche à l'épreuve du handicap* (Bruyères-le-Châtel: Nouvelle Cité, 2016).

11   Christian Salenson, *Christian de Chergé. A Theology of Hope* (Collegeville, Minnesota: Liturgical Press 2012).

12   Such engagement needs to happen in all spheres of society, but some, including the many areas relating to the religions, are proving especially challenging in the contemporary world. For a profound Catholic approach to interreligious engagement see Michael Barnes SJ, *Interreligious Learning: Dialogue, Spirituality and the Christian Imagination* (Cambridge: Cambridge University Press, 2012).

13   John Swinton has written extensively on disability, for example his *Becoming Friends of Time: Disability, Timefulness, and Gentle Discipleship* (Waco, TX: Baylor University Press, 2016).

14   Aberdeen is unique among British universities in having such a centre. In Northern Ireland, Belfast Bible College has been running a course of theological study engaging with disability and is offering theological training to people with learning disabilities. From 2017 their Centre for Intellectual Disability and Ministry became a separate entity, but with close ties to the College. See www.belfastbiblecollege.com/tio-developments. Among those involved is Jill Harshaw, author of *God Beyond Words* (London: Jessica Kingsley Publishers, 2016).

15   We are grateful to John O'Brien, one of the Nottingham founders, for this account.

16   See https://rosecastle.foundation.

17   This is the result of relationship with Lyn's House through a steering group member. There have been some other spin-offs from Lyn's House, perhaps the most notable being an initiative by the Brett Foundation, Maidenhead. It was providing food for those in Maidenhead who could not afford it, helping between 100 and 150 families every week. Their founder, Nigel Cohen, has written of his first visit to Lyn's House:

   'When I came across Lyn's House in Cambridge it opened my eyes to understand how much more we could do than simply providing food to people in need… It was apparent from the moment I stepped foot inside the house that this was a charity with a difference. The atmosphere was relaxed and welcoming. There was a warm "buzz". Everyone was engaged, either in conversation or in an activity (such as drawing or singing): no one was alone. I immediately felt I was part of a very special family of people who cared deeply about each other… I was "buzzed": I came back to Maidenhead overflowing with ideas. I knew we did not have the resources to do what Lyn's House was doing so well. Instead, we started by inviting all the residents at a local home for people with learning disabilities (Coghlan Lodge) to dinner. We had access to a small shop in the heart of Maidenhead, where we could heat food and dine with our guests. We sent a handwritten invitation to each of the residents. We learned later that many had never received an invitation to a party before, and were thrilled. The carers at the home brought half a dozen of the residents to the party: very unsure what they would find. We, too, were very unsure how the evening would go… Within a matter of just minutes, we knew we had done the right thing; it was not just our guests who were having a great time, it was also us. The happiness was infectious: it spread to everyone there.

18   Not the least of the advantages of this model is its relation to sources of funding. In the UK the state is obliged to provide for physical care and support, and therefore can limit the funding it provides to those legal obligations. This leaves little flexibility for care providers who wish to build a fuller community life, unless they can access other funding. Lyn's House has no dependence on state funding but seeks to raise money from other sources and inspire volunteer work that can complement what the state provides. This fourth model takes this complementarity further, and is realistic about the necessity, given current constraints, to combine public and private funding for the sake of the common good.

19   Micheal O'Siadhail, *The Five Quintets* (Waco, TX: Baylor University Press, 2018).

20   *The Five Quintets*, ibid. pp.327–38.

Lyn's House Practicalities

James Gardom

The Lyn's House model arose from the perception that the residential community model historically at the heart of the L'Arche movement might be very hard to set up. The regulatory structures around residential communities for vulnerable adults are formidable, and assembling the money and expertise to do this was beyond the capacity of the steering group. In order to invite people to give up their current care arrangements and join such a residential community we needed to be in a position to state with confidence that the community would last their lifetime. This would require considerably greater financial and institutional stability than we could offer. It has also become clear over the time the project has been running that people with learning disabilities are not generally looking to live in community at this point in history, any more than people without learning disabilities.

The model we have developed, of a Christian residential community offering hospitality and friendship to people with learning disabilities has a number of practical advantages. Here we will describe the arrangements and highlight some of those advantages.

What is set out here applies to the past six years of Lyn's House, and although the House is moving to a new location where some of the practicalities will be different we nonetheless hope that our experiences so far might be helpful to those considering any similar kind of project.

Finances

Lyn's House is remarkably inexpensive to run. The costs can be divided into (1) the house, (2) food and (3) transport.

The House

We are very fortunate that the owner supports the project by allowing us to rent the house at roughly two thirds of its market value. The residents pay roughly the market value of the four rooms they inhabit. That rental more or less equals what the owner of the house receives, with a little bit over for utilities. This means that we effectively receive the parts of the house and garden used for Lyn's House hospitality free of charge. These are a large kitchen, a large studio, a small prayer room and the garden. To this extent the basic existence of the house is cost neutral.

However, there are housing costs. Residents are, in principle, responsible for paying Council Tax. If all the residents were students this would not be a problem, as students are exempt. If all the residents were working in well-paid jobs this would not be a problem. Difficulties arise where there is a mixture of students and non-students, and where the non-students are in low-paid occupations. The non-student residents become responsible for much or all of the Council Tax of the whole building, irrespective of their income, and irrespective of how much of the building they occupy. The steering group has made arrangements with the non-student residents to cover the additional Council Tax that they are paying because they are sharing a house with students, and because of the band of Council Tax into which they fall. The total cost of this is around about £1500 a year.

The house we occupy is not large enough to fall under the Houses in Multiple Occupation regulations which significantly simplifies the arrangements for fire protection, etc.

We are very fortunate to have an active landlord's representative who responds rapidly to maintenance needs. She is an exacting person, and a certain amount of money is spent each year returning the house to a pristine condition, and dealing with the wear and tear and emergency maintenance issues arising from the unusual pattern of use for the house.

We have not had to make any adaptations to the house to make it accessible. We are fortunate that the layout of the house enables residents to have their own private space as well as the shared space of the project. We are fortunate also that there is a room that can be set aside for prayer and discussion, enabling friends who need a less noisy environment than the main studio to withdraw, and also making it possible for the community and the friends to pray together in a separate space.

Residents carry their own property insurance. The landlord has her own insurance. We have not been able to obtain public liability insurance for the operation of Lyn's House, because our organisation has been so informal, to date, that there has been no entity that could be insured (or, we believe, sued).

Food and Entertainment

The residents receive money, sometimes in advance and sometimes in arrears to pay for the food that is shared at the suppers and at the parties. We also spend small quantities of money on art materials, DVDs, and other things to ensure that the hospitality is enjoyable to everyone. The total cost of this is around about £1000 a year.

Transport

Friends are usually brought to suppers and to parties in taxis, and Lyn's House organises and pays for these. We have an account with a local taxi firm, and we use a book of forms. This enables us to keep track of costs and to know who was brought when and by whom. This costs roughly £300 a month in term time, when Lyn's House is operational.

Structures

The organisational structures of Lyn's House are, at the moment, a matter of custom and mutual trust rather than any kind of constitution. Continuity through the years is provided by the steering group which meets, usually with residents present, and sometimes with friends and parents, about six times a year. The steering group receives new members by mutual agreement, keeps notes of its decisions, and shares out the tasks for the coming months. Someone from the steering group attends the weekly planning meeting at Lyn's House once a month, usually the Monday after the Sunday of a tea party, so that concerns about particular friends can be shared. Each resident has a connection with a member of the steering group, so that concerns can, in principle, be raised one-to-one.

Members of the steering group have particular responsibilities for, for example, financial planning, protection issues, liaison with the landlord, day-to-day finance and worship.

The steering group runs a single community bank account into which residents' rent and donations are received, and from which house rental and other expenditures are paid.

The key responsibilities of the steering group include (1) recruitment, (2) protection responsibilities, (3) fundraising, (4) guidance and encouragement to the residents, (5) forward planning and (6) prayer.

Recruitment

Recruitment of friends has never been difficult. At least in Cambridge the families of people with learning disabilities form a network, and this was our initial recruiting ground. Now that Lyn's House is up and running members of the steering group and others quite regularly come across families who are looking for the kind of friendship and support that Lyn's House offers, and we characteristically invite them along to tea parties, and see, as time goes on, whether there is willingness and an opening for more regular attendance at suppers. We have not felt that we have the competence to deal with mental illness alongside learning disability.

Recruitment of residents has proved more difficult. It has been a more or less constant source of anxiety since the beginning of the project. We have recruited from local theological colleges, from graduate students of the University of

Cambridge (with particular representation from the Faculty of Divinity), via local churches and by word of mouth. The community is necessarily quite transient, which means that we are almost always on the lookout for new residents. It has proved just possible to run the house with only two active members, but this was an inappropriate strain on those residents.

A significant body of volunteers has developed around Lyn's House, and to some extent the variation of resident numbers and engagement can be handled through the increased or diminished use of these volunteers.

When a potential resident appears, we invite them to a tea party so they can meet the current residents and friends, and the member of the steering group first contacted will have a preliminary discussion with the potential resident to explain the arrangements and answer any questions. If there is a will to proceed the potential resident writes a letter of application to the steering group, nominates a couple of referees, and is interviewed by two members of the steering group who have not yet had any connection with the potential resident. The potential resident will also meet with current residents and their feedback is sought. If everyone is agreed, we start the DBS checking process, and agree a date to move in. A rental contract is signed.

We take responsibility for the appropriate Right to Rent checks under the 2014 Immigration Act, usually by photographing the passports and residence permits.

Protection Responsibilities

The Diocese of Ely has generously agreed to be our sponsoring body for the purposes of DBS checks. All residents have received this before they are permitted to be on their own with any friend of the house. All new residents and new volunteers undergo the DBS checking process. For the period before the arrival of the DBS certificate they and the other residents are committed to ensuring that they are never alone with a vulnerable adult. Residents and volunteers are given guidance on protection issues. There is a designated protection officer on the steering group who is contacted if there are any concerns arising from the behaviour of residents, volunteers, guests or friends, or from reports that raise concern about things happening outside Lyn's House. We receive advice from the Diocese, and make strong efforts to deal with problems quickly, personally and transparently.

One aspect of the deepening relationships between the house, the residents and the friends has been growing trust, and the deepening reality of the friendships that we share. This means that painful issues can be and are addressed. Not all of these are protection issues, but it is a good sign that the friends wish to discuss relationships, marriage, mortality and sexual attraction. It is also a good sign that more informal meetings can take place in the pub, the cafe or at church, but the protection issues raised by these genuine friendships are significant. We have never had any concerns, and this is partly because we have discussed individuals and issues in detail at joint meetings of the residents in the steering group.

Fundraising

Lyn's House, at the moment, costs around £8000 a year to run. The rent paid by the residents covers the cost of the house, and of the utilities. The steering group has to raise funds for food, transport, equipment and entertainment. The informality of our structures has made it quite difficult for us to receive donations from institutions, except where those institutions have a strong personal relationship with members of the steering group. Cambridge colleges, local churches and charitable foundations have been generous. In this case a significant component of the fundraising has been personal contributions by members of the steering group, and family and friends of the residents and friends.

Guidance and Encouragement of Residents

In principle every resident is assigned a member of the steering group as their point of contact and mentor. How well this has worked out is very dependent on the individual relationships created. Residents are invited to the steering group meetings, and this provides an opportunity to discuss concerns. Regular Study and Reflection days, often with a focus on the development of particular skills, have also been helpful. However, on a number of occasions the communication between the residents and the steering group has effectively broken down. The reasons for this include (1) a sense that the steering group has not responded to expressions of concern, (2) reluctance, as a Christian community, to be explicit in expressing concerns and (3) a sense of being overwhelmed by the additional demands created when the community is not working well. It is possible that the age disparity between the residents and the steering group may be a contributory factor. The steering group has tended to assume that silence indicates that all is well, and we have occasionally been dismayed to find that it implies quite the opposite.

Forward Planning

The steering group meets with residents before the beginning of each term to consider plans for the following term. Cambridge planning horizons are relatively short and things can happen very quickly. Plans for increasing or decreasing the number of dinners, increasing, decreasing or varying the weekend activities, recruitment drives, visits to colleges or other L'Arche communities, to the cinema, birthday parties are all discussed in this way. The basic principle is that we can do precisely as much and no more as we have energy and enthusiasm to undertake. We seek to be responsive to requests and suggestions from friends.

Prayer

The steering group is committed to praying for Lyn's House, and all meetings begin and end with prayer. A number of our sessions together with the residents have been focused on praying for Lyn's House, and the steering group has always encouraged the residents to have a regular time of shared prayer each day. Although correlation cannot establish causation, the most worrying times in the house have correlated with times when this discipline was proving hard to sustain. Opportunities for prayer within the dinners and events continue this connection, and we are all at our happiest and most confident with Lyn's House when prayer is frequent, shared and peacefully expressive of our relationship with God.

The Residents

Over the years our residents have been roughly 50 per cent students and 50 per cent in employment. They need to have enough income to pay the rent, enough energy to sustain the programme of the house, and enough engagement with faith and theology to understand the vision of equal friendship which lies at the heart of Jean Vanier's practice, and of Lyn's House. Some residents have recruited new residents through church and friendship networks. The Christian Flatshare website has proved fruitful, as Lyn's House can be seen as an unusual kind of flatshare.

We have not set a creedal or church membership test for residents, but self-identification as Christian, and active engagement with the Christian life has been part of what we are looking for in residents. A willingness to live with other Christians whose patterns of faith and prayer may be different from one's own seems also to be very important.

We have found that a reasonable degree of personal robustness is necessary for those living within Lyn's House, and therefore we have resisted the possibility of being a therapeutic community for residents.

Practical Guides

Over the years we have developed a number of practical guides for suppers and parties, and these can give a vivid sense of the organisational demands and the preparation needed for these events, as well as some indication of what they actually feel like. They are intended partly as guidance for anyone who may wish to try something similar, and partly as reassurance – this all takes some doing, but it is, with goodwill, perfectly doable. As well as the information which follows, more detail is available to residents and the steering group would be happy to make the detailed documents available to anyone interested in running a similar project. We are indebted to Patrick McKearney and Giulia Conto for these documents which set out accepted practice in the house.

Organising a Dinner, as Host

Before

ARRANGING THE VOLUNTEERS, GUESTS, ETC.

Normally there will be one person responsible for arranging which hosts, guests and volunteers are coming on which days. If you are unsure if that is being done then please ask someone on the steering group.

WHO IS COOKING, ORGANISING PRAYERS, ETC.

It is your responsibility to make sure that food is brought and cooked, and that prayers are organised.

The dinners follow a fortnightly cycle. Normally, at the end of the previous dinner with the same people, the host will have asked the volunteers coming next time who is prepared to bring food, be the lead cook, and do the prayers. This will be recorded on the 'Current Rota'.

If there is nothing there (either because someone forgot, it is the first dinner in a term, or because you are in a time of irregular dinners) then it is your responsibility to get in touch with the volunteers to make sure these tasks are done. Well in advance of the dinner, look at the Current Rota for details of which volunteers are coming. More details are provided in the particular guides about how to advise volunteers about what they need to do for each of these tasks.

Their contact details should be in the Gmail Contacts. Get in touch with the person responsible for communication if not. If there are no volunteers then please get in touch with the Rota Organiser to check what is happening.

FOOD

If a meal has not been agreed in advance, then you will need to decide on a meal and make sure that the food is bought.

PRAYERS

You may want to be in conversation with the person organising prayers. If they have never done it before, or if they ask for advice, then you should be able to give them guidance on how the prayers run, and on what people like.

REMINDING GUESTS

On the day, some guests and their carers need reminding that the dinner is happening. This is the responsibility of the host. The relevant information is held with the guests' details.

TRANSPORT

Some guests also need transport to be arranged. This is the responsibility of the host. The relevant information is held with the guests' details.

If it is our responsibility, then this normally involves organising a taxi.

Guest Wellbeing

Before the dinner, if you do not know the guest well, or have not hosted them before, then check over their needs for the dinner. These will be available in the house records.

5:30pm–6pm: Arrive at the house and open up the back door by 5.30pm at the latest to let the volunteers in. Make sure you know who is in charge of the cooking, and that they get going. Make sure you know who is in charge of prayer, and that they're ready when needed.

6pm–6:30pm: Make sure that the guests have arrived and are OK. In particular, check any necessary precautions. For instance, if someone is in danger of over-eating, check what they ate earlier in the day.

6:30pm–7pm: Ensure that prayer time happens. If the person has not prepared anything different, then you can always follow our very normal format.

7pm–8:30pm: Enjoy dinner, ensure it goes smoothly, and that everyone is OK. It is your job to keep an eye on time for the guests. Make sure they are ready to leave when their transport arrives (generally at 8.30pm). Some need more preparation in advance.

After

Cleaning

Ensure the volunteers stay to help you clean the kitchen thoroughly.

Payment

If you haven't done it before, then make sure that the volunteer who brought and bought the food is reimbursed.

Arranging Next Time

Sit down with the volunteers to go over the Current Rota for the next dinner in the series. Make sure that there is someone down under the headings: bringing food, cooking, prayers. Make sure that you agree on (and write down) a suitable meal choice for next time.

Checking for Any Issues

Ask the volunteers if there are any issues that you need to follow up. This could be a problem you need to take to the steering group. It could be a safeguarding issue (if so, please follow the safeguarding policy). It could be something you need to ask their carer/parent about. It could also be that you learn something new about a guest and need to change one of the reference documents as a result.

Night Prayer

Often, volunteers stay to say night prayer. Prayer books are available in the house.

Organising a Party, as Host

Two Weeks Before

About two weeks before the party, you need to be in touch with everyone on our books about the upcoming event.

Most people can be reached by simply emailing the whole of Lyn's List. However, some guests will need to be contacted by post.

All you need to send by email or by post is an invitation.

To allow people to plan in advance, include information about the next party *after* this one in the invitation. You can also include this information in the dinner term card.

You might want to send out a separate email to the steering group and all volunteers asking if a couple of people can come early and stay late to help set up and clear up. This is especially important if not all the residents are attending the party.

On the Day

GUEST PREPARATION

Some guests need reminding about the party on the day. The relevant information is held with the guests' details.

Some guests need transport arranged for them – and this may well be a different form of transport to that they use to come to the dinners. The relevant information is held with the guests' details.

HOUSE PREPARATION

The public part of the house needs to be very clear and pretty clean. You should set up the main reception room so that there is space for the food to be laid out, and so that there are lots of places to sit down.

Keep the kitchen pretty clear. On the table put drinks and cups. In the main reception room, put the food.

RUNNING THE PARTY

During the course of the party you don't need to do anything in particular, except make sure it is all following its course nicely. There are some areas it's worth keeping an eye on:

- Do the guests need anything? Some find it hard to get themselves food or drink, or might need some help communicating with people. Sometimes guests are left alone for large periods of time and that's not good.

- Are there any risks? Guests can be a risk to themselves and others, and others may be a risk to them. Look in the reference documents for more information on this. But you shouldn't assume that other adults around are keeping an eye on this. It's your responsibility.

- Is there enough food, drink, cups etc.? Make sure to keep all of this well stocked. You can do a quick dishwasher run of cups, or have someone washing them as you go. We run out surprisingly quickly.

CLEARING UP

Encourage some others to stay around afterwards if you can. It's a good opportunity to clean the public part of the house fully.

Our Accumulated Wisdom for Welcome and Community

E.S. Kempson

Creating a Welcome

What follows is accumulated wisdom from half a decade of creating a welcoming home at Lyn's House. I hope that compiling it might perpetuate and expand that good work. This has been an amazing community to be a part of and I am excited to see how it and perhaps similar projects grow and develop in the years to come. Since it has changed my life for the better, I expect that it will do so for many more.

Pointers on Communication[1]

Even when we recognise the full humanity of people with intellectual disabilities, showing it in our actions takes some care and learned skill. It does not, however, require overlooking or minimising genuine differences between individuals. After all, it is these very differences that so often shape what we have to offer each other. For this reason, keep in mind two key things when communicating with people with learning disabilities: (1) their relative lack of power (particularly in the sense of personal autonomy) and (2) their relative lack of some kinds of understanding and/or ability to communicate.

As an adult, if we want to go out for an evening, we understand what that would require in money and transportation. We know how to order drinks or food and keep ourselves safe. For our intellectually disabled friends, they don't have the same autonomy. Imagine having to ask a carer before you go out. You don't know if they will say 'yes' or 'no', and you may not understand the reasons for their answer. That fact makes your relationship to your own intentions uncertain, in a way that is not the case for a more autonomous person.

One way of thinking about this is to realise that people with learning disabilities have experienced the state of powerlessness associated with childhood for much longer than we have – for maybe fifty years. There can be a degree of awareness of that difference, and shame associated with it. It also puts a person in a carer role in a position of power. But adults with intellectual disabilities are not children in grown bodies. Adults with intellectual disabilities have to cope with adult concerns that children are often shielded from. For instance, the death of their parents, questions of romance and being sexually mature, needing to find financial support, and dealing with governmental services. They are more varied in their abilities and inabilities, meaning the generalised approach one can take to stages of childhood do not apply. There is no single way to interact, for each person has her/his own special difficulties, points of connection, and places of vulnerability or joy. Additionally, they cannot always sustain certain sorts of interaction for very long, and may feel put on the spot if a conversation that went well for five to seven minutes is forced to last for fifteen. Finally, children often have a sense of their own ongoing development and change; 'I can't do that now but I WILL be able to as I grow up.' Adults with intellectual disabilities, on the other hand, are often aware of their own limits as unlikely to change, and the greater power others have over them.

So if we are relating to someone with learning disabilities, we will want to reduce the imbalance of power, not assuming more than necessary. We want to retain as little control as possible, and to give the other person as much as possible. Like anyone else, they enjoy being appreciated and contributing something meaningfully to what is happening. How might we do all this?

- *Listening:* This is really the key. We can practise listening to more than just the words people say, and attending with more than just our ears. We can pay attention to how someone uses their voice, their hesitation, agitated or excited speech, and repetitions or peculiar phrases. We can notice preoccupation and lack of interest when on a subject – they may have something quite different on their mind, or be expressing fear or distress. When we pay attention to body language, how someone moves and sits, what they do with their arms, how they eat, and where they look, it can help to say what we understand her/him to mean or be feeling (e.g. 'You're looking away a lot – would you like to do something else?'). Asking families and carers for help with interpreting things we haven't understood, such as simple sign language or characteristic phrases, has also been a help.

- *Creating a less verbal environment:* Many adults are comfortable with highly verbal and fast-moving socialising. This often excludes people with learning disabilities who have less facility or limited stamina for such conversations. To keep from dominating with words, we can try to enter imaginatively into different ways of communicating, and think about social interaction in more physical and less verbal ways. Not all conversation has to 'get somewhere.' We can notice how people appear to be comfortable communicating and connect that with games, activities, ways of moving or sitting in the room, and different rooms. A simple game that needs few words, like Jenga, can work well, as can doing helpful tasks together, like mixing batter or taste-testing ingredients. Silliness can be a great communicator of joy and affection. One alternative to conversation is singing. This can take many forms – singing along to a well-known musical film or pop songs, community singing using the piano, songs with actions or dance, simple chants.

- *Providing real choices within structured boundaries:* It is good to think in advance about choices that core friends are presented with, and try to organise things so that they have real choices. In terms of hosting core meals, tea parties, and other gatherings, having real choices does not mean having no limits. It can be helpful to think of what is involved in any kind of hospitality in our own homes – we set the structures and boundaries, and this is not 'paternalistic' towards our guests. At the same time, we can be open to choices we didn't anticipate. It's often empowering (and fun) to say 'yes' to unexpected suggestions unless there is a reason for saying 'no'. However, housemates and volunteers are not expected to violate their own personal boundaries. As one housemate remarked, 'Learning that it is all right to say "no" to someone was a huge step forwards.'

- *Establishing routine and familiarity:* Too many changes and too much unexpected novelty disempowers people with learning disabilities because they are less quick to comprehend and master new situations. If we can create regularity and familiarity, keeping things broadly the same, this gives them security and also freedom at the same time: security of the familiar and freedom of knowing how to engage. This can be done through language (telling the same joke or stories), routines (activities in a predictable sequence, e.g. tea, activity, prayer, dinner, goodbyes), arrangements of furniture, familiar faces (and a pattern of introduction for new faces), known food and drinks, and so on. Using repetition and ritual provides familiarity, structure and security, out of which people are able to act more autonomously. At prayer time, having known prayers, songs and patterns of sharing all help those with intellectual disabilities to engage more deeply.

- *Building your knowledge of individuals:* Every person is different. Building up detailed, accurate background knowledge of the people we are hosting and befriending after meals will help us connect with them. It will also save them the often difficult process of explaining themselves to new housemates and volunteers. Some of this will be details of family, living circumstances, age, and medical and dietary needs. We can ask carers, parents and others who have known the person longer for advice. It is practically helpful to have records: these must be kept securely and be up to date. Just as important is knowledge of interests, talents, likes and dislikes, faith, personality, favourite films, songs, places, holidays, foods, activities, friends, and so on. Quick debriefs after a core meal or event are a good way to keep everyone on the same page and records accurate.

- *Appreciating what core friends offer:* We have probably all had the experience of receiving friendship, care, help, support or comfort from people with intellectual disabilities. They can share in our joys and sorrows just as we can in theirs. With core friends, saying what we enjoy about the meals together, that we are happy to see them again and will miss them until next time, all this builds one's own appreciation as much as the core friend's sense of being appreciated. Becoming more aware of how and when this takes place, and communicating that awareness, directly or indirectly, can restore balance as well as developing deeper relationships.

- *A word on difficulties:* Difficult topics naturally emerge in conversations in Lyn's House. One difficult area where we have experienced this in conversation is about sex and intimate relationships. Some core friends find talking with people their own age is an opportunity to bring up questions and concerns. Such discussions can be handled well if done delicately, but it is important that no one should feel pushed to discuss topics they do not wish to, including volunteers and housemates as much as core friends. It is also important to consider the wishes of carers and families, who may have different approaches to these and other topics. They can be a good source of guidance.

   Another recurrent theme is grief and fearing the death of loved ones. This was especially poignant when one of our core friends passed away. In my experience, the core friends have a full grasp of death, and it is best to sympathise with the bereaved friend rather than minimise the situation. We can sit with them in their feelings, offer to hear a memory or say a prayer, and then help them return to the group, even if their sadness comes with them. It is comforting to know that others feel your loss.

   Difficulties can arise in areas of behaviour. We have had incidents of core friends refusing to go home (unrelated to any safeguarding concerns) and needing to be firm about boundaries in relation to touching.

This brings us to the importance of safeguarding vulnerable adults. For their protection, all housemates and volunteers have a background safeguard check (DBS in England and Wales – there are similar services in Northern Ireland and Scotland),[2] and are taught how to recognise signs of a safeguarding incident, how to respond, and who to report it to. A member of the steering group is the official safeguarding officer who ensures proper practices are followed. All the good of a community could be undone if it becomes a site or cover for exploitation and abuse, even if this is through ignorance or negligence.

Nuts and Bolts of Specific Events

Over the years, events at Lyn's House have varied as lessons have been learned. Below is a brief overview of our approach to the main events that make a welcoming home and a healthy community life.

Morning prayer is when the housemates join in prayer, drawing on the strength of God's love and growing in fellowship with each other. It is most important that morning prayer is at a time and in a style that all housemates agree to. At Lyn's House it has varied between three and five mornings a week, allowing for understandable absences. Usually, it has been liturgical, a variation of morning prayer in the Anglican Franciscan prayer book, but this could change. Over the years, a time of silent contemplation lengthened and shortened and space has been given for intercessions. In my year, we started at 7:30am and finished at 8:00am. We found that leaving the last ten minutes for aimless talk over coffee and tea (see the discussion of spare time in Chapter 3) was crucially important to the health of the community, especially in times of strife.

Core meals developed a set pattern.

5:30pm – set up by two housemates and one to three volunteers. One has brought food for dinner and is in charge of cooking throughout.

6:00pm – welcome tea as one to three core friends arrive.

6–6:45pm – talk and/or activity time, e.g. cooking, baking, Jenga, colouring, show and tell, telling stories, etc.

6:45pm – prayer in the living room (cook remains in kitchen with anyone who opts out of prayer).

7:05pm – dinner, usually with a healthy helping of laughter.

7:30pm – dessert, followed by more chat or activities.

8:15pm – departures and tidying up. It is important not to neglect the friendships among housemates and volunteers as well, and so it is good to take some time after the core friends leave to debrief and get to know each other, while tidying. At times this extends into another cup of tea or drink together.

Prayer at a core meal needs to be accessible for core friends. Thus, building familiarity and avoiding complexity is good, as is adjusting or shortening prayer time as it is underway, as seems fit. We have found a simplified *lectio divina*[3] is one option that has worked well. The leader reads a Bible story and each person takes a turn saying what they heard or liked in the story. The same can be done with an illustration of a story, picking out what each person likes in the picture, or everyone having several pictures. Taizé[4] chants are popular. Core friends, if given the opportunity, might make their own suggestions or even lead. The most popular structure, I found, was opening with a Taizé song, then everyone taking turns sharing one happy thing they are thankful for (passing an olive wood cross as a talking stick), then we'd repeat the song and each speak of a sadness or worry of our own to ask God's help. We might sing again, then we'd share a hope, asking for some good for another person, and then finally close with the Taizé song again. I was repeatedly struck by how our core friends would bring up concerns they never mentioned over tea, and how honest the volunteers and housemates were in their contributions.

Weekend tea party is two hours (3:00pm to 5:00pm) so as not to over-stretch core friends. Everyone is invited (including carers and former housemates), and this is the best event for a new guest to attend. Transport is arranged according to need. Housemates prepare the space, drinks and a few savoury snacks, while a plethora of baked goods are brought in a bring-and-share style. Birthdays may be celebrated, songs sung, garden games played, and so forth. If there are new or departing members, a time of prayer and reflection is valuable. A whole-group gathering in one form or another during the afternoon, even if only for ten minutes, keeps the sense of shared community strong, more than a series of individual friendships. We try to make sure no core friend is left alone or ignored in a corner.

Additional gatherings such as film nights and arts afternoons have worked best when they are two hours long and have at least one housemate or volunteer for every two core friends. These have been a great opportunity for volunteers to take control of an event and contribute from their interests and talents. One long-standing volunteer has an artistic flair, and has led arts days of painting, stamping Christmas cards, and felting pictures, to name a few. For film nights, providing popcorn and pizza is always a big hit, and musicals and popular children or young adult films mean a good time is had by all (e.g. *Paddington, The Sound of Music, Frozen, Aladdin*).

Housemate bonding might include day trips to nearby towns, film nights, or just having the Monday house dinner out. These are best when devised by the housemates, either as a sign of good fellowship or as a time to create it. At times, inviting long-standing volunteers adds to the benefit.

Housemate induction is a crucial time to pass on wisdom from previous generations of the community, build connection between the current members, and share a vision for the year to come. Induction covers basic introductions and builds towards greater sharing of motivations and hopes for time in the house. Visioning and concrete discussions of best practices and expectations belong together, so that hard-won lessons of previous years are not lost. The steering group is an important presence in holding the wisdom of years past and passing it on to new members as time goes by.

Training days benefit everyone involved. A training day could be a simple session on communication, or the history of L'Arche and Lyn's House, with the added bonus of building relationships between housemates, volunteers and the steering group.

Public talks have taken the benefits of Lyn's House beyond those who have time to volunteer or visit, such as to church communities, colleges, local authorities or the general public. These may discuss the project itself, the plight of the intellectually disabled more generally, the history of L'Arche and Jean Vanier, or some combination thereof. We could also provide a practical session for others interested in improving their relations or ministry with the intellectually disabled too. Recruitment and donations may come of this, but that is not the immediate point. The point is to share the Lyn's House story, that such love in community is possible, worthwhile and valuable, and to pass on the wisdom that has been learned.

Behind-the-Scenes Responsibilities

Creating a residential Christian community and their events that centre people with learning disabilities involves significant behind-the-scenes operations, such as financial concerns, informational responsibilities and maintaining a clear vision. At Lyn's House, these responsibilities have most naturally fallen to members of the steering group because: their long tenure means they can provide continuity; and their relative distance from running events gives them a big-picture view of the project.

Note, this does not mean the steering group is like a distant board of trustees which convenes occasionally to make decisions and then disbands in between without intervening responsibilities. (If the project becomes a registered charity, there would be a board of trustees and roles could overlap.) Neither are they like headteachers checking in on residential students, nor managers keeping an eye on their employees. On the contrary, they are adults on a par with the housemates and volunteers. They all volunteer their time and talent without material remuneration, each contributing different necessary tasks to the community as a whole. Accidentally adopting an asymmetrical dynamic has led to broken trust at points in Lyn's House's history, as housemates felt overworked, without support or guidance, and the steering group lamented finding itself ignorant of the inner workings of the project. This can be avoided if the steering group treats the housemates, and by extension volunteers, as active partners in the project's work and conceptual planning, rather than as the labour carrying out their vision.

To avoid similar breakdowns, we have found it valuable for the steering group to have a clear understanding of its own responsibilities and its procedures for accomplishing them, whether that means delegating them to others or doing it themselves.

- *Perpetuating the spirit:* Our steering group founded Lyn's House because they were caught by Jean Vanier's vision of life lived together with people who have intellectual disabilities. The character of that vision – how it has developed during its life in Cambridge, its central principles, practices and memories – all this is held by the steering group as they seek to share it with new members of the community. Inductions, recruitment, shared liturgies at tea parties, and public engagement have been invaluable to this end, as have shared reading lists and discussion days where members talk over their developing vision.

- *Keeping records:* To maintain the ethos, we have worked to preserve wisdom and knowledge gathered over the course of the project, so that the wheel is not reinvented every few years. Information on running the house, events, contact information and core friend details, once organised and securely stored, can be shared and taught at induction or training days, as relevant. Ideally, our steering group designates its preferred system and method for this so that they, housemates and volunteers can easily add to it.

- *Maintaining the house:* As in any situation where the residents do not own their residence, questions have arisen regarding financial and material responsibility. When all the usual legal and financial norms are followed, including drawing up rental agreements that clearly stipulate the accountability and provision for rent, utilities, Council Tax and maintenance, confusions are easily avoided. No one benefits when a 'friendly understanding' turns out to have been a misunderstanding with negative consequences and no clear recourse. Handling property matters (e.g. bills, repairs, keys.) with professional conduct and official forms (e.g. bills paid, keys supplied and repairs made promptly) has not de-personalised our community. It provides a clear bulwark and framework within which relationships can function well.

- *Safeguarding:* One of our steering group members is the official safeguarding officer, who sees to it that background checks are conducted on all housemates and volunteers and who also provides them with guidance in recognising and reporting safeguarding incidents. Occasional guests are not checked as long as the housemates and volunteers ensure the guest is not left alone with core friends. Any additional legal requirements and recommended best practices are implemented as appropriate.

- *Finances:* By overseeing the project's finances, our steering group provides housemates with funds for meals and core friends' transportation. It is technically possible for projects like Lyn's House to function at almost zero cost. If the housemates cover their rent and utilities, then the only costs are food and transportation. Our biggest cost is providing taxi transportation to core friends who need it. If volunteers, carers or others had cars and they were willing to give lifts, this would reduce costs. Other than that, there is the cost of the dinners, which we have kept to between £12 and £15, though not infrequently a volunteer cook offers to simply donate the ingredients without remuneration.

  In our case, because of the size of the house and its Council Tax, the steering group has also covered the house's utilities, covered gaps in rent when housemates have not been replaced, and made up differences in Council Tax when it was inequitable. We have found it indispensible for these policies and procedures to be clearly laid out and followed by all involved. Otherwise, it results in inconsistent practices being unfairly applied.

- *Fundraising:* In our experience, fundraising provides vital support, even when the running costs are low. In the best circumstances, this involves building relationships with individuals, communities and organisations (e.g. churches and other religious groups, local charities, educational institutions.). While housemates and volunteers have given talks and presentations to various groups, it has mainly been the steering group's responsibility to build these relationships and to provide financial security for the project as a whole.

- *Publicity and communications:* Running our events requires frequent communication with volunteers, core friends, their carers, and among housemates. Ultimately, we have decided it is too onerous to ask the housemates to do this on top of their hosting responsibilities, and the steering group has delegated communications to a hired individual.

  Publicity is a part of our project's ministry; telling the story of Lyn's House spreads the good news. Training events have helped to share the knowledge we have gained from the project. Additionally, these events have naturally drawn forth individuals who were interested in volunteering or becoming housemates. Sometimes, straightforward publicity is needed (e.g. on flat-sharing sites), or a website and social media presence. Even when the steering group delegates these tasks, its continuing attentiveness has been invaluable to see that all is going well.

- *Recruiting:* The process of recruiting new housemates for us has involved a written application, prospective visits (to the house, tea parties or meals), meeting one or more current housemates, and an interview with members of the steering group. Indeed, this process of discernment signals an intention to be reflective in each step taken to develop the concept of 'Lyn's House'. It has been important for the process to be transparent and the information regarding cost and time commitments provided to be complete and consistent between applicants. Similarly, when choosing among applicants it is considerate not to leave people without a decision for great lengths of time, or to imply spots are secured before decisions have been made.

  When possible, the steering group has sought to attend to the composition and balance of the house. We have found a mix of genders to be advantageous for hosting meals, though the ability to live well alongside others is of greater importance. Living in community and running Lyn's House involves more responsibility and demands more stability than typical living arrangements. It has been a marvellously healing place to reside. The goal is ultimately more stability among the housemates as a cohesive group, than either the under-functioning or over-functioning of individuals. Finally, when housemates have continued for multiple years, involving them in the decision-making process regarding new housemates has contributed to the home's cohesion.

- *Leadership:* Clearly, with all these responsibilities, the steering group as a group leads Lyn's House as a project. Since we have never designated a specific leader within the steering group, they lead *as a group*. Explicitly designated individuals are then chosen to fulfil or delegate each of the roles above, their work being accountable to the group as a whole. If a leader were chosen, this single individual would need to be aware of all the moving pieces, their purposes, and how they interact with each other. Such a position would ideally prevent crucial tasks being accidentally forgotten or poorly executed, preserve hard-won wisdom, and ensure the consistency of practice that prevents unfairnesses from developing.

- *Celebration:* One final and joyful part of the steering group as leader-in-group-form has been that it leads the community in celebration and appreciation. Communal times of prayer and appreciation are often the most joyful of the year. Whether it is taking volunteers for a Christmas dinner, holding departing housemates in prayer, feting a core friend, or sharing news of a project secured by the committee's hard work, celebration is in order. Through all the twists and turns, the resolute perseverance of the steering group over half a decade has been instrumental to what Lyn's House has become. None of this would have happened without them, and it is remarkable how much love has been shown, relationships grown, and how far we have come.

Finally, I reproduce here, in full, advice from a list contributed by Matthew Harbage.

Matt's Top Ten Lessons Learnt from Living in Community

1. Agree expectations amongst the community

    i. Including – guests staying over; romantic relationships within the house; whether you have to move out if you no longer decide to help with the community's goals; how long people are committing to; chores; how often you will eat together; money.

    ii. And chat over the things below together...

2. Have goal(s) exterior to the community. It was popular at one point for Christian communities to form just to be a community to live a Christian life. Maybe that works, but I've found you need something to help focus the community, put arguments behind you, and remind you why you came together with this bunch of people.

3. Communication is hard when you've got more than three people; it's worth agreeing a fixed evening/afternoon once a week to get together to talk about practical things about the house, talk about people being away/guests, and plans to achieve the community's goals.

4. Remember your limitations – we are all so limited in our capacities. Be gentle with each other, and yourself, and be realistic about what the community's goals should be and how often you might get together to serve those goals. Make time for rest and potentially space away from the community house.

5. Pray together – it's a spiritual thing; praying together helps bind us together, stopping 'the Tempter', as it were, dividing the community and getting in the way.

6. Talk about a vision together – you need to agree, straight away, some expectations (Point 1) but throughout your life as a community it can be really exciting to dream together about where you are going as a community. You might not all agree on a vision, and that's fine, but over time some common ideas for a vision will hopefully emerge. Remember forming a community and being a community is a journey – one where people may join, and leave, where the goals may shift over time. Be open to the Spirit leading you in new directions, but also hold on to your core reason for being together.

7. Ground yourself personally – don't neglect your own, personal prayer/ worship life – or think you can make up for a lack of personal prayer/ worship because you're a praying community. Don't forget friends outside the community. This helps to ground us when we're feeling low, lonely, or need help with direction.

8. Be accountable as a community – have a small group of older/wiser Christians who can help guide the community in the good times and mediate should any disagreements arise (which they probably will!).

9. Get to know Jean Vanier's writings e.g. *Community and Growth* – or others; there is a whole wealth of experience out there. You might want to check out Taizé, 'New Monasticism' and 'Rules of Life'.

10. A heads up on forgiveness – living with someone usually means you discover the things that you like about them, and things that really get on your nerves. It cuts both ways, and if you are honest and open with one another, you can learn a lot about yourself (both strengths and weaknesses). This is an amazing opportunity to love one another, and to bring yourself honestly before God when you pray, warts and all. It is an opportunity to love one another unconditionally – to show one another the love of God even when you don't think the person in front of you deserves very much. You will probably fail a lot at loving one another so forgiving one another is therefore an essential gift in community: forgiving yourself for your faults, and others theirs, and forgiving one another when you fail to love each other as you should.

11. Yes, this top-ten goes up to 11 – one further gift worth cultivating in community: celebration! Celebrate the little things, and the big things. God loves to bless His children and you will have much to be joyful for I'm sure as you serve him together!

This list arose out of experiences from living in Lyn's House (2013–14) and being part of the theological college Westcott House. It was originally written for my brother who was considering forming a Christian community in 2016.

Endnotes

1 Expanded from notes devised by Judith Gardom and Deborah Hardy Ford, drawing on themes from a presentation by Patrick McKearney.
2 DBS stands for Disclosure and Barring Service.
3 *Lectio divina* or 'Divine reading' is a way of slowly reading and meditating on scripture.
4 These originate with the ecumenical Christian community in Taizé, France.

Bibliography

American Psychiatric Association, *Diagnostic and Statistic Manual of Mental Disorders: DSM-5*, 5th ed. (Arlington, VA: American Psychiatric Association Publishers, 2013).

Arndt, William F. and F. Wilbur Gingrich, *A Greek–English Lexicon of the New Testament*, 2nd cd. (Chicago: University of Chicago Press, 1979).

Authorised Daily Prayer Book of the United Hebrew Congregations of the Commonwealth (with New Translation and Commentary by Chief Rabbi Sir Jonathan Sacks, (London: Collins, 2006).

Barnes, Michael, SJ, *Interreligious Learning: Dialogue, Spirituality and the Christian Imagination* (Cambridge: Cambridge University Press, 2012).

Bartlett, Peter and David Wright, *Outside the Walls of the Asylum: The History of Care in the Community 1750–2000* (London: Athone Press, 1999).

Baum, Markus, *Against the Wind: Eberhard Arnold and the Bruderhof* (Rifton, NY, and Robertsbridge: Plough Publishing House, 1998).

Baumann, Gerd, *Contesting Culture: Discourses of Identity in Multi-Ethnic London* (Cambridge: Cambridge University Press, 1996).

Baumeister, Roy, 'Effects of Social Exclusion and Interpersonal Rejection: An Overview with Implications for Human Disability', in *The Paradox of Disability*, ed. Hans Reinders (Cambridge: William B. Eerdmans Publishing Company, 2010), pp. 51–9.

Bell, Sandra and Simon Coleman (eds), *The Anthropology of Friendship* (New York: Berg, 1999).

Berrios, G.E. and H. Freeman (eds), *150 Years of British Psychiatry, 1841–1991* (London: Gaskell/Royal College of Psychiatrists, 1991).

Bodenhorn, Barbara, '"He Used to Be My Relative": Exploring the Bases of Relatedness among Inupiat of Northern Alaska', in *Cultures of Relatedness: New Approaches to the Study of Kinship*, ed. Janet Carsten (Cambridge: Cambridge University Press, 2000).

Bonhoeffer, Dietrich, *Life Together* (London: SCM, 1954).

Bonhoeffer, Dietrich, *Life Together and Prayerbook of the Bible: Works, Volume 5* (Minneapolis: Fortress Press, 1996).

Bowers, Faith (ed.), *Let Love be Genuine* (London: Baptist Times, 1985).

Bowers, Faith, 'The Story of Build', *Baptist Ministers' Journal*, April 1993.

Bowers, Faith, *When Weak, then Strong: Disability in the Life of the Church* (London: Bloomsbury Central Baptist Church, 2008).

Brigham, L. *et al.* (eds), *Crossing Boundaries: Change and Continuity in the History of Learning Disability* (Kidderminster, BILD Publications, 2000).

Brisenden, Simon, 'Independent Living and the Medical Model of Disability', *Disability, Handicap, and Society* Vol. 1, No. 2 (1986): 173–8.

Brock, Brian, 'Praise: The Prophetic Public Presence of the Mentally Disabled', in *The Blackwell Companion to Christian Ethics*, ed. Stanley Hauerwas and Samuel Wells, 2nd ed. (Oxford: Wiley-Blackwell, 2011).

Brock, Brian and John Swinton (eds), *Disability in the Christian Tradition: A Reader* (Grand Rapids, MI: William B. Eerdmans, 2012).

Brown, W.P. (ed.), *Character and Scripture: Moral Formation, Community, and Biblical Interpretation* (Grand Rapids: Eerdmans, 2002).

Brown, William P., 'Wisdom's Wonder: Proverbs, Paideia, and Play', *The Covenant Quarterly* (2010), pp.13–24.

Bruderhof, the, *Foundations of Our Faith and Calling* (Rifton, NY, and Robertsbridge: Plough Publishing House, 2012).

Buber, M., *Between Man and Man*, trans. R.G. Smith (London: Kegan Paul, 1947).

Carey, Matthew, *Mistrust: An Ethnographic Theory* (Chicago: Hau Books, 2017).

Chesterton, G.K., *Eugenics and Other Evils* (London: Cassel, 1922).

Claassens, Julie, Leslie Swartz and Len Hansen (ed.), *Searching for Dignity: Conversations on Human Dignity, Theology, and Disability* (Stellenbosch: SUN MeDIA, 2013).

Common Worship: Daily Prayer (London: Church House Publishing, 2011).

Corbishley, Mary S., *Corby: Teacher of the Deaf for Fifty Years* (Rushden, Northants: Stanley L. Hunt, 1980).

Creamer, Deborah Beth, *Disability and Christian Theology: Embodied Limits and Constructive Possibilities* (Oxford: Oxford University Press, 2009).

Davis, Lennard J. (ed.), *The Disability Studies Reader*, 2nd ed. (London/New York: Routledge, 2006).

de Vinck, Christopher, *The Power of Powerlessness* (Grand Rapids: Zondervan Publishing House, 1988).

Desai, Amit and Evan Killick (eds), *The Ways Of Friendship: Anthropological Perspectives* (New York: Berghahn Books, 2013).

Digby, Anne, *Madness, Morality and Medicine: A Study of the York Retreat, 1796–1914* (Cambridge: Cambridge University Press, 1985).

Duranti, Alessandro, *The Anthropology of Intentions: Language in a World of Others* (Cambridge: Cambridge University Press, 2015).

Edgerton, Robert B., *The Cloak of Competence* (Berkeley: University of California Press, 1993).

Edwards, Jannette and Marilyn Strathern 'Including Our Own', in *Cultures of Relatedness: New Approaches to the Study of Kinship*, ed. Janet Carsten (Cambridge: Cambridge University Press, 2000).

Emerson, Eric, 'Models of Service Delivery', in *Learning Disability: A Life Cycle Approach*, ed. Gordon Grant *et al.* (Maidenhead: Open University Press, 2010), pp.118–19.

Emerson, Eric and Keith McVilly, 'Friendship Activities of Adults with Intellectual Disabilities in Supported Accommodation in Northern England', *Journal of Applied Research in Intellectual Disabilities* 17, no. 3 (1 September 2004), pp.191–7.

Ford, David F., *Christian Wisdom: Desiring God and Learning in Love* (Cambridge: Cambridge University Press 2007).

Foster, Richard, *Celebration of Discipline: The Path to Spiritual Growth* (London: Hodder & Stoughton, 1980).

Foucault, Michel, Richard Howard and David Graham Cooper, *Madness and Civilization: A History of Insanity in the Age of Reason* (London; New York: Routledge, 2009).

Fox, Michael V., 'Amon Again', *JBL* (1996) pp.699–702.

Frydrych, Tomáš, *Living under the Sun: Examination of Proverbs and Qoheleth* (Leiden: Brill, 2002).

Garfinkel, Harold, 'Studies of the Routine Grounds of Everyday Activities', *Social Problems* 11, no. 3 (1 January 1964), pp.225–50.

Garland-Thomson, Rosemarie, 'Misfits: A Feminist Materialist Disability Concept', *Hypatia* 26, no. 3 (2011), pp.591–609.

Giubilini, Alberto and Francesca Minerva, 'After-Birth Abortion: Why Should the Baby Live?' *Journal of Medical Ethics* 39 (2012): 261–3.

Goffman, Erving, *Stigma: Notes on the Management of Spoiled Identity* (New York: Simon and Schuster Inc., 1963).

Gordon, Paul, *An Uneasy Dwelling* (PCCS Books, 2010).

Gravell, Carwyn, *Loneliness and Cruelty: People with Learning Disabilities and Their Experience of Harassment, Abuse and Related Crime in the Community* (London: Lemos&Crane, 2012).

Gunether, K., 'The politics of names: rethinking the methodological and ethical significance of naming people, organizations, and places', *Qualitative Research* 9, 4 (2009), pp.411–21.

Haigh, Rex, *Therapeutic Communities: Past, Present and Future*, ed. Penelope Campling (London: Jessica Kingsley Publishers, 1999).

Hardy, D.W. and D.F. Ford, *Jubilate: Theology in Praise* (London: Darton, Longman and Todd Ltd, 1984).

Harshaw, Jill, *God Beyond Words: Christian Theology and the Spiritual Experiences of People with Profound Intellectual Disabilities* (London: Jessica Kingsley Publishers, 2016).

Haslam, Molly, *A Constructive Theology of Intellectual Disability: Human Being as Mutuality and Response* (New York: Fordham University Press, 2012).

Hauerwas, Stanley, *Suffering Presence: Theological Reflections on Medicine, the Mentally Handicapped, and the Church* (Notre Dame, IN: University of Notre Dame Press, 1986).

Hauerwas, Stanley, Jean Vanier and John Swinton, *Living Gently in a Violent World: The Prophetic Voice of Weakness* (Downer's Grove, IL: InterVarsity Press, 2008).

Heschel, A.J., *The Sabbath: Its Meaning for Modern Man* (New York: Farrar, Straus and Giroux, 2005).

Hilton, M., N. Crowson, J. Mouhot and J. McKay, *A Historical Guide to NGOs in Britain: Charities, Civil Society and the Voluntary Sector since 1945* (Basingstoke: Palgrave Macmillan, 2012).

Holy Bible, New Revised Standard Version (London: SPCK, 2011).

Hryniuk, Michael, *Theology, Disability and Spiritual Transformation: Learning from the Communities of L'Arche* (Amherst: Cambria Press, 2010).

Jackson, Robin, *Discovering Camphill: New Perspectives, Research and Developments* (Floris Books, 2011).

Jenkins, Richard, *Questions of Competence: Culture, Classification and Intellectual Disability* (Cambridge University Press, 1999).

Kavanagh, Patrick, *Lough Derg – A Poem* (London: Martin Brian and O'Keeffe, 1978).

Kimbriel, Samuel, *Friendship as Sacred Knowing: Overcoming Isolation* (Oxford: Oxford University Press, 2014).

Kristeva, Julia and Jean Vanier, *Leur regard perce nos ombres. Échange* (Paris: Fayard, 2011).

Lacey, Paul A. and Anne Dewey (eds), *The Collected Poems of Denise Levertov* (New York: New Directions Publishing, 2013).

Laidlaw, James, 'A Free Gift Makes No Friends', *Journal of the Royal Anthropological Institute* 6, no. 4 (1 December 2000), pp.617–34.

Landsman, Gail, *Reconstructing Motherhood and Disability in the Age of Perfect Babies* (New York: Routledge, 2008).

Mathieu, Marie-Hélène, *Never Again Alone! The Adventure of Faith and Light from 1971 until Today* (Bloomington, IN: WestBow Press, 2014).

Mattingly, Cheryl, *Moral Laboratories: Family Peril and the Struggle for a Good Life* (Berkeley: University of California Press, 2014).

Mauss, Marcel, *The Gift: The Form and Reason for Exchange in Archaic Societies* (London: Routledge Classics, 2002).

McCartney, Dan G., 'The Wisdom of James the Just', *Southern Baptist Journal of Theology* (2000) pp.52–64.

McCloughry, Roy and Wayne Morris, *Making a World of Difference: Christian Reflections on Disability* (London: SPCK, 2002).

McKearney, Patrick, 'L'Arche, Learning Disability, and Domestic Citizenship: Dependent Political Belonging in a Contemporary British City', *City & Society* 29, no. 2 (1 August 2017), pp.260–80.

Moore, Charles E. (ed.), *Called to Community: The Life Jesus Wants for His People* (Rifton, NY, and Robertsbridge: Plough Publishing House, 2016).

Nouwen, Henri, *The Road to Daybreak: A Spiritual Journey* (New York: Doubleday, 1988).

Nouwen, Henri, *The Return of the Prodigal Son: A Story of Homecoming* (London: Darton, Longman and Todd, 1992).

Nouwen, Henri, *Can You Drink the Cup?* (Notre Dame, IN: Ave Maria Press, 1996).

Nouwen, Henri J.M., *Adam, God's Beloved* (Maryknoll, NY: Orbis Books, 2007).

Nouwen, Henri with Michael J. Christensen and Rebecca J. Laird, *Spiritual Direction: Wisdom for the Long Walk of Faith* (London: SPCK, 2011).

O'Brien, John, 'Supported Living: What's the Difference?' (1993), http://eric.ed.gov/?id=ED360801.

O'Conor, Ward, *Dr John Langdon Down and Normansfield* (The Langdon Down Centre Trust, 2009).

O'Siadhail, Micheal, *Collected Poems* (Tarset: Bloodaxe Books, 2013).

O'Siadhail, Micheal, *The Five Quintets* (Waco, TX: Baylor University Press, 2018).

Oliver, Michael and Colin Barnes, *The New Politics of Disablement* (Hampshire: Palgrave Macmillan, 2012).

Packull, Werner, *Hutterite Beginnings: Communitarian Experiments during the Reformation* (Baltimore: The Johns Hopkins University Press, 1995).

Pailin, David, *A Gentle Touch* (London: SPCK, 1992).

Pockney, R., 'Friendship or Facilitation: People with Learning Disabilities and Their Paid Carers', *Sociological Research Online*, Volume 11, Issue 3 (2006), pp.1–9.

Pols, Jeannette, 'Washing the Citizen: Washing, Cleanliness, and Citizenship in Mental Health Care', *Culture, Medicine and Psychiatry* 30, no. 1 (1 March 2006), pp.77–104, https://doi.org/10.1007/s11013-006-9009-z.

Pols, Jeannette and Ingunn Moser, 'Cold Technologies versus Warm Care? On Affective and Social Relations with and through Care Technologies', *ALTER-European Journal of Disability Research/Revue Européenne de Recherche Sur Le Handicap* 3, no. 2 (2009), pp.159–78.

Potter, David, *Through Changing Scenes* (Carlisle: Paternoster Press, 2001).

Race, D.G. (ed.), *Learning Disability: A Social Approach* (London: Routledge, 2001).

Randall, Ian, *Spiritual Revolution: The Story of OM* (Milton Keynes: Authentic Media, 2008).

Randall, Ian M., 'Church Community is a gift of the Holy Spirit': The Spirituality of the Bruderhof Community* (Oxford: Centre for Baptist History and Heritage, 2014).

Randall, Ian M., *A Christian Peace Experiment: The Bruderhof Community in Britain, 1933–1942* (Eugene, OR: Wipf and Stock, 2018).

Rapp, Rayna and Faye D. Ginsburg, 'Enabling Disability: Rewriting Kinship, Reimagining Citizenship', *Public Culture* 13, no. 3 (2001), pp.533–56.

Redley, Marcus and Darin Weinberg, 'Learning Disability and the Limits of Liberal Citizenship: Interactional Impediments to Political Empowerment', *Sociology of Health & Illness* 29, no. 5 (July 2007), pp.767–86.

Reed, A. and C. Reed, *Memoirs of the Life and Philanthropic Labours of Andrew Reed, D.D., with Selections from His Journals* (London: Strahan and Co., 1863).

Reinders, Hans, *Receiving the Gift of Friendship: Profound Disability, Theological Anthropology, and Ethics* (Grand Rapids/Cambridge: William B. Eerdmans Publishing Company, 2008).

Reynolds, Thomas, 'Love Without Boundaries: Theological Reflections on Parenting a Child with Disabilities', *Theology Today* 62 (2005), pp.193–209.

Reynolds, Thomas, *Vulnerable Communion: A Theology of Disability and Hospitality* (Grand Rapids, MI.: Brazos Press, 2008).

Rezende, Claudia Barcellos, 'Gifts of Food: Sociability and Friendship among English Middle Class People', *VIBRANT – Vibrant Virtual Brazilian Anthropology* 4, no. 2 (2007), pp.5–26.

Sachs Zion, Naom and Shawn Fields-Meyer, *A Day Apart: Shabbat at Home* (Shalom Hartman Institute, 2004).

Saint Augustine (Translation and notes by Henry Chadwick): *Confessions* (Oxford: Oxford University Press, 1992).

Salenson, Christian, *Boulversant Fragilite: L'Arche a l'Epreuve du Handicap* (Nouvelle Cite, Bruyeres-le-Chatel, 2016).

Salenson, Christian, *Christian de Chergé. A Theology of Hope* (Collegeville, MN: Liturgical Press 2012).

Schwáb, Zoltán, 'Is Fear of the Lord the Source of Wisdom or Vice Versa?', *VT* (2013) pp.652–662.

Schwáb, Zoltán, 'I, the Fool: A 'Canonical' Reading of Proverbs 26:4–5', *JTI* (2016) pp.31–50.

Searles, H. F., *Collected Papers on Schizophrenia and Related Subjects* (London: Karnac Books, 1965).

Shakespeare, Tom, *Disability Rights and Wrongs Revisited* (London: Routledge, 2013).

Shakespeare, Tom and Nicholas Watson, 'The Social Model of Disability: An Outdated Ideology?' in *Exploring Theories and Expanding Methodologies: Where We Are and Where We Need To Go*, vol. 2, Research in Social Science and Disability (Amsterdam; London: JAI Press, 2001).

Shaw, Ian J., *The Greatest is Charity: The Life of Andrew Reed, Preacher and Philanthropist* (Darlington: Evangelical Press, 2005).

Shulevitz, Judith, *The Sabbath World: Glimpses of a Different Order of Time* (New York: Random House Inc, 2011).

Singer, Peter, *Practical Ethics*, 3rd ed. (Cambridge: Cambridge University Press, 2011).

Smith, Daniel G.W., 'Rituals of Knowing: Rejection and Relation in Disability Theology and Meister Eckhart', *International Journal of Philosophy and Theology* 79, no. 3 (2018): 279–94.

Soskice, Janet Martin, *The Kindness of God* (Oxford: Oxford University Press, 2007).

Spink, Kathryn, *The Miracle, the Message, the Story: Jean Vanier and L'Arche* (London: Darton, Longman and Todd, 2005).

Swinton, J., *Becoming Friends of Time: Disability, Timefullness, and Gentle Discipleship* (Texas: Baylor University Press, 2016).

Swinton, John, 'From Inclusion to Belonging: A Practical Theology of Community, Disability and Humanness'. *Journal of Religion, Disability & Health*, Vol. 16, No. 2 (2012), pp.172–190.

Vanier, J., *Community and Growth* (London: Darton, Longman and Todd, 1989/2007).

Vanier, Jean, *Drawn into the Mystery of Jesus Through the Gospel of John* (London: Darton, Longman and Todd, 2004).

Vanier, Jean, *An Ark for the Poor: The Story of L'Arche* (Ottawa: Novalis, 2012).

Vanier, Jean, *Becoming Human* (Toronto: House of Anansi Press Inc., 2008).

Vanier, Jean, *The Heart of L'Arche: A Spirituality for Every Day* (London: SPCK, 2013).

Vanier, Jean, *Signs of the Times: Seven Paths of Hope for a Troubled World* (London: Darton, Longman and Todd, 2013).

von Rad, Gerhard, *Old Testament Theology*, Vol. 1 (Edinburgh: Oliver and Boyd, 1962).

Wehmeyer, Michael *et al.*, *The Story of Intellectual Disability* (Baltimore, MD: Paul H. Brookes Publishing, 2013).

Welshman, John and Jan Walmsley (eds), *Community Care in Perspective* (Basingstoke: Palgrave Macmillan, 2006).

William C. Gaventa, *Disability and Spirituality: Recovering Wholeness* (Waco, TX: Baylor University Press, 2018).

Williams, Paul, 'Residential and Day Services for Adults', In *Learning Disability: A Social Approach*, edited by David Race (London: Routledge, 2002).

Williams, Rowan, 'The Body's Grace', in Eugene Rogers, Jr. (ed.), *Theology and Sexuality* (Oxford: Blackwell, 2002).Wittgenstein, Ludwig, *Philosophical Investigations: The German Text, with a Revised English Translation*, ed. Gertrude Elizabeth Margaret Anscombe (Wiley-Blackwell, 2001).

Witherington III, B. *Matthew*, Smyth & Helwys Commentary Series (Macon GA: Smyth & Helwys, 2006).

Woodburn, James, 'Egalitarian Societies', *Man* 17, no. 3 (1982), pp.431–51.

Woodfin, Carol, *An Experiment in Christian Internationalism* (Macon, GA: Baptist History and Heritage Society, 2013).

Wright, David and Anne Digby (eds), *From Idiocy to Mental Deficiency: Historical Perspectives on People with Learning Disabilities* (London: Routledge, 1996).

Wright, David, *Mental Disability in Victorian England* (Oxford: Oxford University Press, 2001).

Yong, Amos, *Theology and Down Syndrome: Reimagining Disability in Late Modernity* (Waco, TX: Baylor University Press, 2007).

Young, Frances, *Face to Face: A Narrative Essay in the Theology of Suffering* (Edinburgh: T & T Clark, 1990).

Young, Frances M. (ed.), *Encounter with Mystery: Reflections on L'Arche and Living with Disability* (London: Darton, Longman & Todd, 1997).

Young, Frances, *Arthur's Call: A Journey of Faith in the Face of Severe Learning Disability* (London: SPCK, 2014).

The Contributors

David F. Ford was born in Dublin. He is Regius Professor of Divinity Emeritus in the University of Cambridge and a Fellow of Selwyn College. He is married to Deborah Hardy Ford. He has published very widely and his current research and writing includes work on: the Gospel of John; theology, modernity and the arts; Scriptural Reasoning; and reconciliation. He co-chairs the Rose Castle Foundation, a centre for reconciliation, inter-faith engagement and conservation.

Deborah Hardy Ford is an ordained Anglican minister living and working in Cambridge. She has worked for many years as a chaplain at Addenbrooke's Hospital and has a psychotherapy and pastoral supervision practice. She has studied English, Social Sciences, Theology and Psychotherapy and is the co-author of a book about her father, Daniel W. Hardy: *Wording a Radiance: Parting Conversations on God and the Church.* Deborah is an associate priest at St Andrew's Cherry Hinton.

James Gardom first worked with people with learning disabilities in Oxford, before training for ordination. After working in Zimbabwe in a theological college, he became vicar of the parish which contains Lyn's house. (Lyn was his first churchwarden.) He is Dean and Chaplain of Pembroke College Cambridge. He is married to Judith.

Judith Gardom is a PhD candidate in Criminology at the University of Cambridge, writing on the roles that reading plays for men in prison. She works with the University's Prisons Research Centre on other research projects in prison settings including the Personality Disorder pathway for offenders. Her background is in Philosophy and Theology, which she has taught at an Anglican theological college in Zimbabwe and in the UK.

E.S. Kempson is a PhD candidate in the Faculty of Divinity, University of Cambridge, with previous degrees in theology and religion from the University of Oxford, Yale Divinity School, and the University of Virginia. Emily lived as a housemate in Lyn's House for one year. Her academic research topics include constructive and biblical theology, Augustine, and contemporary truth-theories. She is also a licensed lay preacher in the Church of England.

Patrick McKearney is a Research Associate and Affiliated Lecturer in the Department of Social Anthropology at the University of Cambridge. As well as having previously lived in Lyn's House, he has conducted anthropological research on the role of care, ethics, and belonging in L'Arche communities in the UK.

Suzanna R. Millar is a Teaching Fellow in Hebrew Bible and Old Testament at the University of Edinburgh. Her current research interests include the Wisdom Literature, the Book of Job, and the role of the environment and animals in the Hebrew Bible. She previously worked at Leeds University, and before that, completed her PhD on the Book of Proverbs at Cambridge University. While in Cambridge, she lived in Lyn's House for two and a half years.

Theresia L. Paquet has cared for her disabled brother throughout her life. Born in South Africa, she has experienced services for people with disabilities living in several different countries. With a PhD in Social Policy she co-founded Mannawell, a non-profit organisation caring for and celebrating people with disabilities. As a Court of Protection visitor she protects people under the Mental Capacity Act. Her brother and Christian faith inspire her compassion. She is married to Ulrich.

Philip S. Powell works as Training Manager with the Jubilee Centre. Born and raised in India, he has lived in the UK since 1998. He was a resident in the Lyn's House community for three years and has previously lived in Christian community in South Africa and The Netherlands. He has a Master's degree in International Relations and has also studied international law. He lives in Cambridge with his Dutch wife Renate.

Ian Randall comes from the north of Scotland. He is a Baptist minister and has had local church pastorates, has taught in theological colleges in London and Prague, and has been a hospital chaplain and a college chaplain. His research and writing have mainly been in the areas of church history and spirituality. Ian is a research associate of the Cambridge Centre for Christianity Worldwide. He is involved in spiritual direction ministry.

Daniel G.W. Smith previously studied theology at Durham University and is currently finishing his PhD at the University of Cambridge, which focuses on the contribution of the thirteenth–fourteenth century theologian Meister Eckhart's thought to disability theology. He lived in Lyn's House for two years and has also lived in a L'Arche community.